Assessing DevOps

For Information Technology, Business and Industry

A Definitive Guide to:

Assess DevOps *Quantitatively* for your IT
Understand Emerging Areas for DevOps Assessments
Extend DevOps Principles to Business and Industry

Manas Shome
Raghubir Bose

Self-published by the authors, Manas Shome and Raghubir Bose
Copyright © Manas Shome and Raghubir Bose
All rights reserved

Manas Shome and Raghubir Bose assert the moral right to be identified as the authors of this work.

This is a non-fiction work. Names, characters, places and incidents, if any, are either the product of the authors' imagination or are used fictitiously and any resemblance to any actual person living or dead, events and locales is entirely coincidental. Further, the content herein solely represents the personal opinions and views of the authors, and does not belong to or represent that of any other individual or organization irrespective of whether the authors have worked for or not.

Any associated intellectual property other than the copyright of this book itself, that may arise solely or primarily due to work done on basis of the content in this book, would be treated as an act of infringement of such intellectual property as belonging to the authors (as part of the organization that they work for, as the case may be).

This book is sold subject to the condition that it shall not, by any way of trade or otherwise, be lent, resold, hired out, or otherwise circulated without the authors' prior written consent, in any form of binding or cover other than in which it is published and without a similar condition including this condition being imposed on the subsequent purchaser and without limiting the rights under copyright reserved above, no part of this publication may be reproduced, stored in or introduced into a retrieval system, electronic or otherwise, or transmitted in any form or by any means (electronic, mechanical, photocopying, recording or otherwise), without prior written permission of the copyright owner, except in the case of brief quotations embodied in critical articles or reviews with appropriate citations.

In loving memory of my parents,
Who brought the world to me.
(Manas Shome)

To all the believers of DevOps.
(Raghubir Bose)

Table of Contents

TABLE OF CONTENTS	**III**
TABLE OF FIGURES	**V**
ACKNOWLEDGEMENT	**1**
INTRODUCTION	**2**
DERIVING DEVOPS FOR ASSESSMENT	**5**
Relevance from an IT Assessment Perspective	6
Why an Organization needs DevOps Assessment	8
Concept of the DevOps Pipeline	10
ENGINEERING PRACTICES FOR DEVOPS	**12**
Importance of Practices in view of Assessment	16
DEFINING THE CULTURAL ASPECT	**18**
Definition of Culture as relevant to Assessment	21
How Propensities Define People Patterns	21
THE BIG PICTURE: WHAT TO ASSESS	**29**
Prioritizing the Portfolio(s) for Assessment	32
WARMING UP WITH A PRE-ASSESSMENT	**38**
The Pre-Assessment Questionnaire	38
The Readiness Scoring Model	55
Generating the Pre-Assessment Report	57
READING THE PRE-ASSESSMENT REPORT	**60**
GOING QUANTITATIVE	**64**
A Brief Note on Evaluating the Quantitative Methods	64
Modifying CPM for Quantitative IT Analysis	66
THE DETAILED QUESTIONNAIRE	**71**
FINDING OUT THE CRITICAL PATH	**80**
ANALYZING THE CRITICAL PATH	**91**
DERIVING THE TARGET IT PROCESS	**100**
Stories for the Target IT Process	100
DevOps Implementation Stories	103

QUANTIFYING PEOPLE ARCHITECTURE	**106**
ARTICULATING TECHNOLOGY FLOW	**118**
DERIVING THE KEY METRICS	**121**
PROCESS METRICS	122
PEOPLE METRICS	125
TECHNOLOGY METRICS	127
HOW TO: THE STEPS TO CONSULTING	**133**
ASSESSMENT REPORT OUTLINE	138
CASES IN DEVOPS ASSESSMENT	**141**
ENTERPRISE GOVERNANCE FOR A LARGE INSURANCE ORGANIZATION	141
DIGITAL PLATFORM FOR A GLOBAL MEDIA AND INFORMATION FIRM	144
INTEGRATION AND BI PORTFOLIO FOR A LARGE INSURANCE COMPANY	147
ASSESSMENT RECAP STEP-BY-STEP	**149**
SELECT FOCUS AREAS FOR IT ASSESSMENTS	**156**
CHAOS ENGINEERING	156
AIOPS: DEVOPS DRIVEN BY AI	163
SECURITY ENGINEERING	167
DATAOPS: DEVOPS FOR DATA	170
BRANCHING AND MERGING STRATEGY	178
CONTAINER STRATEGY AND DEVOPS	183
CLOUD STRATEGY AND DEVOPS	187
DEVOPS FOR LEGACY MODERNIZATION	193
EXTENDING DEVOPS TO BUSINESS	**198**
AGILITY AS THE RATIONALIZED OBJECTIVE OF ENTERPRISE IT	198
DEFINING THE ENTERPRISE VALUE CHAIN	199
MAPPING BUSINESS METRICS TO IT METRICS	201
DEVOPS FOR SELECT INDUSTRY VERTICALS	**206**
RETAIL AND CONSUMER PACKAGED GOODS (CPG)	206
MEDIA, PUBLISHING AND INFORMATION SERVICES	207
BANKING, FINANCIAL SERVICES AND INSURANCE	208
MANUFACTURING	210
LIFESCIENCES AND HEALTHCARE	211
TELECOMMUNICATION AND CABLE	212
ENERGY AND UTILITIES	213
TECHNOLOGY AND TOOLS LIST	**216**
GLOSSARY	**221**
REFERENCES	**228**

Table of Figures

Figure 1: Simplified Representation of a DevOps Pipeline 10
Figure 2: Dimensional impact due to Engineering Practices 12
Figure 3: DevOps as a Set of Engineering Practices 15
Figure 4: Cultural criteria based on team propensities 18
Figure 5: Organizational Layers 29
Figure 6: Simplified View of DevOps Readiness Report 32
Figure 7: Representative Heatmap for 7 Portfolios of an organization 33
Figure 8: Portfolio Heatmap Matrix 35
Figure 9: Representative Pre-Assessment Outcome Structure 40
Figure 10: Sample Pre-Assessment Report 58
Figure 11: Interpreting the Report Section-wise 61
Figure 12: Notation for event and activity 67
Figure 13: Example of network with one initial and multiple final state events 69
Figure 14: Example of the As-Is Process Architecture 85
Figure 15: Example of the To-Be Process Architecture 97
Figure 16: People Architecture Diagram for As-Is 106
Figure 17: Role-wise People Propensity Scores for As-Is 109
Figure 18: People pattern for Low-Low-High Propensity Combination 111
Figure 19: Simplified As-is People Architecture 111
Figure 20: To-Be People Pattern - Option (a) 112
Figure 21: Simplified People Architecture for Option (a) 113
Figure 22: To-Be People Pattern - Option (b) 113
Figure 23: Simplified People Architecture for Option (b) 113
Figure 24: Variations to time estimates due to People Propensities 115
Figure 25: Technology/ Tools architecture representation 119
Figure 26: Metrics structure for DevOps 122
Figure 27: Mapping to Process Metrics 132
Figure 28: Steps for Consulting 136
Figure 29: Possible Resilience curve variations for Chaos Test 157
Figure 30: Traditional versus Container based Deployment Approach 184
Figure 31: Containers and Function of a Full Stack Engineer 184
Figure 32: Visualization of a Container 185
Figure 33: Enterprise Value Chain 200

Acknowledgement

The book is an outcome of the work we have done with various organizations; we are thankful to all the people in such organizations who pushed us in innovating ways and means to optimally assess their information technology landscapes so that target states can be accurately and deterministically predicted.

The knowledge that we assimilated through the conferences and forums – both academic and industry-based – has been invaluable for us in coming up with this book. We are thankful to the numerous academicians, teachers, corporate leaders and professionals whose talks and insights have been undying inspirations to the content of our book.

We would like to express gratitude to our "Ninja" team in the organization we currently work in – Chiranjib Bhattacharjee, Devjeet Sarkar, Moumita Bose, Abhijit Das, Swati Saha and Dipankar Basak – who have provided us important inputs that have substantially influenced shaping up of our book. We would also like to mention our gratitude to Anwesha Chakraborty, Saurav Roy, Chayan Mullick and Ramesh Sharma who formerly were part of our team and have significantly influenced our work.

Behind this team is the relentless support of the leadership in our organization in terms of investments and infrastructure, thereby enabling us to innovate and work without having to face and deal with day to day operational challenges.

Last but not the least, we extend our sincere thanks to our respective spouses (Sumana Shome; and Moumita Bose) – our toughest critics – and our daughters (Asmita Shome; Rupkatha Bose and Ruplekha Bose) – our loving distractors who forced us to take breaks and think afresh every time – who all made it a journey for us worth taking!

Manas Shome and Raghubir Bose

Introduction

We, Manas and Raghubir, have been working in the area of DevOps – both in terms of consulting (whereby DevOps assessment becomes so important for us), and implementing DevOps on the ground – for multiple large to truly global organizations. We both have more than twenty years of experience in the industry, apart from pursuing interests in painting, trekking, music, mythology, philosophy and meditation (whew!). We do believe that doing DevOps (and of course, practicing Agile) is more to do with the latter interests from which we derive our inspiration to take it to our IT workspace.

Purpose of writing this book

In course of our work on DevOps, we found that most of the assessments done to evaluate the state of DevOps and provide recommendations to achieve an improved state, typically are very qualitative in nature, and subject to heuristics in terms of finding out multiple "likely" solutions to a given problem. What gets recommended leaves a lot of gap on what and how exactly DevOps needs to be implemented on the ground. Additionally, while such assessments sometimes do use value stream analysis for the IT life cycle process to bring in a quantitative approach, they may not adequately address the people and technology perspectives and impact of DevOps in the target state on these two dimensions.

Given that we devised a way to quantitatively approach the problem of assessment to eliminate most, if not all, the heuristic factors – more so including the people and technology dimensions – the purpose of the book is to guide you in understanding the aforesaid approach and hence, enable you to think deterministically (as opposed to non-deterministic approaches resulting in multiple outcomes to a given problem) while you do such IT assessments.

Who is the book for?

This book is for you if you have an intermediate understanding of IT processes – in terms of how IT project or IT product life cycles work – and typical challenges encountered in IT with respect to how IT implementations are done.

We believe that the book would immensely help you if you are an IT consultant, advisor or architect working with one or more organizations to define their DevOps roadmap(s). A basic understanding of concepts in mathematical modelling and quantitative techniques would be an added advantage. You may be planning to do a DevOps assessment for an organization, or create and define your own DevOps assessment model to assist one or more organizations in such assessments. You are an IT leader – say, a CxO, VP, IT director or a departmental head – who requires a deep understanding of how to bridge the gap between your IT strategy and what needs to be done on-the-ground. And lastly you are a business leader or strategist who needs to understand how your business strategy – with all the industry-specific flavors – should map to your IT strategy itself in the perspective of DevOps and related fields; given that in today's world, business value is substantially and directly derived from IT performance.

What this book is not about

The book is not about introducing you to DevOps or teaching DevOps. The book does not teach what is IT consulting or what is being a great IT consultant or an IT strategist. The book does not talk about IT or business assessments in general. The book does not provide a really long list of questions that you may ask during assessments (though sufficient templates are provided) – as questions vary widely across organizational contexts, and that may be too prescriptive at times – however, equips you to frame the right questions in specific formats to be asked during an assessment.

The book covers specific approaches for DevOps assessment that aim to be quintessentially quantitative and deterministic, and based on specific practices of the authors. It can at least serve as a launching pad for getting started on thinking about DevOps assessments in quantitative terms in order to obtain deterministic, as opposed to "multiple ways to resolve a problem", outcomes; and how to extend such principles in mapping business to IT.

What's New in this edition?

While the earlier edition covered the workflow and the quantitative framework for assessing IT for DevOps in detail, in this edition we have further covered the following:

a. Understanding Why an organization needs DevOps assessment
b. Understanding the "Big Picture" on what to assess
c. Understanding and deriving people patterns from cultural propensity scores
d. The steps of executing a consulting assignment for an organization
e. Select focus areas in IT for DevOps assessments
f. Extending DevOps principles to business and across industry verticals
g. Cases in DevOps assessment

> We have kept the style of writing this book quite informal. Look out for boxed content such as in here, as quick reference of main points to remember or of caution. We have also taken the liberty to interchangeably use certain words based on the context, say "people" and "culture"; "organization" and "enterprise"; "technology" and "tools"; "story", and "activity"; et al. Guess, use of such words would be a breeze for you to comprehend as the reader. Feel free to write to us at assessingdevops@gmail.com for questions and feedback. We will try our best to reply to your email at the earliest.

Deriving DevOps for Assessment

From the perspective of IT, DevOps as a literal term is all about how to bring the different teams in IT, categorized namely as 'Dev' (developers, testers, et al; people who own and manage the actual functional software application being written) and 'Ops' (operations teams who own and manage the infrastructure and workflows through which the software is changed and executed), are brought together to work in a cohesive manner. The roots go back to a set of historical events whereby a need was felt to get these teams working together to achieve higher agility and resilience in how software is built, deployed, executed and controlled.

When we started working on DevOps a few years back, we saw that implementing DevOps on the ground across organizations was more to do with how to bring together not only a set of people to effectively collaborate, but also to optimize the processes in the IT life cycle and to bring in technology led automation that would force the people to work together over a set of chained workflows.

Our inspiration lies in our studies of the mythology and philosophy. We observed through our studies that **Agility** – the capability to not only be fast, but also to be able to change the direction (read, to respond to changes) – has been the key factor in say, winning wars. Examples spanning across mythology (Battle of Kurukshetra in the Mahabharata, or the tale of David and Goliath in the Bible) and history (invasions of Persia and India by Alexander, or the Battle of Normandy during the World War II) show that deploying small tightly knit (read, highly collaborative and trust-based) teams backed by a culture of technology and automation, as relevant to such times, become the most effective ingredients for victory.

Relevance from an IT Assessment Perspective

We found out, as others in the industry would have done earlier, doing DevOps was about achieving just one thing first:

> ## IT Agility

That essentially meant, (a) how fast your software moves from requirements stage to production rollout over a change cycle, and (b) how fast you can bring it back to a change cycle if such a need is felt while running in production, say due to a failure that needs to be fixed or an improvement suggested by a user of the software. This further leads to reducing rework, reducing wastage, improving software quality, improving reliability of the processes that define the software life cycle, improving customer experience across the value chain (IT to business) and all other terms that you would have already come across pertaining to this paradigm in IT.

Hence, when we were asked as practitioners of DevOps to assess IT and come up with how DevOps can be done, the first tenet for us was to optimize IT in terms of people, process and technology so as to achieve maximum IT agility. However, this can only succeed if agility happens not only for Dev, but also for Ops. In fact, taking one step forward, we found that bringing in business – teams who define the requirements on what software has to be built or changes are to be done – into the scope of agility, can bring in true IT agility.

> ## IT Agility = Dev Agility + Ops Agility + Business Agility*

* However, for the purpose of keeping things simple, we would first confine ourselves in assessing DevOps for IT to the two constituent teams, namely Dev and Ops. In later chapters we would explore how adding business agility to the equation extends the principles to the enterprise.

But the question for us was, how do we assess and plan to optimize IT in terms of people, process and technology so that everything end to end takes substantially less time to complete in a definitive and predictable manner across the software life cycle? This is especially a challenge given that any such change would entail uncertainties in people behavior and culture.

The answer for us was to look at planning (and suggest doing) DevOps in terms of a set of engineering practices; heavily involving technology led automation that would not only enforce, but also acceptably enable the people involved in the IT process to work together faster, and that too, over an optimized set of processes vis-à-vis "the old way of doing things".

Now let us quickly summarize the three basic tenets as described above. These tenets form the basis of our assessment approach as outlined throughout the rest of the book, hence would pave the way on how to assess (and suggest ways to do) DevOps for IT:

1. **The primary objective of DevOps is to achieve IT Agility**
2. **Achieving IT Agility is to achieve both Dev Agility and Ops Agility** (leaving aside the notion of Business Agility for the sake of simplicity for now)
3. **DevOps can be assessed (and executed) as a set of engineering practices**

The last one above further shows us how DevOps can not only be assessed, but also provide insights to suggest methods of improvement as part of such assessment, in definitive terms; some of such methods involving quantitative techniques so that the output can be in most of the cases, if not always, deterministic (as opposed to heuristic or subjective) in what needs to be done and how.

While we do talk of primary objective being IT Agility for DevOps, aspects such as improved software quality, IT system resilience and reduction of IT operational costs are also being described to be equally important objectives of DevOps. The way we see it is, the more we try to achieve higher IT agility, the more we need to establish such aforesaid factors in parallel for all the bells and whistles to work together and deliver outcomes "first time right", else it is not possible to achieve IT agility in true sense.

Why an Organization needs DevOps Assessment

An organization may be simplistically viewed as an entity that runs a set of core business processes (with it auxiliary or supporting processes including third-party interfaces) aided by its IT processes as the backbone. Factors such as uncertainty due to business cycles in any given industry, consumer demands for faster and better services, competitive pressures to win over consumers and regulatory requirements, have led to organizations seeking high efficiency, consistency and predictability in their IT systems and processes.

Organizations range from small and lean startups to large multinationals spanning across the globe. Given the business complexities arising out of the aforesaid factors and varying organizational sizes, we have seen that organizations – in a bid to be "consistently high performing" – need to have their IT assessed in terms of DevOps for the following reasons; the list may not be exhaustive though:

- **IT process latencies and inefficiencies start with people** – the Dev and the Ops teams – who apparently work with conflicting objectives; the former wanting to push in as many changes to the system as possible, and the latter worried about system stability and control. Hence, IT as a discipline needs to be analyzed in terms of how people behavior affects processes and technology, which hence calls for a DevOps assessment.

- A given industry may be driven by specific needs; say, meeting consumer demands faster and better (retail), on-time regulatory compliance (insurance), high resilience to widespread physical or over-the-air networks (telecommunication), faster services to consumers with high availability and security (banking and financial services), efficiencies in managing energy consumption (energy and utilities), or rich content value delivery to consumers without any latency (media and information services). For all such varying reasons, a need to enable consistently high throughput for IT changes and managing such changes with minimal disruption to consumers in the least possible time – the core objective of DevOps – organizations, irrespective of the industry, need to continuously assess their state of IT in terms of DevOps.

- A relatively small to medium organization may be looking at a **"grow fast and grow consistent" strategy**, that may need to have their IT assessed to evaluate how fast they can push new products and services with acceptable quality standards – consistently being able to reach its consumers over time across select channels – without any substantial impact to its margins; even if it comes at the expense of short term impact on say, IT security and regulatory compliance. Such an organization would need to understand how IT can deliver the value in terms of agility and availability.

- For a large multinational with say a **"maintain market leader position" strategy**, the focus would again be on high IT agility, however within the confines of high security, reliability and strict regulatory compliance across the geographies it operates in; even at a short term impact on say, margins. Such an organization would need to understand how IT can deliver the value in terms of agility, security and reliability.

- **For an organization who finds that other similar organizations in the industry are on their way to be "high performing"** – substantiated by respective adoption of DevOps at various stages – it may want to further find out its state of IT vis-à-vis DevOps adoption, and what needs to be done to close the gaps to arrive at a given desired state of DevOps. In this case however, the competition or better performing organizations in the given industry typically become the benchmark. Hence the approach entails a risk whereby as DevOps is practiced differently for different organizations within the confines of their respective organization cultures, the assessment may be construed by the industry players to provide a "one size fits all" outcomes.

- **For an organization who has already adopted DevOps**, a continuous DevOps assessment may be envisaged for steadily improving the value that IT delivers to business. More so with the advent of people behavioral studies and technology evolution, such outcomes can be leveraged for better and faster IT performance. Such an approach would be more relevant for organizations who are leaders in their respective industries, and strive to set examples in new ways of delivering IT value to business.

Concept of the DevOps Pipeline

Implementing DevOps is about changing people structures and behavior in an organization (or, a specific team in context to start with) to align to an optimized process flow enabled using a set of technologies and tools, typically in form of one or more toolchain(s).

Such an arrangement involving the three dimensions of people, process and technology defines what is called the "DevOps Pipeline". Hence, to assess DevOps it is important to understand the concept.

A formal definition

A DevOps Pipeline is defined as a collection of discrete, deterministic and finite automata covering some or all aspects of software engineering discipline from conceptualization to production, in a forward (say, to deploy software) or reverse (say, to provide feedback for performance) sequence, that enables orchestration of the aforesaid three dimensions so that the time to deploy the identified product, functional solution or project that moves through it, is minimized.

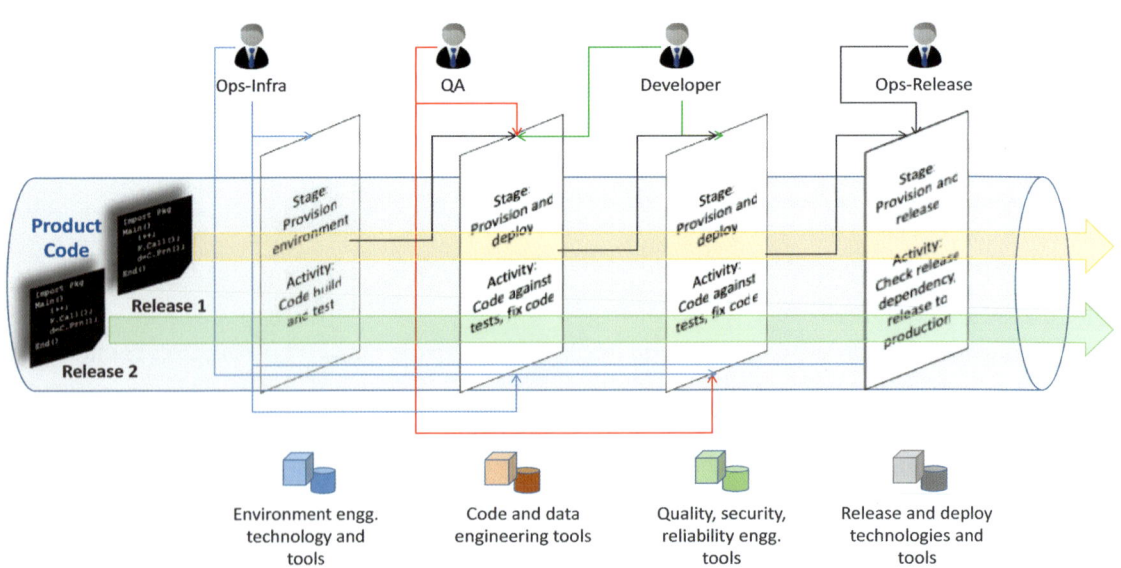

Figure 1: Simplified Representation of a DevOps Pipeline

In simpler terms, a DevOps Pipeline can be construed as a collection of automated tasks whose execution is orchestrated by a controller, typically called a Continuous Integration Server, incorporating one or more of the following IT functions:

- Integration
- Quality
- Reliability
- Build
- Release
- Deployment
- Provisioning
- Monitoring
- Service operations
- Security
- Feedback loops

There can be other software engineering practices that can add to this pipeline.

Note that "Automata" (plural for "automaton") is a set of self-operating machines – the term being used formally in the field of computer science and discrete mathematics – that take inputs, process the inputs, and generates one or more output(s). This typically involves solving a problem through following a pre-determined sequence of operations or responding to a set of pre-determined instructions; the response being based on inferences drawn by matching the inputs with such pre-determined patterns.

Engineering Practices for DevOps

The engineering practices for DevOps define the process discipline that needs to be established through a set of technology based automation across one or more processes of the IT life cycle. Creating such automation reduces variability in execution of such processes due to human cultural aspects, hence brings in deterministic behavior and substantial predictability in how IT gets done.

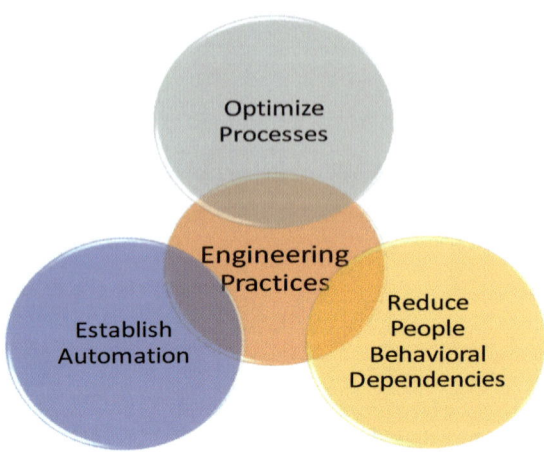

Figure 2: Dimensional impact due to Engineering Practices

Further, establishing such automation enables bringing in more parallelism across multiple process execution through optimizing dependencies and waiting times across such processes. This optimizes utilization of multiple IT team roles, say application owners, developers, testers, release managers, et al, so that more gets done in relatively less time which is the very essence of achieving IT agility.

We may consider the following to be categories of engineering practices to start with. You are free to add to this list to create your own based on how fine grained you may want to assess DevOps as a set of such practices. The relevant traditional role primarily responsible for each of the practices is indicated in the format *"[Traditional role name]"*.

- o **Requirements engineering** *[IT product owner / lead]*: Engineering practices that may include optimizing processes and establish automation to capture and manage requirements either coming in from production cycles or as feedback from users, translating requirements from informal to structured formats, categorizing and prioritizing requirements (say, into functional and non-functional types), and integrating them for traceability to the rest of the IT life cycle.

- **Code engineering** *[Developer]*: Practices that may include how efficiently and beautifully code can be created or written. It essentially deals with say, bringing in higher modularity to code (so that it is easy to maintain and reuse), redefining code writing styles and architectures (say, microservices) that optimize storage and execution requirements of the code, establish application security, and potentially bring in automation to code writing (say, starting with model driven code development) and checking for errors to save developer's time and identify code issues early on.

- **Data engineering** *[Data architect / modeler]*: Practices that may include how efficiently data can be managed and maintained. It is all about optimizing database schemas, optimizing how unstructured data may be managed for easy retrieval and usage, accessing and using relevant data (and database) through establishing right types of integration to applications, automating data archival and reservation as part of IT workflows, managing data redundancy optimally, manage data migration seamlessly, establish data security, et al.

- **Quality engineering** *[Tester / QA team]*: Practices that may include ensuring quality of applications "first time right" with minimal developer's rework; hence, practices such as test driven or behavior driven development resulting in in-sprint automation (enabling tests and code development at the same-go or "Sprint" in Agile terms), embedding all-round test automation as part of code builds, et al, would be relevant. Security testing, as part of the overall security strategy given the focus on security across the IT value chain, may also be included as part of quality engineering; associated branches such as "DevSecOps" or "SecurityOps" may be the scope of study for such practices.

- **Reliability engineering** *[QA / infrastructure test team]*: Practices that may include ensuring performance and resilience of the technical infrastructure that makes DevOps possible as a practice; it ensures that the IT technical backbone works without unacceptable degradation of performance at any point of time. For example, building in the monitoring systems for such infrastructure to reactively or predictively capture failure events, defining and establishing rule-based self-healing mechanisms for such infrastructure, automated identification of issues in DevOps led architecture implementations, et al, would be relevant. "DevSecOps" or "SecurityOps" practices may be further included as part of the practice from the perspective of IT infrastructure security perspective. "Chaos engineering" is a specific practice as part of reliability engineering practices that can help build higher resilience in the IT systems on a continuous basis; however, note that this discipline may also span across other engineering practices based on the types of IT failure that an organization wants to proactively address in production (possibly starting with pre-production processes).

- **Build and release engineering** *[Operations / release team]*: Practices that may include how seamless build and release cycles for applications can be established; establishing continuous integration (CI) and continuous delivery (CD) frameworks over the Software Development Life Cycle (SDLC) using automation tools integrated over a tool chain is of significance. Other engineering practices such as quality engineering may be embedded as part of build and release cycles. Also, reliability engineering may be applied over such build and release frameworks themselves to measure resilience of the frameworks and take corrective action on failures.

- **Environment engineering** *[Operations / infrastructure team]*: The practices deal with how hardware (or virtualized) infrastructure and environments that hold applications and data, either in non-production or in production, can be seamlessly provisioned, managed and optimized; this may incorporate on-demand environment provisioning, ensure optimal environment resource utilization, destroy existing environments (and re-create if required). Achieving infrastructure immutability to preserve environment behavior (say, retaining production-like configurations) and at the same time, reduce specific environment retention dependencies during the IT life cycle, is of significance.

- **Service operations engineering** *[Operations / production support team]*: The practices deal with managing changing requirements and addressing issues post-rollout of applications into production. They may comprise of monitoring production systems to detect events (say, system performance outliers), automated triggering of relevant events as incidents, automated incident resolution, triggering of problem and change management workflows through suitable feedback loops, and trace back to the SDLC for code based fixes.

- **Security engineering** *(IT security team; application, infrastructure and data security teams)* – The practices lie at the center of Dev and Ops practices, and include all aspects of ensuring security across the layers of application, data, technology and infrastructure. This would entail practices for establishing application security, both for source code and executables at run time; data and database security; security of IT environments and technologies or tools; and infrastructure security. Applying security patches and related upgrades, security governance, security testing, chaos engineering (in terms of handling ad hoc security failures), and continuous vulnerability (and other security events') monitoring are some of the operational aspects of such practices.

From a typical implementation perspective, the aforesaid engineering practice categories can be represented as follows:

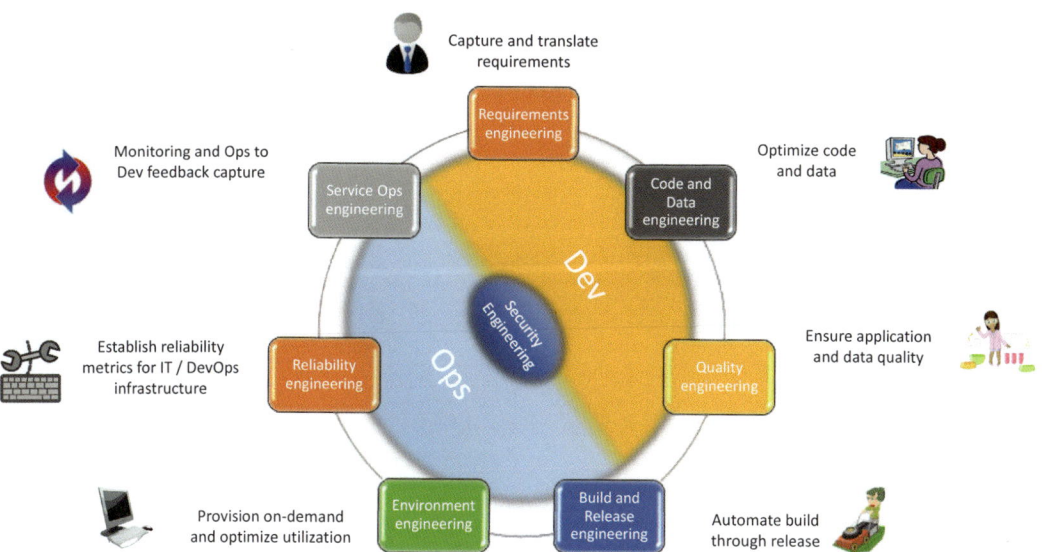

Figure 3: DevOps as a Set of Engineering Practices

Note that we have combined code engineering and data engineering in one box; as code and data (and corresponding databases) are both the core build subjects for IT, practices pertaining to them may typically be implemented in tandem to support synchronizing of changes, if relevant. For instance, implementing microservices architecture based approach for java (code) may need corresponding structural changes to the underlying database schemas and the data itself.

Further, if an organization wants to start from Dev side of its structure, it may start its DevOps implementation journey from one of the boxes shown around "Dev" in the above figure and go clockwise towards Ops. Alternatively, an organization may want to start their DevOps journey from one of the "Ops" side boxes and go anti-clockwise towards Dev. For Ops to Dev – where the organization wants to tackle say, optimizing production support processes and introduce self-healing systems for handling incidents, it may start work on Service Ops engineering practices and either go clockwise (if it wants to streamline the related Ops practices for infrastructure and site reliability), or go anti-clockwise (if it wants to streamline Ops to Dev feedback loops for more efficient change management and problem fixes). Hence, the actual flow of such practices would depend on where the organization may want to start their DevOps journey.

Importance of Practices in view of Assessment

The aforesaid six engineering (plus one, including security engineering) practices form the basis of assessment. While we are defining DevOps to be having the sole objective of reducing IT cycle time, this needs to happen across disparate processes in the IT life cycle. Bringing in the concept of engineering practices across the IT life cycle defines the areas in which the reduction of cycle time can be assessed step by step, either by treating each of the practices individually for assessment, or taking two or more practices into consideration together with respect to the sequence in which they can be executed; say, bringing in more parallelism in executing these practices, of course depending on the dependencies between them, can contribute significantly in reducing the cycle time.

Further, as we will see later, defining each practice brings in homogeneity across a set of similar activities being done as part of the larger IT process, thereby enabling us to apply common or similar quantitative parameters for assessing the practice, hence providing a deterministic method for our assessment approach.

Defining the Cultural Aspect

While optimizing the IT process in terms of cycle time and assessing the technology landscape used for automation across the process are quite important – given that we are dealing with IT – the people cultural aspect becomes the most important factor in deciding whether the implementation of any such process and technology changes would effectively be utilized on ground to bring in the expected benefits to IT. Hence, it is of utmost importance that we define how to model the cultural aspect so that we can effectively quantify, analyze and assess its impact on both the current and desired state of IT prior to actual implementation of such changes.

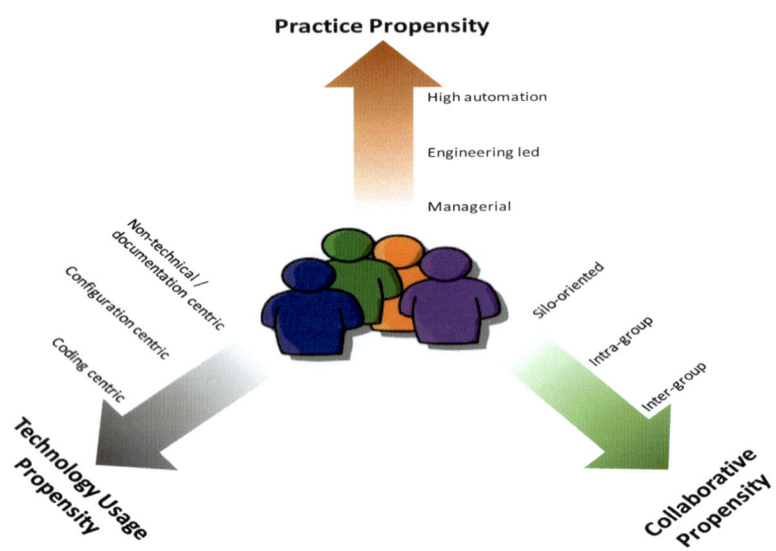

Figure 4: Cultural criteria based on team propensities

As indicated in the above figure, we would define three criteria, or propensities, for assessing the cultural aspect in view of DevOps. Here, "Propensity" is construed as an inclination or natural tendency to behave in a specific way; this may apply either to an individual, or to a group or team. Propensity for a team may align to that of the organization, it can be skewed, or it can be entirely orthogonal. The concept similarly applies to the individual with respect to the team. We have seen that an alignment typically results in high agility, whereas an orthogonality results in loss of agility based how skewed the relative propensities are.

Practice Propensity

Implementing DevOps on ground is all about engineering rigor, hence requiring more of technical problem analysis and solving aptitude in terms of people behavior, as opposed to managerial orchestration of activities. Whereas to an extent the managerial aptitude is important in coordinating any such implementation from a people standpoint alone, the cultural objective is to engineer the systems that can themselves orchestrate the IT processes. Hence, we define practice propensity as the affiliation of the current people (or team) in IT with respect to their given engineering practice (as defined in the previous chapter) being:

a. Primarily managerial oriented
b. Primarily engineering oriented
c. Primarily high automation oriented

Teams that are managerial oriented typically required transformation in one or more people to being engineering oriented so that the DevOps implementations on the ground can be done effectively and are architecturally sound. Teams that are already engineering oriented may strive for higher automation, say to bring in intelligent automation for building self-orchestrated systems.

Technology Usage Propensity

While the above propensity talks about the process based behavioral propensity of the IT team, technology usage propensity provides the technology based behavioral propensity of the team. This essential means, if a team is given a set of technologies (in terms of software tools and applications) to work with, what would be the kind of technology they would typically go for. Though a given engineering practice may impact what types of software can be primarily used for its activities, we find that usage propensity of the team may still bend on a specific technology type, irrespective of whether the team is given such a tool to work with. The propensity is parameterized qualitatively as follows:

a. Non-technical or documentation based tool usage
b. Configuration centric tool usage
c. Coding centric tool usage

As the given team matures more towards DevOps led automation, we find that team propensity in technology usage gradually transforms to usage of tools that are configuration centric. For example, while traditional teams doing manual testing and release management may heavily use documentation based tools such as simple spreadsheets, they gradually adopt higher automation through usage of tools where they can configure test cases and release plan respectively. As they mature more into higher state of DevOps, they would typically use tools where the entire testing and release activities can be coded; this would simplify managing tests and releases as a continuous pipeline of activities respectively. Note that the latter point demonstrates how faster IT cycle times can be achieved.

Collaborative Propensity

This propensity indicates the interpersonal behavioral patterns of IT teams in terms of affinity to collaborate as opposed to working in a silo. We may parameterize the propensity as follows:

a. Silo based
b. Intra-group oriented
c. Inter-group oriented

Note that while the nature of a given activity in a given IT process, and specifically within an engineering practice, may have a bearing on this propensity; the team may still have its own propensity to exhibit such behavior while a group of activities taken together collectively as part of the practice gets executed by it. For example, documenting a record of resolving an environment provisioning issue in a known error database (KEDB) by the infrastructure team may exhibit a simple silo-based behavior, however, the team may exhibit a collaborative behavior either within the team or with other teams while executing all the activities needed to say, provision the environment and recording issues in the KEDB. Moreover, as the IT team attains higher DevOps maturity, we find that the IT systems and tools are brought in to first encourage more of intra-group collaboration, and then gradually bring in more of inter-group collaboration. This further has an impact on the collaborative behavior of the IT team.

Definition of Culture as relevant to Assessment

The above three criteria define and parameterize the culture, first in qualitative terms, and as we will see later, in quantitative terms. The quantitative values to be associated with the parameters would enable us to:

- Define a score that can indicate a composite cultural maturity of the IT team
- Enable us to refine the quantitative estimates on implementing process and technology changes for a given target maturity state of DevOps, based on the impact of culture
- Understand how the team's behavioral pattern based on – or the people pattern – may change in the target state vis-à-vis the current state (in case of greenfield IT cycle whereby no current state exists yet, what people aspects would represent the target state)

Note that the cultural aspect specifically implies the team culture of the concerned IT team as part of the larger organization. We have found that the IT team work culture – more than the socio-cultural or demographic aspects of individual team members – are primarily shaped by the larger organization and the specific processes and technologies that are part of the team's day-to-day work, and is sufficiently exhibited as a combination of the aforesaid propensities.

How Propensities Define People Patterns

The aforesaid three propensities have a profound influence on people structure and interactions, hence not only defining the topologies at any given point in time, but also how such topologies shift across time. Further, it is the people behavior that drives defining (and executing) the IT processes and leveraging associated technologies. Hence, we define not only topologies of IT teams, but the people architecture of the teams. Here we will take a brief look at the people architecture patterns that emerge.

Following provides the patterns that evolve based on given propensity combinations across people in a team. We would use, for convenience, the relative terms "Low" and "High" to define a given combination of propensities. In the later chapter on "Quantifying People Architecture", we would use a method to quantitatively attribute the terms from an assessment perspective.

For the accompanying figures, which we have simplified the representations to depict teams and their characteristics, we have used the following conventions:

- Team(s) under consideration exhibiting the said propensities

- Team perceived optional to exist with other team(s)

- Overlaps denote collaboration

Note that while we have primarily depicted Dev and Ops in the accompanying figures, other groups such as QA are depicted based on specific contexts only. Though not shown in all figures, they may exist as part of Dev or Ops team, or as part of the larger IT team.

Propensity Combination (Practice – Technology Usage – Collaboration)	People Pattern (with Possible Organizational Changes impacting or impacted by the pattern)
Low – Low – Low	The IT team has processes that employ basic or configurable tools requiring little or no manual intervention, and almost no collaboration; application development follows traditional manual waterfall methodology (with developers managing their own releases), and traditional Ops-centric work (typically infrastructure or L1/L2 support) working as an IT group separate from project teams that are in charge of application development. Another scenario is having a separate quality

assurance team (segregated from Dev) that uses manual testing methods.

Organizations typically **convert such Ops team (consisting of say, system administrators) to DevOps team**, however the team still **works in a silo**.

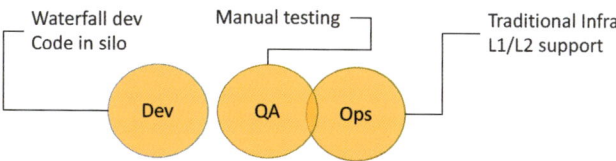

Low – Low – High	The only difference with respect to the above is that, there is a high degree of collaboration between people. This occurs due to closer intra-group interactions within Dev team and/or the Ops team – say, multiple developers working on the same code change, or release teams working closely with each other (say, managing release dependencies). Here, the Ops team primarily collaborates, either within the group and at times with other groups within the team (say, with QA for test environment provisioning, or Dev for releases). Organizations typically convert such Ops team to dedicatedly manage environments and releases, **re-branding it as the DevOps team or embedding them as part of the Dev team**, creating and managing release pipelines. 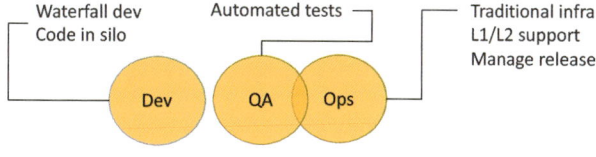

Low – High – High	The IT team does not have an automation engineering mindset, however uses technologies and tools that provide coding facilities, and people are highly collaborative. This is possible in the following scenarios: a. Dev and Ops working as a single IT team – The risk is that, Dev and Ops team **may play "protecting one's own turf" within the same team**. b. Mature Ops team practicing infrastructure-as-a-code – **Ops team with high intra-group collaboration** maintaining all environments and pipelines, but limited interaction with the Dev team. c. Mature Dev team that practices self-service using say, cloud infrastructure and/or containerized services – **Dev team thinks "no Ops needed"**, however organization may still maintain a minimal Ops team for critical support. However, note that in this case the **team's utilization of technologies invested in may be far from optimal**, given that even though there is a high technology usage propensity, it has not resulted in high automation as a practice propensity for the team. 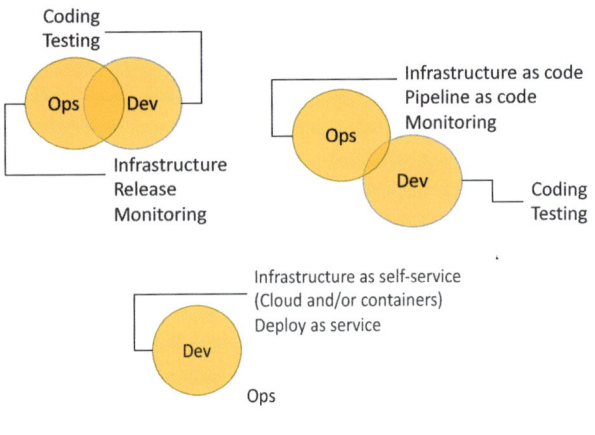

High – High – High	**Very mature DevOps team** that establishes engineering practices across the IT life cycle, with Dev and Ops working together as a single team. May gradually **achieve a "NoOps" state** requiring little or no intervention for a dedicated Ops team, thereby enabling the Ops team to explore newer paradigms such as coded pipelines using learning capabilities for self-healing resilient systems, and reliability engineering. Applications may still be large enough to enforce intra-group collaboration within Dev teams during the development cycles. Such teams later may have **reduced intra-group collaboration as application architectures mature**, thereby shifting towards the below combination (High-High-Low) for the team's propensities. 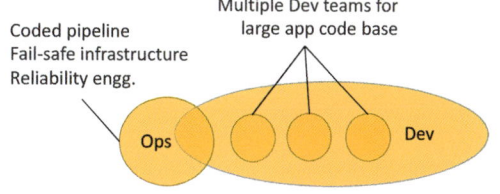
High – High – Low	The IT team executes the processes using **automation toolchains and technology architectures that provide high scalability and flexibility (through say, coding facilities), and high process resilience to failures**. For example, use of well-managed auto-scaling and self-healing container clusters (applications existing as individually manageable services) on cloud, with integrated tool-based test-and-deploy automation by the Dev team.

	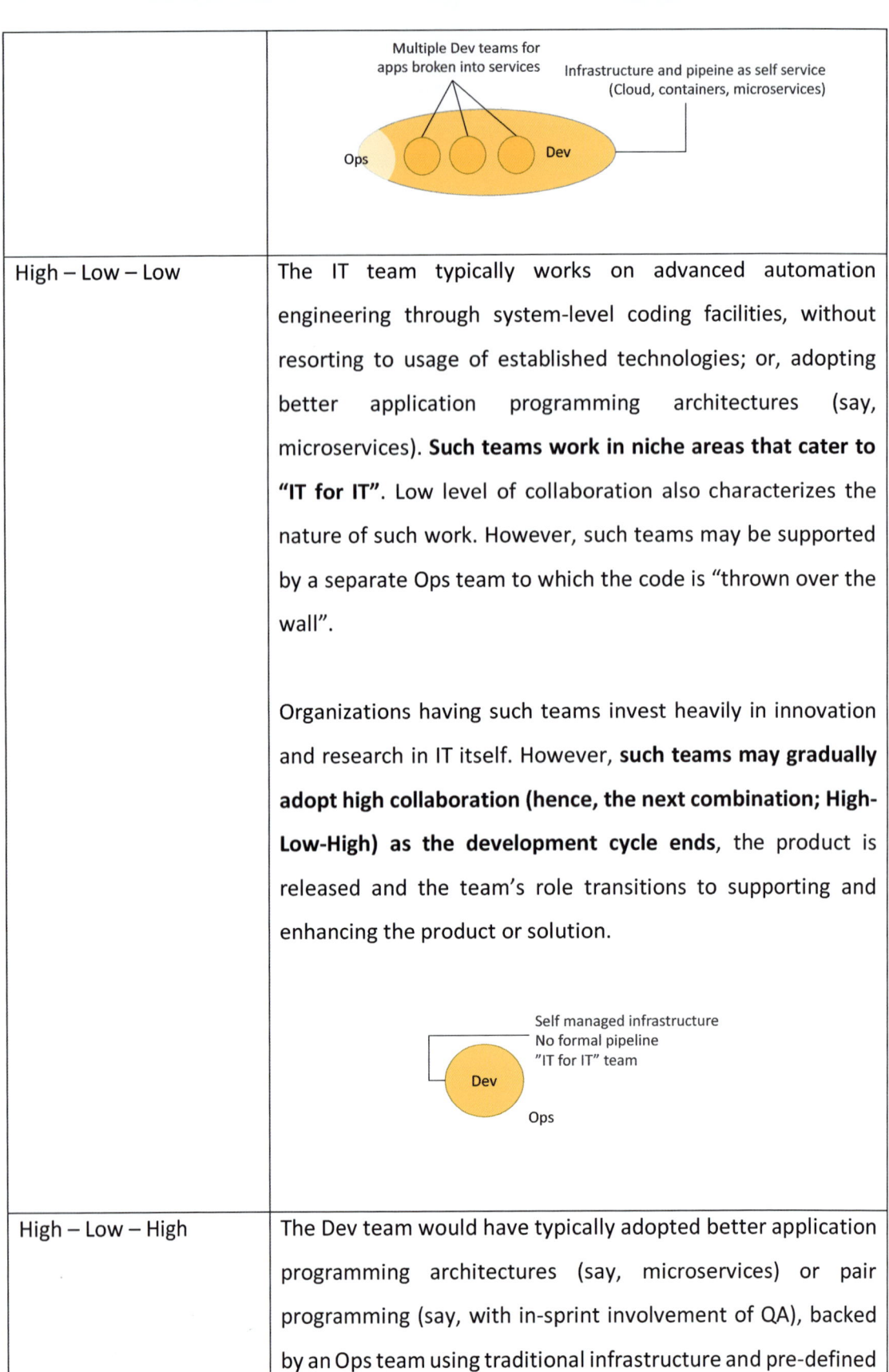
High – Low – Low	The IT team typically works on advanced automation engineering through system-level coding facilities, without resorting to usage of established technologies; or, adopting better application programming architectures (say, microservices). **Such teams work in niche areas that cater to "IT for IT"**. Low level of collaboration also characterizes the nature of such work. However, such teams may be supported by a separate Ops team to which the code is "thrown over the wall". Organizations having such teams invest heavily in innovation and research in IT itself. However, **such teams may gradually adopt high collaboration (hence, the next combination; High-Low-High) as the development cycle ends**, the product is released and the team's role transitions to supporting and enhancing the product or solution.
High – Low – High	The Dev team would have typically adopted better application programming architectures (say, microservices) or pair programming (say, with in-sprint involvement of QA), backed by an Ops team using traditional infrastructure and pre-defined

release processes (see above combination). The Dev team may not employ any formal tools, however all execution may be code or script-based.

Organizations having such IT teams may **gradually enhance the scope of the Ops team to be a "release automation team"** separately to manage multiple releases for such IT teams, or as part of the IT teams, to optimize the release processes through custom coding or scripting.

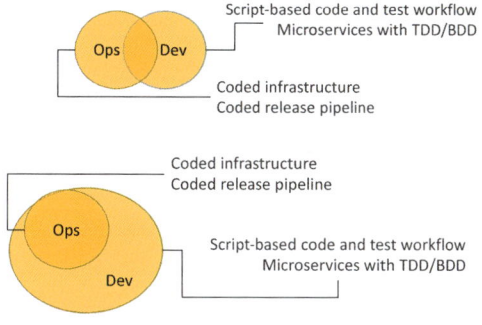

Low – High – Low	The propensity represents IT team working in silo, with very low utilization of the automation technologies and tools at its disposal. This may represent **under-utilization of organization's resources** – both in terms of manpower and technology – leading to high waste in IT processes. The organization may want to do DevOps because "everyone is doing it", and added quite a few DevOps or automation tools in the landscape, expecting that they would address the problems that DevOps seeks to resolve. Use of procured technologies may be disparate without a central pipeline or toolchain that could have reinforced a connected workflow or collaboration.

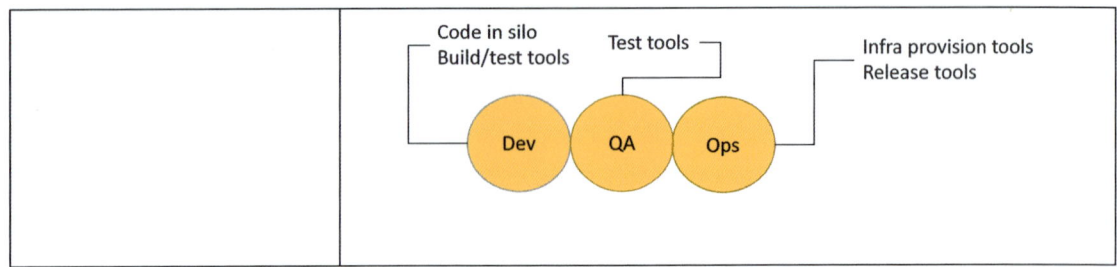

We will revisit the shift from one type of people pattern to another (based on the propensity combinations) and its importance to the organization in context as part of assessment, in the later chapter, "Quantifying People Architecture".

The Big Picture: What to Assess

From the perspective of assessment, we define an organization as an entity that executes a set of processes using a set of entities – each such process being defined by one or more objectives – that together drives the organization's vision. The processes and related IT entities may be depicted as layers as in the following figure, the topmost being Business, connected through interfacing processes and associated data flows:

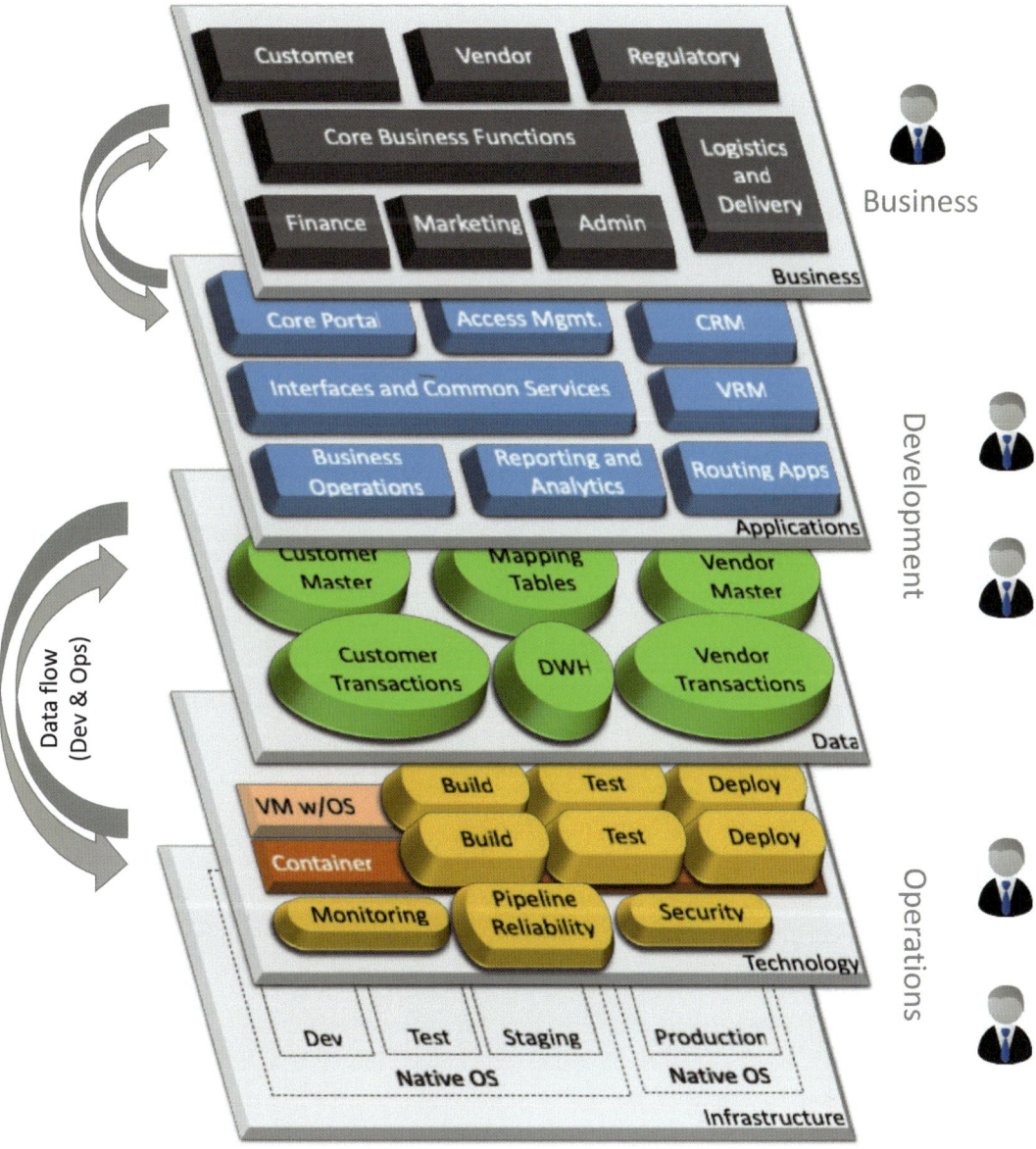

Figure 5: Organizational Layers

The processes in the business layer directs the rest of the organization in achieving its objectives that lead to the vision. From an IT standpoint, the application layer represents the corresponding business functions. The data layer supports the application layer by provision of and update to data, as necessitated by the business. The technology layer defines the technologies, software, tools, network protocols, et al, that enable the applications and data to reside, execute in given ways, and undergo changes sitting within one or more IT environments. The environments themselves – say, development environment, test environments, production environment, et al – are physically realized as part of the infrastructure layer that forms the backbone of the IT systems.

From the perspective of DevOps, the application and data layers are "Dev centric", being typically managed by the developers and quality / test personnel; whereas the technology and infrastructure layers are "Ops centric", being typically managed by operations personnel.

Before delving into any in-depth assessment of any specific system, we define the scope of assessment, given the above definition of the organization. The organization may want to undertake the assessment at any of the following layers:

a. At the business layer for a specific business function, whereby applications, data, technology and infrastructure for the given business function would come under scope of such assessment. This may typically happen if each business function works as an independent business unit who wants to undertake its own DevOps journey. The pitfall for such an assessment is that, the organization may not be able to later rationalize their underlying DevOps pipelines based on the application, data or technology stack, hence introducing cost overheads. For example, there may be three business units having applications on the Java stack, each having its own processes and technologies to manage changes to such applications; such variations would lead to redundant investments in technology and manpower to manage the underlying infrastructure across the three units.

b. At the application layer whereby assessment is undertaken for a given application stack. This may typically happen when the organization is trying to rationalize the technology backbone by application stacks. Whereas this is beneficial in terms of reducing cost overheads due to underlying technologies that can be leveraged, the target architectures for such assessment needs to be flexible enough to accommodate variations and changes to business function specific processes while designing the DevOps pipelines.

c. Assessment at the data layer comprises of looking at processes that define, design, manage and migrate data and related databases. The requirement for such assessment is typically to bring in better data quality, especially when there are frequent changes to the data, or databases need to be converted (say, to a different schema) or migrated (say, to a new database version or system). Other reasons for such assessment would be for ensuring data security, and processes including periodic data archival, data reservation, test bed creation and management, et al. Terms such as "DataOps" define the processes that focus on realizing agility in operations with respect to managing data.

Technology layer itself forms the subject of the assessment whereby the current technologies mapped to business, application or data layer (the basis of assessment as described above) are studied with respect to the current state, and analyzed to arrive at the target state. Based on the target state of technology layer, decisions on the infrastructure layer may be arrived at by infrastructure and IT architecture teams (if the impact of such changes is across enterprise IT, or primary business functions in perspective of enterprise IT).

There are two criteria based on which we decide which portfolio(s) may be taken up first for detailed assessment, and thus prioritize the assessments portfolio-wise (or platform-wise):

a. **DevOps Readiness** – How quickly and seamlessly can the portfolio or platform be on-boarded on to a successful DevOps adoption

b. **Business Criticality** – How important the portfolios are, in perspective of impact to business, in achieving higher IT maturity states in terms of DevOps

Prioritizing the Portfolio(s) for Assessment

In the case of a platform (or the enterprise IT) comprising of a number of portfolios – at the business, application or data layer – the objective here is to first narrow down the scope of assessment to one or few portfolios through prioritization. We typically see that the organization in context may want to limit the assessments to a few portfolios to kick-start (or resume) their DevOps journeys, instead of doing a "Big Bang" assessment of all portfolios and then thinking of which ones to channelize the IT investments to, for downstream adoption of DevOps. Further, an incremental approach of assessing a few (followed by adoption in those portfolios) helps to manage investments more efficiently and track the return on such investments before taking on the next few portfolios.

Composite Outcome	Culture	Process	Technology	Metrics
Frameworks and Standard Practices	🟢 Dedicated governance 🟢 Architectural alignment 🟡 IT security alignment	🟢 Work planning 🟡 Agile tracking 🔴 Centralized IT dashboard 🟢 Knowledge management	🔴 Automated regression 🟢 Issue-to-code traceability 🔴 Auto-resolve incidents	🟡 Lead time to change 🟢 Change success ratio
Operational	🟢 Ops participate In Scrums 🟡 Manage Agile backlogs 🟡 Dev-Ops cross-training	🔴 Requirements to test cases 🟢 TDD / BDD 🔴 Containerized deployment 🔴 ZDD	🟢 CI with coded pipeline 🔴 CD 🟡 Environment on-demand 🟢 Monitoring	🟡 Environment spin-up time 🟢 Incidents due to infra issues 🟢 Mean time to repair / fix

This is a simplified representation only
Actual form of DevOps readiness report is described and represented in detail in the next chapter

Figure 6: Simplified View of DevOps Readiness Report

Once the layer for the assessment has been decided upon, we use the Pre-Assessment Questionnaire – as described in the next chapter – to arrive at a state of DevOps readiness for a given business or application portfolio, a platform (consisting of a group of applications, or business functions) or at the enterprise IT level. In the case of platform or enterprise IT as the scope, we recommend that it to be first broken down into portfolios, and then individual pre-assessment done for each of the portfolios. Doing a pre-assessment for a platform or enterprise IT at one shot, that is generating a single report for all portfolios combined, can skew the outcomes towards portfolios that are perceived to best represent the overall platform or enterprise IT.

Portfolio Heatmap

Once the respective DevOps readiness is assessed individually for the portfolios, we create a heatmap that helps us identify which of them have a higher propensity to adopt DevOps; such portfolios may already have invested relevant technologies, trained and nurtured their workforce on Agile and DevOps principles, and may have defined and somewhat aligned their operating models and processes to such principles.

	Central Customer Portal	Financial Reporting	Enterprise Functions	Enterprise Data Management	Vendor Management	Regulatory Compliance	Business Governance
Technology Stack	React JS, Java/J2EE, Oracle, MS SQL Server	Angular, MVC, C#, Oracle, MS SQL Server	Angular, MVC, MS.NET, Oracle	Informatica, .NET, MS SQL Server, Oracle, OBIEE, Cognos	ASP.NET, TIBCO, Proprietary, MS SQL Server, Oracle	ASP.NET, MVC, Angular JS, JavaScript, JQuery, C#, MS SQL Server, Oracle	ASP.NET, C#, MS SQL Server, Oracle, VB.NET
Culture	1	3	1	3	1	3	3
Process	3	3	3	3	3	3	3
Tech	1	3	1	3	3	3	3
Metrics	3	4	4	3	4	4	4
DevOps Readiness Score	17.7	30.8	18.5	33.8	21.5	30.8	30.8

Weights used for dimensions are as follows: Culture – 3, Process – 2, Technology – 1, Metrics – 0.5
Score for each portfolio is computed as = (weighted average of dimension-wise score) x 10
Dimension-wise scores for each portfolio are computed as integer average of parameters (for each dimension) captured in the pre-assessment questionnaire

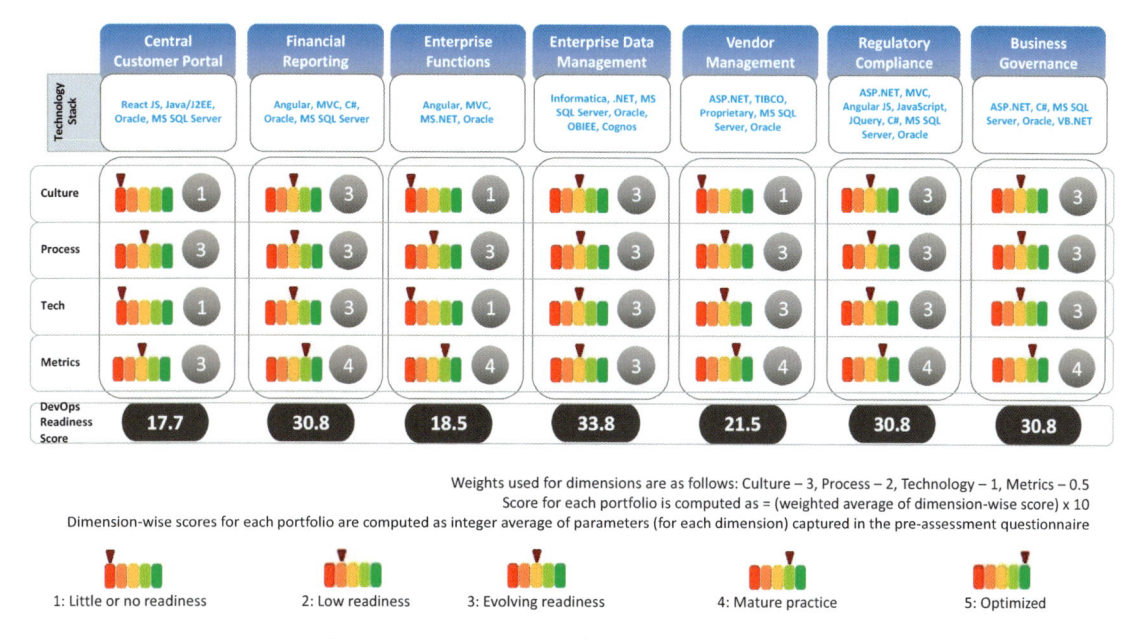

1: Little or no readiness   2: Low readiness   3: Evolving readiness   4: Mature practice   5: Optimized

Figure 7: Representative Heatmap for 7 Portfolios of an organization

To create the heatmap from each of the individual portfolio-wise pre-assessments done, first we compute average scores for each of the dimensions – culture, process, technology, metrics – and then compute a weighted average as the consolidated score of DevOps readiness for the portfolio. The weights assigned may vary with the importance given to each of the dimensions for the assessment; we typically attach higher weights to culture and process, followed by technology, and lastly metrics (given that metrics is only a derived outcome of, and only a governance mechanism to assess, the maturity of the other three dimensions).

$$Ci = \frac{\Sigma(Wj \times Aj)}{\Sigma Wj}$$

where, Ci = consolidated score for pre-assessment of ith portfolio,

Wj = weight of dimension j, Aj = average score for dimension j

(whereby, j => culture, process, technology, metrics)

As an example from the above figure, we computed the score for "Central Customer Portal (CCP)" as follows:

C|$_{CCP}$ = {(Culture weight x Culture score) + (Process weight x Process score)

+ (Technology weight x Technology score) + (Metrics weight x Metrics score)}

/ (Summation of weights) x 10

= {(3 x 1) + (2 x 3) + (1 x 1) + (0.5 x 3)} / (3 + 2 + 1 + 0.5) x 10

= 17.7

The other important input to prioritize which portfolios to consider for the assessment, is the business criticality of the portfolios in terms of complying to the objectives of the business. Criticality may simply be quantified as values that are relatively high to relatively low, for the purpose of arriving at the matrix distribution as described below.

Whereas DevOps readiness identifies the "quick win" portfolios that can be boarded on to a desired state of DevOps relatively easily in terms of people, process and technology; the business criticality says how important is a portfolio to the business in terms of addressing its pain areas that DevOps can solve. Hence, we need both of them to be considered together for each portfolio to infer which one(s) to prioritize.

Portfolio Scatter Graph

Once the aforesaid details are available, we draw a scatter graph across two dimensions; one dimension representing "Ease of DevOps adoption" (DevOps Readiness) and the other representing "Criticality for DevOps adoption" (Business Criticality).

For the aforesaid example of portfolio heatmap, let the portfolio-wise categories respectively be defined as follows:

Portfolio name	DevOps Readiness	Category (>25; Easy)	Business Criticality (1 – 5)	Category (>3; Critical)
Central Customer Portal	17.7	Difficult	5	Critical
Financial Reporting	30.8	Easy	2	Not critical
Enterprise Functions	18.5	Difficult	2	Not critical
Enterprise Data Management	33.8	Easy	4	Critical
Vendor Management	21.5	Difficult	3	Not critical
Regulatory Compliance	30.8	Easy	4	Critical
Business Governance	30.8	Easy	1	Not critical

Plotting the above as a categorized scatter graph:

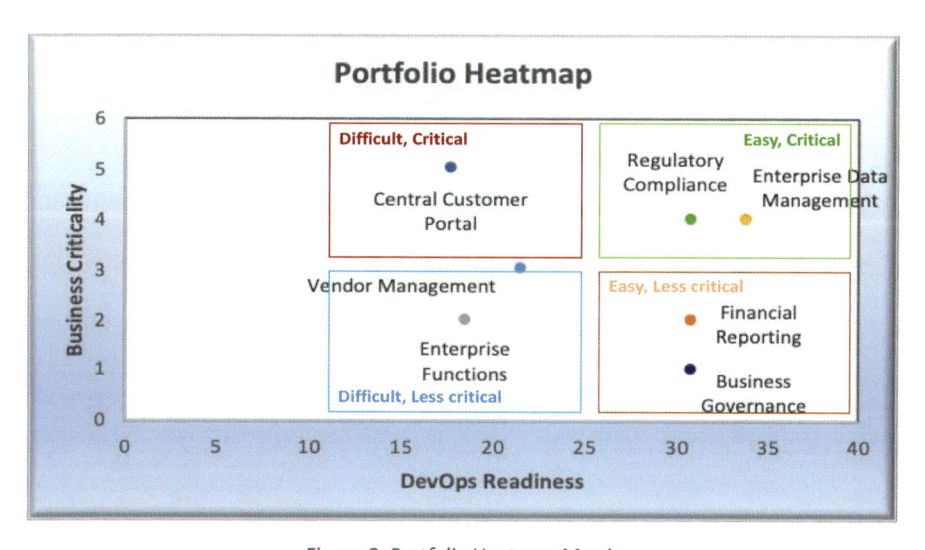

Figure 8: Portfolio Heatmap Matrix

Following is the significance of the respective combination of categories with respect to taking the decision on prioritizing the portfolio for DevOps adoption:

- **Relatively easy, Highly critical** – Prioritizing assessment (and DevOps adoption) for such portfolios typically bring in faster visibility of IT to the organization's business (and the senior management). Successful DevOps adoption for such portfolios create "quick win" business cases to attract further IT investments to drive DevOps programs. An organization taking up such portfolios first for assessment should already have a strong technology layer foundation, and should be well aware of the impact to business once the change takes place due to DevOps adoption. In the above example, Regulatory Compliance and Enterprise Data Management are the identified portfolios.

- **Relatively easy, Less critical** – Prioritizing assessment for such portfolios typically enables "testing the waters" on how well the organization as a whole may react to a DevOps-led transformation, without having a substantial impact to business. Hence, if an organization is going to embrace DevOps for the first time – albeit possibly with some adoption of Agile practices and a few successful "experiments" being done using DevOps toolchains – such portfolios may be the right candidates for the IT team to gain more confidence in adopting DevOps, before taking on more critical portfolios. In the above example, Financial Reporting and Business Governance are the identified portfolios.

- **Relatively difficult, Highly critical** – Such portfolios may be considered later, given that substantial time and effort may be required towards DevOps adoption. Further, the impact to business would be high in terms of an organizational change that DevOps may bring in; for instance, resulting in high business loss due to impact on customer experience caused by application downtime during such change. Organizations having legacy IT systems may have such portfolios which are highly critical to business but are averse to DevOps-led organizational changes to be brought in; either due to people or due to technology considerations. At times, such portfolios may not even be considered for DevOps adoption unless there is a substantial financial impact for not adopting DevOps principles. In the above example, Central Customer Portal is the identified portfolio.

- **Relatively difficult, Less critical** – Such portfolios may also be considered later, or may not be considered at all for DevOps adoption. In the above example, Vendor Management and Enterprise Functions are the identified portfolios.

Once the portfolios are decided upon and identified as above, the in-depth quantitative assessment as described in later chapters below may be applied to such portfolios as the scope of the assessment.

Following are the steps to understand what to assess:

a. **The organization may be perceived as a set of connected layers** – business, application, data, technology and infrastructure; understand where to start among the former three

b. **Identify the portfolios** in the layer

c. **Conduct pre-assessments** to assess DevOps Readiness for the portfolios

d. **Obtain portfolio-wise Business Criticality** to adopt DevOps, by talking to business

e. Based on points c and d above, **create a Portfolio Heatmap** to prioritize which portfolio(s) may be picked up for detailed assessment (and possible implementations downstream)

Warming up with a Pre-Assessment

We typically start with a pre-assessment for DevOps which helps us in "breaking the ice" with the key stakeholders of the organization we are working with, and also to gather the much needed "big picture" on the breadth and depth of the assessment. The captured data is primarily qualitative, with a few specific quantitative details, which serves two purposes:

a. Provide the overall set of objectives that the organization feels to be the reason to get on to the DevOps journey; in case the organization is already doing DevOps, the typical requirement is to understand where it stands vis-à-vis the industry with respect to its objectives, and what can be improved. These objectives, or at least some of them, may be the guidance based on which the detailed assessment would be done.
b. Provide a basis of validating certain aspects of the data that gets captured during the detailed assessment later. We will see later how this works.

However, note that while the pre-assessment captures gaps across different aspects of IT in terms of DevOps readiness, whether a given aspect's gap needs to be addressed or not, and if yes, how it needs to be exactly addressed, are not covered by the pre-assessment. This is done by the detailed assessment.

The Pre-Assessment Questionnaire

We start with a questionnaire that captures the high level details which would help us to understand the scope and assess the state of DevOps readiness of a given portfolio, platform or enterprise IT. While deciding on the structure of the questionnaire, our first objective was to design the assessment outcome that would not only span across people, process and technology, but also cut across the above three dimensions in terms of how ready is the organization in "being DevOps" and in "doing DevOps". The second objective was to arrive at a mathematical model through a simple scoring mechanism that would help us to quickly find out how each of the responses stand relative to each other and provide a composite view of the degree of readiness. Our third objective was to make the questionnaire simple enough for an organization to answer so that it can typically be completed in say thirty minutes' to an hour's time, of course subject to availability of relevant data with the concerned IT team.

Note that no high level questionnaire in a simple format can capture more than a specific view of the state of DevOps; in this case, we decided to look at DevOps readiness as the view.

Given the above objectives, we finalized four factors or dimensions for the readiness assessment:

- **People or culture**: What is the cultural readiness of the people in adopting Agile and move to higher levels of automation

- **Process**: What is the process readiness in terms of reducing waste and work-in-progress across every activity, and reduce activity dependencies to bring in parallelism towards higher IT agility

- **Technology**: What is the technology readiness in terms of addressing higher levels of automation, and possibly moving towards intelligent automation and analytics

- **Metrics**: How are metrics captured, analyzed and utilized to optimize the IT process; what is the state of readiness in terms of moving towards metrics based IT

Cutting across the above dimensions, we decided to form a matrix based assessment outcome addressing the below criteria to give a full view of DevOps:

- **Frameworks and standard practices**: What is the organization's readiness in establishing a foundational structure across the above four dimensions to do DevOps; this is "being DevOps"

- **Operational**: What is the readiness of the activities being done on-ground by the IT team that would help the organization improve the processes in achieving a given state of DevOps; this is "doing DevOps"

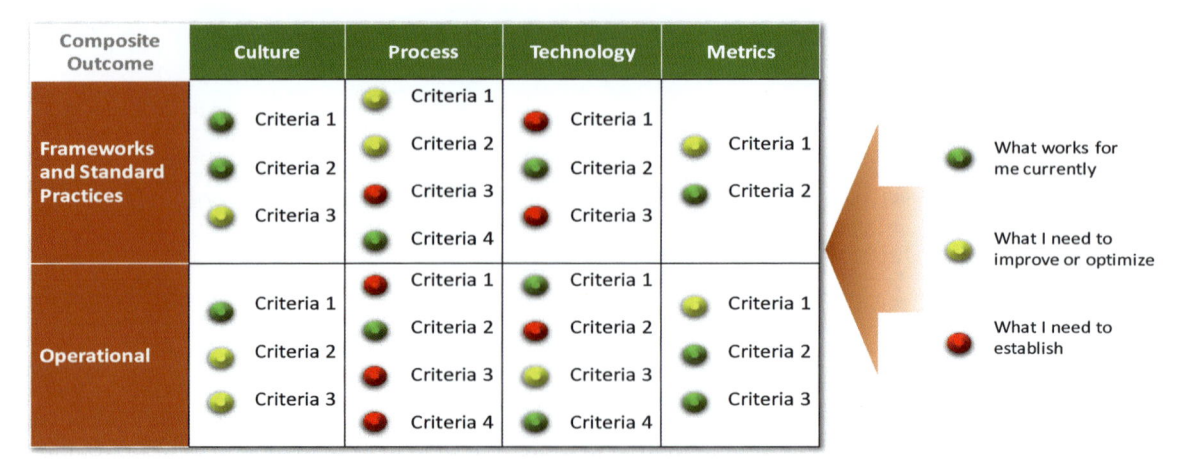

Figure 9: Representative Pre-Assessment Outcome Structure

Given the above, we designed the questionnaire by assigning the questions under five broad categories as follows:

- **Scope and direction**: This is to understand the boundaries of the IT team and processes for which the rest of the questions – under the below four categories – would be answered
- **Culture**: Questions that would address the people practice aspects of IT
- **Process**: Questions that would address the non-people practice aspects of IT in terms of types of activity that are executed
- **Technology**: Questions that would address the automation aspects of IT
- **Metrics**: Questions that capture the essential metrics of IT based on the scope

Based on the above categories, we will now cover typical questions, with associated details, that may be considered for the readiness assessment. It is advisable to restrict the number of questions to as less as possible, while being able to capture as much details as possible; of course for us, we had to design some of the questions in a way that can capture multiple related details as part of the same question. Secondly, we have used fixed values for most of the questions, where applicable, built as drop down lists in a spreadsheet software. From an implementation perspective, this approach helps us to straightaway formulate and use a simple mathematical model instead of having to deal with processing unstructured textual data prior to applying the model. Further, you have to decide on the impact and significance of each question on the overall pre-assessment for which you may want to assign a weightage on a given scale to the question.

Note that the response design and scoring method described for each of the questions below are specific approaches we followed based on our model; you may want to design it differently based on specific objectives and viewpoints of your assessment.

Scope and direction

Question 1: Does the scope cover a single application stack, multiple stacks under a given portfolio, or enterprise?
- Rationale: This is to understand the breadth of the assessment; multiple stacks may require multiple instances of the questionnaire to be filled up if required.
- Response design: Additionally, you may capture the relevant stack details; for example, application stack may be java, .NET, et al; database stack may be Oracle, DB2, et al.
- Scoring is based on difficulty level; the more the stacks we handle, the more is the difficulty level on a given scale.

Question 2: Does the scope cover SDLC, or IT service management cycle (ITSM; once code has moved to production), or both?
- Rationale: This is to understand the depth of the assessment; based on the response, some of the other questions, or part of them, may have higher relevance.
- Response design: If SDLC, you may want to find out if it applies to major or minor releases or both; if ITSM, you may want to find out if the scope is till incident management (with or without problem management in scope), or till the change management process back to SDLC.
- Scoring method: Scoring is based on difficulty level; the more we cover in depth, the higher is the difficulty level on a given scale.

Question 3: What is the locational or geographic distribution of the IT team(s) in scope?
- Rationale: This is to understand the degree of integrated (or disparate) team(s) that are operating as part of the scope.

- Response design: You may capture the location type, say onshore, offshore or captive; further, you may capture the team type operating in each such location, say only Dev (with or without QA as part of the team), only Ops (also, infrastructure team, release team, support team, or a combination of them), or both.
- Scoring method: Scoring is based on difficulty level; the more disparate the team(s) are located, that too of heterogeneous types in terms of IT services covered, the higher is the difficulty level on a given scale.

Question 4: What is the vendor involvement for the given scope?
- Rationale: This is to understand the stakeholder ecosystem. Note that the actual vendor name may not be captured as the intent is to later find out if a given team involves vendor(s) and potentially belong to different organization cultures.
- Response design: You may capture whether only the organization's employees do IT, or there is a single or multi-vendor ecosystem in place; you may further choose to segregate by types of IT services, say Dev, QA, Release, IT Security, et al.
- Scoring method: You may not attribute a score as this is informational only; the data may be used to understand vendor dynamics that may be used later during the detailed assessment as covered in subsequent chapters.

Question 5: What are the top pain areas that DevOps would try to address?
- Rationale: The pain areas would define the broad level objectives with respect to what the detailed assessment would strive to address.
- Response design: You may capture pain areas segregated by the following parameters: IT cycle time, Availability, Maintainability, Scalability, Reliability, IT visibility and IT security.
  - With respect to IT cycle time, you may want to find out if business is aligned to, or at least adjusts to the current release frequency and/or release cycle time achieved by IT, or expects faster time to market possibly leading to escalations depending on the criticality of the application(s) being production deployed.
  - On availability, pain areas may be in pre-production due to environment provisioning delays, or in production due to environment downtime caused by infrastructure issues.

- On maintainability, you may want to find out if issues with maintainability is due to code (for instance, due to high technical debt of code leading to frequent production issues; monolithic code base; or, fragmented code incorporating multiple disparate technical interfaces), or due to environment and related configurations (for instance, due to unavailability of suitable data during test data refresh; or, virtual machine configuration not aligned to production).
- On scalability, issues may be due to code (say, incorporating architecture that cannot handle large volumes of data during peak loads), infrastructure (say, unable to support multiple release cycles if business demands rise) or manpower (say, to quickly support a spurt in IT process automation related projects undertaken by the organization).
- With respect to reliability, pain areas may include inconsistent code behavior due to varying input data loads or data value ranges, varying response times due to environment issues after every release, or production issues due to data integrity problems.
- On IT visibility, fragmented or no centralized IT dashboards to provide visibility across IT operations from say, release through incident management, resulting in substantial governance and reporting effort; or, no centralized tracking of activities across projects or sprints.
- With respect to IT security, pain areas may be due to vulnerability issues caused by code, environment or database.

o Scoring method: Scoring is based on difficulty level; more the aforesaid parameters where pain areas are observed, and higher the criticality of the pain areas, higher would be the difficulty level in addressing them to achieve a given state of DevOps. Note that you may arrive at a composite score based on parameters responded to, to give an overall difficulty score.

Culture

Question 1: Is there a DevOps champion or group to strategize, govern and guide execution of DevOps initiatives?

- Rationale: This is to understand the level of focus of the organization to drive DevOps; however, you may also want to find out that such an individual or group does not practice "DevOps in a silo" that would defeat the very purpose, rather propagate the practices to be adopted by IT teams in context.
- Response design: You may further want to find out, in case such an individual or group has been identified (and operating), the primary role of the individual or group; this is important as for example, if someone from the Dev team acts as a DevOps champion or the Dev team as a whole is driving DevOps, there is a higher possibility of initiating the DevOps journey from the Dev team itself. This may lead to say, a Dev-driven-DevOps view of how DevOps gets done.
- Scoring method: Scoring is based on maturity level; if such an individual or group exists, maturity is medium to high. Moreover, based on the role, Ops-driven-DevOps would have a higher maturity than Dev – typically given that achieving Agile Ops is the essence of DevOps whereas most organizations end up doing only Agile Dev – unless of course the organization has already achieved a "NoOps" state through high Ops automation, hence and is striving to achieve "NoDev", in which case the situation is reversed.

Question 2: Is Agile (if adopted) practiced by Dev along with QA team, as a single team? Do they together participate in Scrums? Does Ops also participate in Agile Scrums?
- Rationale: This is to understand the extent of Agile adoption, if present. Further, working as a single team towards say, a project or product delivery would enable executing multiple IT activity types in a single Sprint, thereby enhancing IT agility.
- Response design: It is a simple Yes/Partially/No response. Additionally, based on if Agile is adopted, the question can further explore what type of Agile is practiced; say, collocated or distributed. Further, if Ops participates, you may want to find out which team – infrastructure, release, application support – participates.
- Scoring method: Scoring is based on maturity level; Agile adoption, to any given degree, would entail a higher score on maturity that non-Agile. An Ops participation in Agile would entail a still higher maturity score. Further, you may segregate the score based on degree or type of Agile adoption.

Question 3: If Agile is adopted, how are activities tracked?

- Rationale: This is to understand the mode of tracking activities; this gives visibility to the seriousness of Agile as a practice, and tool based integration (provided, a tool is leveraged) that may be made possible for determining team performance through automated dashboard on people metrics.
- Response design: The response may be say, Scrum board for project Sprints and/or Kanban for continuous flow of work. More informal modes, say using a spreadsheet or email based tracking may also be practiced.
- Scoring method: Scoring is based on maturity level; more formalized the tracking is – possibly with suitable tool based automation – higher the maturity score.

Question 4: Is there an established Architecture Review Board (ARB)?
- Rationale: This is to understand if there is a centralized ARB that defines the enterprise architecture, maintains its conformity to organization's policies and DevOps as a philosophy, and helps IT teams map their IT landscape to the architecture at the ground level.
- Response design: It is a simple Yes/Partially/No response. Additionally, you may want to capture whether the ARB only defines the enterprise architecture and communicates it to the downstream IT teams, or also takes ownership to map it to individual projects, either taking a sample of such projects based on a given criteria or across all projects.
- Scoring method: Scoring is based on maturity level; assuming that the ARB exists in the organization, more the involvement of the ARB in complying projects (or, systems) to the defined enterprise architecture, higher is the maturity score.

Question 5: Is there an established IT security group that manages security policies and implementations?
- Rationale: This is to understand if there is a centralized IT security group to bring in focus on security as an embedded aspect of DevOps. The organization, in that case, may have readiness to implement automation around DevSecOps as a practice, or revisiting securityOps as a service for supporting fast changes to IT security implementations.
- Response design: It is a simple Yes/Partially/No response. Additionally, you may want to capture whether the group only defines the policies and communicates it to the

downstream IT teams, or also takes ownership to map the policies to individual projects in terms of say, security compliance and testing.

- Scoring method: Scoring is based on maturity level; assuming that the group exists in the organization, more the involvement of the group in addressing security needs of projects (or, systems) in compliance to the defined security policies, higher is the maturity score.

Question 6: Are team members working on an IT project, either say in development or application support, cross trained across multiple roles – Dev, QA and Ops functions? Better still, are they specifically trained in Agile and/or on DevOps?

- Rationale: This is to understand the people readiness in terms of competencies related to multiple IT roles; this would enable teams to function effectively as a single team and bring in substantial parallelism in executing role specific tasks, hence higher agility.
- Response design: With respect to cross-role competencies, you may want to capture which areas among Dev, QA and Ops functions are covered. Further, with respect to Agile and DevOps, you may want to capture what methods are being covered; for example, Agile Scrum and managing backlogs, CI, CD, implementing CI and/or CD on cloud, infrastructure as code, pipeline as code, et al.
- Scoring method: Scoring is based on maturity level; the wider the training coverage, both across roles and across Agile and DevOps, the higher is the maturity score for the IT team in context.

Question 7: Does the IT team dynamically self-organize – say, performing different roles across Dev and QA, and Ops – to adjust to varying workloads and changing requirements?

- Rationale: This is to understand the readiness in actually "doing DevOps" whereby we assess if team members are adequately cross-trained across roles, and are hence have put such training into actual practice.
- Response design: It is a simple Yes/Partially/No response. Additionally, you may want to find out if dynamic team organization is facilitated by someone such as a project lead or Scrum Master, in which case new people joining the team get time to accustom themselves to such cultural aspects, in case they are not yet exposed to earlier.

- Scoring method: Scoring is based on maturity level; the wider the role-wise coverage practiced typically in the same Sprint (assuming Agile way of working), the higher the score.

Process

Question 1: Is there a process handbook or reference document that outlines how IT projects need to be done?
- Rationale: This is to understand the focus of the organization in defining their IT processes in terms of adopting Agile and achieving higher IT agility through DevOps. Such document serves as an enterprise-wise guideline and reference that IT team need to adhere to while executing respective projects.
- Response design: You may want to find out if such document includes Agile principles and practices – that too only for Agile Dev, or also for Agile Ops – and process guidelines for establishing and supporting DevOps-led automation.
- Scoring method: Scoring is based on maturity level; inclusion of Agile practices and further on DevOps, would entail higher scores on maturity in defining such process guidelines.

Question 2: What are the technology-led paradigms practiced by the organization, as aligned to DevOps practices?
- Rationale: This is to understand what are the actual DevOps practices on-ground that typically involves automation, in the organization.
- Response design: The response may be solicited as a list of practices including but not limited to say, the following – a. Automated requirements to Agile stories translation, b. Model driven auto-generated code development, c. Test driven development (TDD) or Behavior driven development (BDD), d. Blue-green zone based zero downtime deployment on immutable infrastructure, e. Continuous monitoring based incident triggers, f. Automated incident resolution for infrastructure issues, et al. You may also want to go one step ahead and capture the degree of adoption of each practice. However, note that you need to appropriately quantify each as a definite score; hence, too many values may complicate the underlying model for evaluation.

- Scoring method: Scoring is based on maturity level; the more the practices implemented on-ground, the higher the maturity score.

Question 3: What are the process management tools used by the organization, which potentially help in establishing integrated DevOps practices?

- Rationale: This is to understand what are the tools used that support establishing Agile and/or DevOps practices. This provides a view to how ready the organization is, and is thinking of process integration and people collaboration, in terms of pursuing DevOps.
- Response design: The response may be solicited as a list of tools including but not limited to say, catering to the following areas – a. Collaborate and track activities; say, Agile stories, b. Knowledge management or document repository, c. Dashboard for IT releases through incident management, d. Tracking of incidents and service requests, et al. You may also want to further capture the degree of adoption and integration for each tool. However, note that too many values may complicate the underlying evaluation model.
- Scoring method: Scoring is based on maturity level; the more the process tools implemented on-ground, and possibly the more they integrate as part of the tool ecosystem, the higher the maturity score.

Question 4: How are IT costs, possibly including return on investments (ROI) tracked as part of the IT life cycle?

- Rationale: This is to understand the focus on cost optimization vis-à-vis IT, which typically is one of the primary drivers for organizational decision making on business-to-IT.
- Response design: You may want to find out if costs are tracked at all; if yes, then whether such analysis and reporting is done as a set of static data points to business, or they provide what-if analytics for decision making, or better still, they not only provide analytics but also feedback on IT through automated change workflows.
- Scoring method: Scoring is based on maturity level; the more the rigor in tracking costs and extracting analytics and hence, data-led decision making, the higher is the maturity score.

Technology

Question 1: What are the technologies/ tools used in the organization, as aligned to DevOps-led automation?

- Rationale: This is to understand what are the current investments done by the organization in terms of DevOps-led automation; this provides, a. how well the organization is ready to adopt DevOps from a technology perspective, b. what are the tools that may be kept in mind in case the to-be technology architecture for DevOps need to be arrived at and proposed, and c. gauge what would be the typical usage propensity of the IT team in terms of tools, hence providing useful insights to the aspect of culture.
- Response design: You may want to find out the technology/ tool names segregated by automation paradigms such as, a. CI, b. CD, c. Managing source code and binaries, d. TDD/ BDD, e. Environment provisioning, f. Automated incident resolution, et al.
- Scoring method: Scoring is based on maturity level; the more the number of tools or toolchains leveraged across the aforesaid paradigms, the higher is the probable readiness of the organization to align to DevOps practices, and hence higher the score.

Question 2: What are the technologies/ tools being planned for usage or procurement in the organization, as aligned to DevOps-led automation?

- Rationale: This is to understand what is the focus of the organization with respect to future investments or planning for technology in terms of DevOps-led automation; this provides views on, a. how the organization perceives DevOps-led automation as, and b. what are the tools that may be kept in mind in case the to-be technology architecture for DevOps need to be arrived at and proposed.
- Response design: You may want to find out the technology/ tool names segregated by automation paradigms such as, a. CI, b. CD, c. Managing source code and binaries, d. TDD/ BDD, e. Environment provisioning, f. Automated incident resolution, et al.
- Scoring method: You may not attribute a score as this is informational only; the data may be used to understand the organization's planned view of technology architecture for DevOps.

Question 3: In what type of environment(s) are applications deployed – both pre-production and production – and technically how?

- Rationale: This is to understand what is the focus of the organization with respect to future investments or planning for technology in terms of DevOps-led automation; this provides views on, a. how the organization perceives DevOps-led automation as, and b. what are the tools that may be kept in mind in case the to-be technology architecture for DevOps need to be arrived at and proposed.
- Response design: You may want to find out the technology/ tool names segregated by automation paradigms such as, a. CI, b. CD, c. Managing source code and binaries, d. TDD/ BDD, e. Environment provisioning, f. Automated incident resolution, et al.
- Scoring method: You may not attribute a score as this is informational only; the data may be used to understand the organization's planned view of technology architecture for DevOps.

Metrics

For all the questions that you may ask on metrics, the rationale is to find out, (a) how aligned is the organization's business expectations and IT performance, and (b) whether the organization has a focus on following metrics driven IT process as a practice.

Question 1: What are the key metrics (with respective values) that the organization measures?
- Response design: You may want to find out the following metrics as the key ones:
  - From IT cycle time perspective, (a) frequency of releases vis-à-vis what the business expects, (b) lead time to incorporate a change starting from requirements coming in and the IT change, either in application or infrastructure, being pushed to production
  - From quality perspective for the application or infrastructure in context of change, (a) change success ratio in production versus pre-production, (b) mean-time-to-repair [MTTR] and mean-time-between-failures [MTBF] in production
  - From reliability perspective, the above quality metrics applied to the DevOps-led automation infrastructure
- Scoring method: Scoring is based on maturity level; the better the metrics look from an IT cycle time, and quality and reliability characteristics, the higher the respective scores. "Better looking" metrics with respect to the above ones here necessarily imply on a

relative scale, (a) higher release frequency, (b) shorter lead time to change, (c) higher change success ratio, (d) shorter MTTR, and (e) longer MTBF.

Question 2: If the given scope covers SDLC, what are the top SDLC metrics (with their respective values)?

- Response design: You may solicit the response asking what are the metrics and what are their respective values. However, we have seen that most organizations either may not be aware of the right metrics from a DevOps perspective, or may not want to share relevant metrics. Either way, we define the following as top five SDLC metrics, with option for the organization to add more to this list:
  - Percentage of tests automated – We have observed that organizations typically quote values with respect to functional regression test automation; figures on non-functional tests typically are not responded with
  - Ratio of functional defects versus non-functional defects
  - Percentage of build failures with respect to total builds post code commits – We have observed that since it shows the propensity of developers to code "first time right", actual figures may not be shared by respective IT teams; moreover, it may also be difficult to measure this in case the code build process is not automated
  - Average cycle time to prepare or refresh test data for test beds
  - Average cycle time to provision a pre-production environment
- Scoring method: Scoring is based on maturity level; the better the metrics look, the higher the respective scores. Defining "better looking" metrics in this context would be relative; on a general notion, higher the extent of automation, lower the number of defects and quality issues, and shorter the cycle times, better looking are the respective metrics. After attributing individual scores to each of the metrics, you may want to define a composite score using suitable weights for each to arrive at the SDLC metrics readiness.

Question 3: If the given scope covers ITSM, what are the top ITSM metrics (with their respective values)?

- Response design: You may solicit the response asking what are the metrics and what are their respective values. However as with the above question on SDLC metrics, we have seen that most organizations either may not be aware of the right metrics from a DevOps perspective, or may not want to share relevant metrics. Either way, we define the following as top ITSM metrics, with option for the organization to add more to this list:

- Percentage SLA (Service Level Agreement) compliance for production incidents
- Break-up of incidents with respect to, (a) infrastructure issues, (b) application code, or data or database related issues, and (c) issues due to other factors such as IT security, data privacy, regulatory compliance, et al
- Percentage incidents auto-resolved using software incorporating rule engine based or intelligent algorithms

o Scoring method: Scoring is based on maturity level; the better the metrics look, the higher the respective scores. Defining "better looking" metrics in this context would be relative; on a general notion, higher the extent of automation, lower and less frequent the number of failures and quality issues, and shorter the cycle times, better looking are the respective metrics. After attributing individual scores to each of the metrics, you may want to define a composite score using suitable weights for each to arrive at the ITSM metrics readiness.

Question 4: What are the top reliability metrics (with their respective values), both as applied to application or infrastructure subject to a given change, or the DevOps-led automation infrastructure (if such already exists) itself?

o Response design: You may solicit the response asking what are the metrics and what are their respective values. However as with the above questions, we have seen that most organizations either may not be aware of the right metrics from a DevOps perspective, or may not want to share relevant metrics. Either way, we define the following as top reliability metrics, with option for the organization to add more to this list:

- For the application or infrastructure that is undergoing or has undergone change, reliability metrics would typically be (a) performance in terms of I/O cycle times, number of database queries, et al, under varying loads, and (b) impact of production failure on business in terms of cost, time to market, customer experience index, et al, (c) percentage traceability of production issues to code or configurations
- For the DevOps-led automation infrastructure itself, reliability metrics would typically be (a) tool or toolchain availability across SDLC or ITSM pipeline, (b) performance of

the tool or toolchain under varying loads, for example, performance of the CI server based on number of builds across multiple developer nodes, and (c) impact of tool or toolchain failure on time to market

o Scoring method: Scoring is based on maturity level; the better the metrics look, the higher the respective scores. Defining "better looking" metrics in this context would be relative; on a general notion, higher the performance and availability of systems, shorter the cycle times, and lower the cost impact on business, better looking are the respective metrics. After attributing individual scores to each of the metrics, you may want to define a composite score using suitable weights for each to arrive at the reliability metrics readiness.

Pre-Assessment Questions Ready Reckoner
Scope and Direction
1. Does the scope cover a single application stack, multiple stacks under a given portfolio, or enterprise?
2. Does the scope cover SDLC, or IT service management cycle (ITSM; once code has moved to production), or both?
3. What is the locational or geographic distribution of the IT team(s) in scope?
4. What is the vendor involvement for the given scope?
5. What are the top pain areas that DevOps would try to address?
Culture
1. Is there a DevOps champion or group to strategize, govern and guide execution of DevOps initiatives?
2. Is Agile (if adopted) practiced by Dev along with QA team, as a single team? Do they together participate in Scrums? Does Ops also participate in Agile Scrums?
3. If Agile is adopted, how are activities tracked?
4. Is there an established Architecture Review Board (ARB)?

5.	Is there an established IT security group that manages security policies and implementations?
6.	Are team members working on an IT project, either say in development or application support, cross trained across multiple roles – Dev, QA and Ops functions? Better still, are they specifically trained in Agile and/or on DevOps?
7.	Does the IT team dynamically self-organize – say, performing different roles across Dev and QA, and Ops – to adjust to varying workloads and changing requirements?

Process

1.	Is there a process handbook or reference document that outlines how IT projects need to be done?
2.	What are the technology-led paradigms practiced by the organization, as aligned to DevOps practices?
3.	What are the process management tools used by the organization, which potentially help in establishing integrated DevOps practices?
4.	How are IT costs, possibly including return on investments (ROI) tracked as part of the IT life cycle?

Technology

1.	What are the technologies/ tools used in the organization, as aligned to DevOps-led automation?
2.	What are the technologies/ tools being planned for usage or procurement in the organization, as aligned to DevOps-led automation?
3.	In what type of environment(s) are applications deployed – both pre-production and production – and technically how?

Metrics

1.	What are the key metrics (with respective values) that the organization measures?

2.	If the given scope covers SDLC, what are the top SDLC metrics (with their respective values)?
3.	If the given scope covers ITSM, what are the top ITSM metrics (with their respective values)?
4.	What are the top reliability metrics (with their respective values), both as applied to application or infrastructure subject to a given change, or the DevOps-led automation infrastructure (if exists) itself?

The Readiness Scoring Model

With respect to the above section, the questions can be categorized as following for the purpose of scoring. Note that questions for which the scoring method is typically informational may not contribute to the scoring model, however may provide useful insights to the IT process that can be say, used during the detailed assessment or be used to understand constraints to the current process.

Questions requiring only one response (for example, question 2 under "Scope and direction" given above) – Each response maps to a specific score on a given scale, either on difficulty level or on maturity level. The question itself would typically carry a weightage, signifying its relevance in pre-assessment, with respect to the entire questionnaire.

$$Si = Wi \times Ri$$

where, Si = Score for the question, Wi = Weight, Ri = Rating based on selected response

You may want to compute percentage score (Sp) to benchmark against the maximum score possible (assuming that the maximum score corresponds to highest readiness):

$$Sp = \frac{Si}{Wi \times Rmax}$$

where, Rmax = Maximum rating (for response indicating highest readiness)

Questions requiring multiple responses across multiple heads (for example, question 1 under "Technology" given above) – Some of these questions may further be broken down into further questions to preserve homogeneity of the response type. Assuming that each such question, after such necessary adjustments, has a set of responses that are homogeneous in nature in terms of the scoring scale, each response may have a specific score on the scale and a given weightage with respect to the overall question. Further, the question itself would have a weightage with respect to the entire questionnaire.

$$Si = Wi \times \Sigma Ri$$

where, Si = Score, Wi = Weight, Ri = Rating for each response

$$Sp = \frac{Si}{Wi \times \Sigma Rmax}$$

where, Rmax = Maximum rating (for each response indicating highest readiness)

Questions requiring two (or multiple) level of dependent responses (for example, question 2 under "Culture" given above) – You need to decide whether the scoring would be attributed to the first level response, or second (or subsequent) level response; given what level of detail you want to consider for scoring. Here, the second level response would be dependent on what is selected as the first level response, third level response (if applicable) is dependent on second level response, and so on. We typically observe that sticking to the first, or at most the second level response is optimal enough for pre-assessment. Further the levels you consider for scoring, chances of the responses becoming quite heterogeneous with respect to the scale increases, thereby making it difficult to rationalize the responses over a single scale suitable for comparative scoring.

$$Si = Wi \times Ri$$

where, Si = Score, Wi = Weight, Ri = Rating based on selected response at the given level

$$Sp = \frac{Si}{Wi \times Rmax}$$

where, Rmax = Maximum rating (for response indicating highest readiness at given level)

A Note on Assigning Weights

Weights may be assigned to questions for up to two levels:

Question with one answer to be evaluated would have one weight assigned based on the significance of the question on the overall pre-assessment.

- For example, based on organization prerogatives, you may decide to assign questions on metrics such as release frequency or release cycle time to have a relatively higher weightage – say 5 in scale of 1 to 5 – in case the organization's end objective is reducing IT cycle time. If the organization's primary objective is on improving software quality, the question on change success ratio would have higher weightage. If the organization needs to ensure strong application security while changes are deployed, you may assign a higher weightage for the question on maturity of the IT security group.

Question with multiple answers to be evaluated would have individual weights assigned to each answer, and an overall weight for the question itself towards its significance on overall pre-assessment.

- For example, for the question on top pain areas, if the organization has a focus on improving application or infrastructure availability, you may assign somewhat higher weights, say 5 in a scale of 1 to 5, for individual responses pertaining to availability, scalability and reliability; as these factors would directly impact the given focus area. Others are still important, however can be assigned slightly lower weights, say 3 or 4 on the same scale. Given that the question on top pain areas itself is very important from overall evaluation perspective, you may assign a higher weight, say 5, to the question.

Generating the Pre-Assessment Report

Based on the aforesaid score – the percentage score being typically considered as the scoring gets rationalized across questions with heterogeneous response types – the report can be generated. We have used color coded shapes to indicate readiness as follows:

Green – Substantial readiness; well established or practiced

Yellow – Partial readiness; need to improve and may need focus

Red – Little or no readiness; need to improve substantially, need focus

As an example, we generated the following report for an organization we worked with:

Dimension	Culture	Process	Technology	Metrics
Frameworks and standard practices	Dedicated governance 🟢	Planning readiness 🟢	Regression tests automated 🟢	Release frequency — 20%
	Architecture alignment 🟢	Agile tracking 🟢	Auto-resolved incidents 🔴	Release cycle time to production — 20%
	IT security alignment 🟡	Incident and service request tracking 🟢	Production issue to requirements traceability 🟡	Change success in production — 100%
		Knowledge management 🟢		Pre-prod NFR defects 🟡
		Centralized IT dashboard 🔴		Cycle time for test data preparation 🔴
		Continuous IT cost analysis 🔴		Build success rate 🟡
Operational	Agile-Dev practice 🟢	Automated requirements translation 🔴	Continuous integration 🟢	Environment provisioning cycle time 🟢
	Ops participation for Agile-Ops 🟡	Dynamic code quality 🟢	Continuous deployment 🟢	Production SLA compliance 🟢
	Managing Agile backlogs 🟢	Assisted / optimized coding 🔴	Source code repository 🟢	Incidents due to infrastructure issues 🔴
	Self organizing IT team 🟡	In-sprint automation with TDD/BDD 🟡	Dashboard 🔴	Incidents due to code/DB issues 🔴
	Dev-QA-Ops cross competency 🟢	Zero downtime deploy 🟢	Environment provisioning 🟢	Incidents due to other issues (security, et al) 🔴
	Agile/DevOps competency 🟡	Containerization 🟢	Continuous monitoring 🟢	App failure downtime impact 🔴
		Automated incident resolution 🟢	Auto-resolve incidents 🔴	Infrastructure failure downtime impact 🟡
		Automated problem to change 🟢		Time-to-repair in production incl. code fix 🟢
		Automated portfolio analysis to change 🟢		Mean-time-between production failures 🔴
		AI / bot-driven orchestration 🟢		

Figure 10: Sample Pre-Assessment Report

We went with the above format for the report. For us, it has worked quite well across organizations that we assessed, however we recommend you to modify it in a way that better depicts the prerogatives of the organization in doing DevOps.

You may also want to compute average scores for each of the dimensions – culture, process, technology and metrics – as an additional step for a portfolio-wise assessment as mentioned in the previous chapter. For doing this for each of the dimensions, we assigned the following values based on color codes for each of the parameters for the given dimension:

Green – 3   Yellow – 2   Red – 1

We then computed the simple average (you may further assign suitable weights based on the significance of the parameters in your organization) of the parameters to arrive at a value between 1 and 3. We further rounded off the figure thus obtained, as the score for the dimension; thereby ensuring that the value would only be 1 (substantial readiness for the dimension), 2 (partial readiness) or 3 (little or no readiness).

$$Sd = \frac{\Sigma_n Sp}{\Sigma n}$$

where, Sd = score for the given dimension,
(whereby, d => culture, process, technology, metrics);
Sp = score (1, 2 or 3) based on color code for a given parameter p;
n = number of parameters for the dimension d

The dimension-wise averages so obtained may be further used to compute the overall DevOps Readiness score as has been already explained in the previous chapter.

Reading the Pre-Assessment Report

There are two ways to read and interpret the pre-assessment report:

A. Focusing section-wise to drive IT improvements

Here, we identify the broader level readiness for a given section of the report, and interpret the overall readiness of the section in terms of specific aspects. This would help in getting the "big picture" view of the given section, so that the organization can choose to prioritize focus on specific aspects within it. Here, a section would imply a combination of a dimension (culture, process, technology, or metrics) and a criterion (frameworks and standard practices, or operational). For example, in the figure below, the section ["Process" vis-à-vis "Frameworks and Standard Practices"] shows somewhat good or moderate DevOps readiness in laying out the foundational policies and standards for processes; for example, planning and tracking policies of Agile programs are established, however there is no single IT dashboard to ensure how programs are moving from conceptualization till rollout. However, the section ["Process" vis-à-vis "Operational"] shows that the DevOps readiness of processes as practiced on-ground is low; for example, in-sprint automation using say TDD/ BDD, zero downtime deployment, and automated incident resolution or change management workflows are either not practiced or partially done without the right rigor. Hence, the organization may want to prioritize such specific aspects in the latter section to improve its state of IT, and make necessary investments in those areas.

Such an interpretation is typically helpful for organizations who have already embarked on their DevOps journey, understand how each of the dimensions impact each other, and want to pin point specific areas that need focus and investments. Hence, this approach is primarily used by stakeholders who want to take it to their higher management in an organization to garner specific funding for IT based on the progress made and improvements envisaged. In this case, the stakeholders already have an understanding of, or have an affinity to, the section for which such focus is envisaged. For example, an application owner may want to garner investments for improvements in practices from a technology perspective through tool or toolchain upgrades or purchases to achieve higher levels of automation, whereas a vendor manager responsible for specific Agile projects may look at more investments to build people competencies in terms of DevOps-led cultural practices. Again, a release manager may want to have more investments to establish policies and frameworks for application release processes prior to investing in technology.

Dimension	Culture	Process	Technology	Metrics	
Frameworks and standard practices	Dedicated governance	Planning readiness	Regression tests automated	Release frequency	20%
	Architecture alignment	Agile tracking	Auto-resolved incidents	Release cycle time to production	20%
	IT security alignment	Incident and service request tracking	Production issue to requirements traceability	Change success in production	100%
		Knowledge management		Pre-prod NFR defects	
		Centralized IT dashboard		Cycle time for test data preparation	
		Continuous IT cost analysis		Build success rate	
Operational	Agile-Dev practice	Automated requirements translation	Continuous integration	Environment provisioning cycle time	
	Ops participation for Agile-Ops	Dynamic code quality	Continuous deployment	Production SLA compliance	
	Managing Agile backlogs	Assisted / optimized coding	Source code repository	Incidents due to infrastructure issues	
	Self organizing IT team	In-sprint automation with TDD/BDD	Dashboard	Incidents due to code/DB issues	
	Dev-QA-Ops cross competency	Zero downtime deploy	Environment provisioning	Incidents due to other issues (security, et al)	
	Agile/DevOps competency	Containerization	Continuous monitoring	App failure downtime impact	
		Automated incident resolution	Auto-resolve incidents	Infrastructure failure downtime impact	
		Automated problem to change		Time-to-repair in production incl. code fix	
		Automated portfolio analysis to change		Mean-time-between production failures	
		AI / bot driven orchestration			

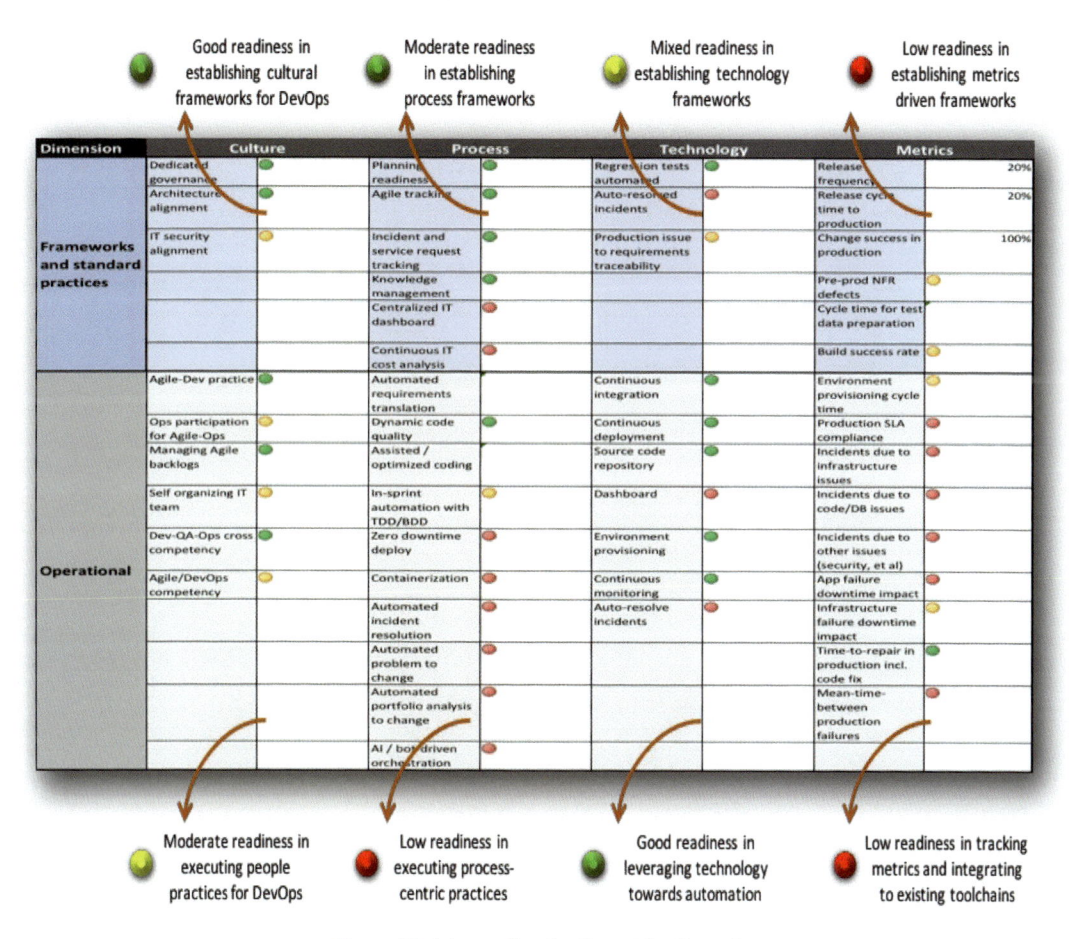

Top annotations:
- Good readiness in establishing cultural frameworks for DevOps
- Moderate readiness in establishing process frameworks
- Mixed readiness in establishing technology frameworks
- Low readiness in establishing metrics driven frameworks

Bottom annotations:
- Moderate readiness in executing people practices for DevOps
- Low readiness in executing process-centric practices
- Good readiness in leveraging technology towards automation
- Low readiness in tracking metrics and integrating to existing toolchains

Figure 11: Interpreting the Report Section-wise

B. Starting with one section and connecting the dots

In this approach, a specific parameter from the report corresponding to the objective of DevOps is being considered by the given organization as the starting point.

One of the most common examples that we have observed is to **increase the release frequency – alternatively reduce release cycle time** for application rollout – to align to business expectations on time to market for say a given set of application features. Hence, in such a case the starting point would be to consider either "Release frequency" or "Release cycle time to production" (refer to top right under "Metrics" in the above figure) respectively. Now the parameters that lead to either of them would need to be identified and considered for improving IT. Say, we shortlist reducing the release cycle time of applications to production as our objective. Hence, the following parameters may be considered by the given organization as leading to this objective; parameters that are in yellow and red states are to be considered for improvement.

Parameter	Rationale	Dimension	Category	State
Agile tracking	Faster response from IT team in addressing bottlenecks	Process	Frameworks and standard practices	🟢
Centralized IT dashboard	Faster response from IT team through better end-to-end release process visibility	Process	Frameworks and standard practices	🔴
Regression tests automated	Faster testing turnaround	Technology	Frameworks and standard practices	🟢
Cycle time for test data preparation	Indicator for faster test provisioning turnaround	Metrics	Frameworks and standard practices	?
Ops participation for Agile-Ops	Faster Ops turnaround for environment provisioning and release execution	Culture	Operational	🟡
In-sprint automation with TDD/BDD	Faster test to dev turnaround in same sprint	Process	Operational	🟡
Continuous integration	Faster build and test turnaround	Technology	Operational	🟢

Continuous deployment	Faster deployment/ release turnaround	Technology	Operational	🟢
Dashboard	Same as for "Centralized IT dashboard" above	Technology	Operational	🔴
Environment provisioning	Faster environment turnaround	Technology	Operational	🟢
Continuous monitoring	Faster response from IT team due to failure event capture early-on	Technology	Operational	🟢
Environment provisioning cycle time	Metrics as indicator for faster environment turnaround	Metrics	Operational	🟡

Question mark (?) indicates data not available

With respect to the above table, the organization may focus on each of the parameters with either yellow or red state, and find out the underlying reasons for such parameter. This enables the organization to identify areas of improvement on their DevOps journey.

This way of interpretation is particularly useful for organizations that either are kick-starting on to their DevOps journey with a specific objective in mind, or want to tackle a specific problem area by identifying (and acting on) the associated parameters that may have respective impacts on the problem area. The latter case may be applicable say, if the organization is constrained on its IT budget, and need to decide on what to invest in based on business priorities, however with the objective of resolving the prioritized problem area to the fullest extent possible by tackling all the associated parameters.

Going Quantitative

We start with the basic objective of DevOps; IT Agility. Hence, our problem statement towards assessing DevOps and finding solutions to an improved state of IT in terms of DevOps would be as follows:

Problem Statement for Quantitative Assessment

What is the current IT cycle time for the IT process in scope, and how can and to what extent the cycle time be reduced so as to reach a desired state of DevOps-led IT?

Given the above, we evaluated quantitative methods that would allow us to represent the IT process as a sequence of tasks – each of which is either automated or done manually, apply specific constraints to the process and optimize it so that the process' cycle time can be reduced to the fullest extent possible with a given set of changes to the constraints. Any change to a given constraint being planned, may need to be agreed upon by the organization while presenting such findings of the assessment; this would have an influence on to what extent can the process be optimized, hence on reducing the process' cycle time. Hence, the only heuristics that apply in terms of adopting a good solution instead of the optimal solution would depend on how far the organization can go towards adopting DevOps practices vis-à-vis the constraints.

A Brief Note on Evaluating the Quantitative Methods

We evaluated several quantitative methods, and a combination of them, with respect to fitment to our assessment approach as given above. Following is a simplified note on some the methods that we evaluated:

Linear programming

To start with, we quantified the three dimensions – people, process and technology – and formulated linear equations based on dependencies across the three. Values for factors related to people and technology were considered as independent variables, and the process factors as dependent variable. Optimizing the values of people and technology factors, if applicable for a specific case, led in turn to optimized set of process factors. However, there were several problems that we faced, a. Too many factors with dependencies across each of the dimensions made the method very complex, and not all factors could be enlisted and/or enumerated, b. The complexity of the equations formulated was very high due to the aforesaid reason, and prone to error, c. For each case, one level of optimization was not enough, and hence led to another set of optimization, and so on; this was cumbersome, and not only prone to error but also subject to a non-optimal solution or no solution at end of the exercise, and d. there is no single optimization criteria; it would vary based on the case in point.

Game theory, may be in conjunction with Markov process

In this case, we considered each activity in the given IT process to have a set of competing requirements in terms of utilizing limited resources. Here, the resources would be people (say, roles that are trying to accomplish a given set of tasks with their own priorities) and technology (say, how a combination of tools forming a tool chain supporting a given deployment strategy, may be preferred over another combination supporting a different deployment strategy). Here again, we are dealing with a set of independent and dependent variables forming a set of equations. The benefit is two-fold, a. There is a single optimization objective, hence less complexity compared to the linear programming method; each process activity needs to find a combination of optimal resource utilization, b. Dependencies across factors within each of the dimensions could also be modelled. However, we had problems of, a. Not being able to create a framework using this method that can generate a sequence of activities to achieve a given state of DevOps, and b. The complexity of equations was still very high due to multiple factors that had to be considered across the dimensions.

Critical Path Method (CPM)

Here we considered optimizing DevOps using a single objective; reducing IT cycle time. CPM as a method allowed us to define and enumerate the entire process architecture for the current state on say, a sequence diagram, and apply optimization techniques using constraints. However, traditional CPM is best suited for cases where, a. The process can be deterministically defined, hence typically is performed by a given mode of automation, and b. Crashing is done considering linear people utilization and cost reduction as constraints. Both the above cases do not quite apply to an IT process whereby respectively, a. Such process may have a mix of human effort and software-led automation, hence cannot be strictly deterministic, and b. Cultural behavior of people and technology are the constraints that need to be applied, which need different modelling approaches. Hence given the above, traditional CPM would need to be modified drastically for fitment to IT processes.

Dynamic programming

This method provides the benefits of both, a. Applying cycle time based optimization, and b. Flexibility in handling multiple final outcomes across paths, given that the technique starts with a right-to-left approach. However, while applying this method to a given IT process for optimization, we found that it induced an additional complexity of managing logistic dependencies across paths, though without being able to adequately handle cultural behavioral aspects. We feel that this method can still be explored with suitable modifications and modelling of the constraints.

With respect to the above methods, we were inspired by CPM to design our own method, however with several modifications and constraint modelling; as we would describe subsequently in this book.

Modifying CPM for Quantitative IT Analysis

Following were the modifications to traditional CPM techniques that we incorporated while modelling our assessment framework:

- o Qualify each event while constructing the network diagram for CPM with the following parameters.

  - Artefact or entity (this is the output of a preceding activity if any, and input to a succeeding activity if any) – Such entity would be of type "Material" (core IT entities such as code, script or environment) or "Information" (supporting entities such as test cases, specification documents, architecture diagrams, et al)

  - State – Initial (hence, without preceding activity), Interim (having both one or more preceding activity and one or more succeeding activity), Final (without succeeding activity)

- o Qualify each activity by not only its duration and relative start time, but also parameters such as the role or team (say, Dev, QA, Ops-Infra, et al) executing the activity, criticality of activity, and either of machine (or, automation) time or process (or, manual) time taken by the activity; this would depend on which criteria you select to use for crashing the path (as outlined later in this chapter under subsequent points)

Event E_n	Activity A_m Activity description	Event E_{n+1}
Artefact name State	Relative start time Lead time, either manual time or automation time Role, Criticality	Artefact name State

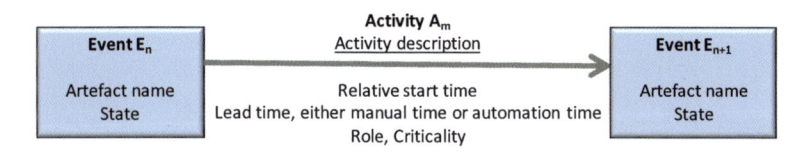

Figure 12: Notation for event and activity

- o Instead of using four time parameters – earliest start time, latest start time, earliest finish time, latest finish time – only one start time along with the activity's duration may be considered to simplify computations; note that since cost may not be typically treated as the primary factor (quantified) for implementing DevOps and given the flexibility to redefine the entire path based on IT cycle time optimization only, each of the start and finish times for each given activity is being rationalized to one value respectively for simplicity

- Idle time is not explicitly considered, given that such time as a break-up would not typically be tracked and shared by any organization

- The relative start time would be computed as follows:

$$T_R = Maximum\ (T_{R-1} + L_{R-1})$$

where, T_R is relative start time of the activity R

T_{R-1} is relative start time of each preceding activity

L_{R-1} is the duration (or, lead time; or, total time) of each preceding activity

In the above equation, note that if an activity has multiple predecessors – some of which may start and/or finish earlier and some later – the predecessors finishing earlier would introduce float time till the others finish and the activity can start; however, for the sake of our assessment, this float may or may not be considered for optimization depending on requirements of the specific case for assessment

Float time can also be introduced by an activity as the time gap created if the activity starts later than its latest completing predecessor; for the sake of our assessment, float times may or may not be considered for optimization depending on requirements of the specific case for assessment

Further note that:

$$L_R = P_R + M_R$$

where, L_R is the lead time (or, duration; or, total time taken) for the activity R

P_R is the machine time (or, automation time) for activity R

M_R is the process time (or, manual time) taken by the activity R

- Only one Initial state event should be considered for a single IT process, however, there can be more than one Final state events for the process

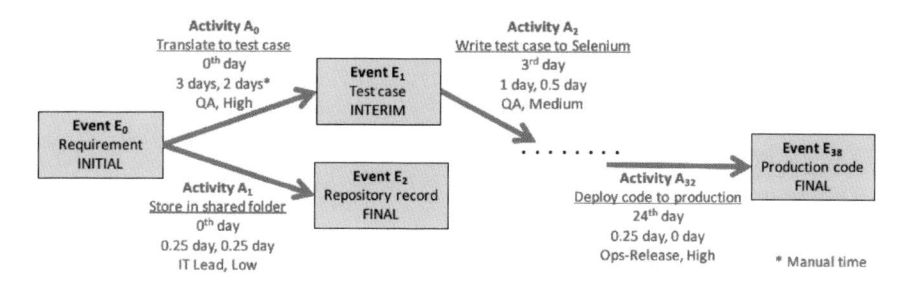

Figure 13: Example of network with one initial and multiple final state events

- o Selection of the critical path would not only depend on the longest duration of the path, but also whether the final state entity is of type "Material" or "Information"; for selection of the critical path in context of an IT process, final state event(s) with only "Material" as final entity type may be considered

  - Other criteria that you may optionally consider may include average criticality of the path (higher the criticality, better the impact of optimization on the IT process), number of distinct roles or teams across the path (note that higher the number, more is the scope of optimizing the path across multiple roles or teams; on the other hand, less the number, more is the depth of optimization that can be achieved for a limited set of roles or teams), manual time taken across the path (higher the time, more the chances of optimization by bringing in automation), average compliance to quality metrics across the path (lower the compliance, higher the need for automation and introducing quality tollgate activities in the interim), et al

  - For each of the criteria that you use to select (and optimize) the critical path, you may need to quantify each one of them and use a combined score over a suitable scale for optimizing the path

- o For estimating the time taken while crashing the path, cultural aspects (as outlined in chapter 4 above) may be modelled quantitatively using a suitable scoring mechanism and factored into the estimates

Note that while we have observed that the above modifications to the traditional CPM works well for multiple assessments, you may tailor the method based on organizational prerogatives and the objectives to do DevOps specifically for a given case.

The Detailed Questionnaire

For the detailed assessment, the questionnaire would quintessentially capture the entire IT process, defined as a set of activities – sequential, parallel or cyclic (for a finite number of times) – each qualified by additional parameters to give insights into the activity's people aspects and technology aspects. The format of the detailed questionnaire may capture the following information based on the above approach:

1. **Activity category** – This may typically be the type of activity or phase for the activity, or the epic in case you are defining activities in terms of Agile stories; for example, "Requirements analysis", "Environment provisioning and management", "Testing", et al

2. **Activity description** – The activity itself (or story, or task in case of following the Agile definition); for example, "Write the build script using Groovy in Jenkins", "Store the software specification document in the document repository", "Execute the regression tests using Selenium", et al

3. **Total time taken** – This is the lead time for the activity from start to finish; for a cyclic or iterative activity, the total time taken to complete the activity (time taken by each cycle or iteration multiplied by average number of such cycles or iterations) – that may be measured with a given unit say, minutes, hours or days – may be considered

4. **Manual time taken** – This is the process time taken by the human operating in the given role to execute the activity in whole or partially (alternatively, machine or automation time – time taken by say, an automation tool or bot to execute the activity in whole or partially) measured in the same unit as total time taken; in case of cyclic or iterative activity, the total manual (alternatively, automation) time taken across such cycles or iterations may be considered

5. **Predecessor activities** – Activity (or list of activities) that are predecessor(s) to the activity in context; note that the initial activity would not have a predecessor

6. **Criticality** – This may specify the significance of carrying out the activity in relation to the entire list of activities; the criticality may either be specified as a discrete value (say, corresponding to high, medium and low), or as a continuous value within a given numerical range in case relatively finer grained analysis based on criticality is required

7. **Role or team** – This is the people aspect of the activity (for example, specifying using acronyms; "Dev" for development team that may either include or omit quality assurance or testing team, "QA" for quality assurance, "Ops-Infra" for infrastructure operations team, "App-owner" for application owner, et al), specifying which role or team owns and executes the activity; in case multiple roles (or teams) execute the activity, you may consider only the primary role (or team) that executes the activity, or alternatively break up the activity into multiple ones corresponding to each role (or team) executing the activity

8. **Input** – The input entity (code, script, environment, document, test cases, et al) required by the activity; in case there is no specific input to an activity, you may want to evaluate if the activity is valid at all for consideration (if not, the activity may either be eliminated or suitably combined with another)

9. **Output** – The output entity generated by the activity; in case there is no specific output from an activity, you may want to evaluate the validity of considering the activity (there are cases where the same entity gets modified by the activity, resulting in the scenario where input = output; in such cases, specify the change done as part of the output specification so that the purpose of having the activity is discernable)

10. **Automation technology or tool used** – This is the technology aspect of the activity, specifying what, if any, tool, script or software is used to automate the execution of the activity; additionally, you may also capture the scope and coverage of automation, for example, Jira (a full-fledged Agile based software development tracking tool) may only be used to track test defects for development projects in an organization, that too for functional test cases (say in this case, 70% test cases being covered) only

You may add on to the above list if you need such additional information (as separate field(s)) as criteria to the quantitative optimization method we would cover in subsequent chapters.

Following is an example of a questionnaire filled up with a sample IT process:

S#	Epic	Story	Total time	Manual time	Predecessor	Predecessor	Predecessor	Predecessor	Criticality	Role / Team	Input	Output	Automation tool
1	SDLC - Requirements Analysis	We create the business requirements specification (BRS) document	5	5	INIT*				Med	Business	Requirement	BRS**	Confluence
2	SDLC - Requirements Analysis	We create the software requirements specification (SRS) from BRS	3	2	1				Med	IT Lead	BRS	SRS**	Confluence
3	SDLC - Requirements Analysis	We identify and include non-functional requirements (NFRs) to the SRS	2	2	2				Med	Architect	SRS	SRS	Confluence
4	SDLC - Requirements Analysis	We post-validate BRS with business users for traceability and coverage	3	3	1				Hi	IT Lead	BRS	BRS	Confluence
5	SDLC - Requirements Analysis	We post-validate SRS using BRS with IT team and architect SME for traceability and coverage	2	2	2	3			Hi	IT Lead	SRS	SRS	Confluence
6	SDLC - Requirements Analysis	We store the BRS and/or SRS in project document library	0.5	0.5	4	5			Low	IT Lead	BRS/SRS	BRS/SRS	Confluence

73

7	SDLC - Requirements Analysis	We identify a requirements repository	0.5	0.5	INIT*			Med	IT Lead	None	Repository	Jira
9	SDLC - Requirements Analysis	We baseline requirements in the repository	1	1	7	5		Hi	IT Lead	Requirement	Requirement	Jira
10	SDLC - Requirements Analysis	We monitor baselined requirements via collaboration	1	1	9			Med	Dev and Ops teams	Requirement	SRS	Jira
11	SDLC - Requirements Analysis	We identify changed requirements and record the changes in repository	1	1	10			Med	IT Lead	Requirement	SRS	Jira
14	SDLC - Requirements Analysis	We analyze (and mark) if the requirement is user-centric or system-centric	3	3	11	12	13	Hi	QA	Requirement	None	Confluence
16	SDLC - Requirements Analysis	For system-centric requirement, we apply TDD to templatize repeatable requirements in TDD format	2	1	14			Med	QA	Requirement	Test case	Jbehave
18	SDLC - Requirements Analysis	We translate the format into test scripts using workflow over a workflow/rules engine or tool	2	1	15	16		Med	QA	Test case	Test script	Jbehave

21	SDLC - Requirements Analysis	We merge the NFRs with functional requirements (FRs) in the repository using a workflow/rules engine or tool	1	0.5	10	19		Med	IT Lead	Test case	Requirement	Jira
38	SDLC - Environment provisioning	We identify mode of template request form (email, service management tool) and basic set of parameters	2	2	INIT*			Hi	DevOps lead	Requirement	Template	ServiceNow
44	SDLC - Environment provisioning	We incorporate parameters for CI - post-commit unit test to build	0.5	0.5	42			Med	Ops-Release	Requirement	Infra as code	Puppet
45	SDLC - Environment provisioning	We incorporate parameters for CT - functional test automation	0.5	0.5	42			Med	Ops-Release	Requirement	Infra as code	Puppet
52	SDLC - Environment provisioning	We identify and prepare environment parameters from dev/test/deploy requirements	1	1	38			Hi	Ops-Release	Template	Infra as code	Puppet
54	SDLC - Environment provisioning	We request for environment through a workflow/ rules engine	0.5	0.5	38			Med	Dev (incl. QA)	Template	Service request	ServiceNow
55	SDLC - Environment provisioning	We validate environment parameters using templates in rules engine	0.5	0	38	53	54	Hi	DevOps lead	Service request	Infra as code	ServiceNow

57	SDLC - Environment provisioning	We approve environment request through workflow mentioning ETA	0.5	0.25	55	56		Med	Ops-Infra	Service request	Service request	ServiceNow
61	SDLC - Environment provisioning	We spin up VM over a VM provider tool directly using GUI or scripts	0.5	0.5	57			Med	Ops-Infra	Infra as code	Environment	Puppet
70	SDLC - Environment provisioning	We post-validate environment (dev team)	0.5	0.5	60	61	68	Hi	Dev (incl. QA)	Environment	Service request	ServiceNow
74	SDLC - Environment provisioning	We revise environment policies and parameters in workflow/ rules engine template	1	0.75	38	70		Hi	Ops-Infra	Template	Infra as code	ServiceNow
75	SDLC - Environment provisioning	We check environment utilization vis-à-vis dev/test cycles for given environment	0.5	0	70			Med	Ops-Infra	Environment	Service request	Zabbix
76	SDLC - Environment provisioning	We provide reminder for environment de-provision (from ops team to dev/test team)	0.5	0.25	70	143	154	Med	Ops-Infra	Service request	Service request	ServiceNow
82	SDLC - Coding	We request for dev environment as a self service request	0.5	0.25	53	54		Hi	Dev (incl. QA)	Service request	Environment	ServiceNow
84	SDLC - Coding	We code application using IDE	3	2.5	70			Med	Dev (incl. QA)	Requirement	Code	Eclipse

91	SDLC - Coding	We check and fix code quality dynamically in-line as part of code checking tool/plug-in integration with IDE	0.5	0.25	84				Med	Dev (incl. QA)	Code	Code	PMD
94	SDLC - Coding	We commit code manually	0.5	0.25	97	98			Hi	Dev (incl. QA)	Code	Code	Git
97	SDLC - Coding	We generate tags manually prior to commit	0.5	0.5	83	84	85	86	Med	Dev (incl. QA)	Code	Commit tag	Git
100	SDLC - Build and package	We build application using language-specific build tool	0.5	0.25	94	95			Med	Dev (incl. QA)	Code	Code	Maven
104	SDLC - Build and package	We unit test code using language-specific build / test tool	0.5	0.25	94	95			Med	Dev (incl. QA)	Code	Test result	Junit
109	SDLC - Testing	We request for test/ QA environment as a self service request	0.5	0.25	53	54			Hi	QA	Service request	Environment	ServiceNow
110	SDLC - Testing	We prepare test plan incl. test scenarios and test cases using Excel (or equivalent)	3	2.5	14				Med	QA	Requirement	Test case	MS Excel / equivalent
114	SDLC - Testing	We prepare functional test scripts [regression] using test automation tool	2	1.5	18	21			Med	QA	Test case	Test script	Selenium

116	SDLC - Testing	We prepare NFR test scripts [performance] using test automation tool	0.5	0.5	19	21				Med	QA	Test case	Test script	HP LoadRunner
127	SDLC - Testing	We execute tests using automation tool - regression	0.25	0	114					Med	QA	Test script	Test result	Selenium
129	SDLC - Testing	We execute tests using automation tool - performance	0.25	0	116					Med	QA	Test script	Test result	HP LoadRunner
140	SDLC - Testing	We record defects in ALM tool	1	0.5	121	127	133	129		Med	QA	Test result	Defect	Jira
143	SDLC - Testing	We (dev team) resolve and close defects in ALM tool (subject to test team validation)	1	0.5	140	141				Med	Dev (incl. QA)	Defect	Code	Jira
155	SDLC - Application release and deployment	We execute release using release automation tool	1	0.5	142	143	152	153		Med	Ops-Release	Service request	Code	Octopus Deploy

* In this case we have considered three initial activities (predecessor as "INIT"), however you may limit it to one for a single IT process

** BRS is "Business Requirement Specification" and SRS is "Software Requirement Specification"

Note that the activities in the above table are not indexed as consecutive integers. In fact, we have selected them from a template of activities that we maintain. We ignored the activities in our template that are not relevant to the given IT process; hence, the corresponding numbers (8, 12, 13, 15, et al) are missing. In case you are identifying your list of activities for your IT process afresh, you may number them sequentially with consecutive integers.

With respect to the fields on capturing activity times, namely "Total time taken" and "Manual time taken", organizations may provide estimated (rather than actual) values respectively, especially where such a time study has not been done. If the process has been executed quite a few number of times, say for a given application stack in context of the DevOps, average value for each activity based on the number of times it has been executed may be considered.

How do you get the questionnaire filled up?

For the organization in context, you may follow any of the following approaches:

Set up an initial meeting with the team who would fill up the questionnaire, to explain the questionnaire and how to fill it up, possibly with an example. You may set up subsequent meetings at given intervals to review how the progress any provide any clarifications required by the participants.

Set up regular meetings with the participants for you to get the relevant information from the participants and fill up the questionnaire yourself. You may get the filled up part reviewed by them, or obtain clarifications if required, in the subsequent meetings.

Combine both the above approaches for different parts of the questionnaire, based on participant interest and availability, and the context. For example, if the primary objective of the assessment is to solve software quality and reliability issues, you may want the participants, especially from the quality team, to fill up their respective activity details themselves (with your guidance). However, you may yourself fill up the Dev and Ops related activities' details in consultation with the respective teams, more so to find out the activities connected to and having an impact on quality related activities, instead of all of Dev and Ops (of course, unless there are unavoidable dependencies) some of which may not be relevant to such context.

Finding out the Critical Path

The critical path forms the basis of the entire detailed assessment; hence it is extremely important to carefully consider what criteria are used for selecting the path. This would be typically based on the objectives and priorities of the assessment.

Let us consider another example of an IT process captured through the questionnaire as outlined in the previous chapter. We would first start with computing the relative start times of the given activities as per the equation given in chapter 7 above. This would enable us to quickly construct the process network diagram and identify all the possible process paths.

For this example, the following table provides the respective relative start times (shown as a gray highlighted column as it is not a part of the questionnaire, but a computed field) with other relevant fields:

S#	Epic	Story	Total time	Manual time	Predecessor	Relative start time	Criticality	Role/ team	Input	Output	Automation tool
A1	SDLC - Requirements analysis	Create (or obtain) the BRS	3	3	-	0	High	QA	Business requirement	BRS	
A2	SDLC - Requirements analysis	Create the SRS from the BRS	2	2	A1	3	High	QA	BRS	SRS	
A3	SDLC - Requirements analysis	Identify and include NFRs as part of SRS	3	2	[A1]	3	High	QA	NFR	SRS	
A4	SDLC - Requirements analysis	Store BRS / SRS in the project document library with versioning	1	1	A2, A3	6	Low	QA	SRS	SRS with version	
A5	SDLC - Requirements analysis	Assess impact to components	2	1.5	A2, A3	7	Med	QA	SRS	Impact matrix	
A6	SDLC - Requirements analysis	For system centric requirement, apply TDD principles and templatize repeatable requirements in TDD format	3	3	A2, A3	8	Med	QA	SRS	TDD format	
A7	SDLC - Requirements analysis	Translate into test cases via a workflow	2	1	A6, [A5]	11	High	QA	TDD format	Test cases	

		using a workflow/ rules engine and feed into Jira								
A8	SDLC - Environment provisioning	Identify mode of request form (email) and basic set of parameters for the given release	1	1	[A1]	0	High	Ops	Existing infra capacity	Basic environment Request form
A9	SDLC - Environment provisioning	Incorporate parameters for infrastructure - CPU, disk space, etc.	0.5	0.5	A8	1	High	Ops	Basic environment Request form	Environment request form (+ infra parameters)
A10	SDLC - Environment provisioning	Incorporate parameters for O/S* - Linux, Unix, Windows, etc.	0.25	0.25	A9	1.5	High	Ops	Environment request form (+ infra parameters)	Environment request form (+ O/S parameters)
A11	SDLC - Environment provisioning	Incorporate parameters for runtime incl. language compiler & runtime, IDE*, zones, etc.	0.25	0.25	A10	1.75	High	Ops	Environment request form (+ O/S parameters)	Environment request form (+ runtime parameters)
A12	SDLC - Environment provisioning	Incorporate parameters for release	0.25	0.25	A11	2	High	Ops	Environment request form (+ runtime parameters)	Environment request form (+ release parameters)
A13	SDLC - Environment provisioning	Incorporate parameters for deployment	0.5	0.5	A12	2.25	High	Ops	Environment request form (+ release parameters)	Environment request form (+ deploy parameters)
A14	SDLC - Environment provisioning	Approve environment request (based on availability) through workflow mentioning ETA*	0.5	0.5	[A20], [A25]	13.25	High	Ops	Filled up environment request form	Approved environment request
A15	SDLC - Environment provisioning	Spin up VM* via Oracle VirtualBox directly using GUI* or scripts	0.25	0.25	A14	13.75	High	Ops	Approved environment request	VM on Oracle VirtualBox
A16	SDLC - Environment provisioning	Spin up VM over public cloud directly	0.25	0.25	A14	13.75	High	Ops	Approved environment request	VM on cloud
A17	SDLC - Environment provisioning	Configure environment in the VM manually (using CLI* scripts and installations)	0.25	0.25	[A15], [A16]	14	High	Ops	VMs	Environment configured VMs
A18	SDLC - Environment provisioning	Validate environment with dev/test team	0.25	0.25	A17	14.25	High	Ops	Environment configured VMs	Validated configured VMs
A19	SDLC - Environment provisioning	Store configuration scripts in project document library	0.25	0.25	A17	14.25	Low	Ops	Environment configured VMs	Configuration scripts with version

A20	SDLC - Coding	Request for dev environment	0.25	0.25	A7, [A13]	13	High	Dev	Environment request form (+ deploy parameters)	Filled up dev Environment request form	
A21	SDLC - Coding	Code application using IDE using in-line code quality check using SonarQube	3.5	3	A18	14.5	High	Dev	Validated configured VMs	Quality checked source code in IDE	SonarQube
A22	SDLC - Coding	Generate tags and commit code manually in Subversion	0.25	0.25	A21	18	High	Dev	Quality checked source code in IDE	Tagged and committed code	
A23	SDLC - Coding	Build (upon unit test) application using Maven through Jenkins	0	0	A22	18.25	High	Dev	Tagged and committed code	Code binary	Maven, Jenkins
A24	SDLC - Coding	Promote application code to QA environment through Jenkins on success build	0	0	A23	18.25	High	Dev	Code binary	QA released code binary	Jenkins
A25	SDLC - Testing	Request for test/ QA environment	0.25	0.25	A7, [A13]	13	High	QA	Environment request form (+ deploy parameters)	Filled up QA environment request form	
A26	SDLC - Testing	Prepare functional test scripts [regression & integration] using Selenium integrated to Jira	0.5	0.25	A18	14.5	High	QA	Validated configured VMs	Functional test scripts	Jira
A27	SDLC - Testing	Prepare NFR test scripts [performance] using HP LoadRunner integrated to Jira	0.25	0	A18	14.5	High	QA	Validated configured VMs	NFR (performance) test scripts	Jira
A28	SDLC - Testing	Execute tests using automation tool - regression & integration	0.25	0	A26	18.25	High	QA	Functional test scripts	Functional tested code binary	Selenium
A29	SDLC - Testing	Execute tests using automation tool - performance	0.25	0	A27	18.25	High	QA	NFR (performance) test scripts	Perf. tested code binary	HP LoadRunner
A30	SDLC - Testing	Defects recorded in ALM* tool	0	0	A29	18.5	High	QA	Tested code binary	Defects	Selenium, Jira
A31	SDLC - Testing	Defects are resolved and closed by dev team in ALM tool (subject to test team validation)	1.5	1.25	A30	18.5	High	Dev	Defects	Final code binary	
A32	SDLC - Application	Identify business change or	2	2	[A1]	-4	Med	RM*	Business requirement	Business changes	

	release and deployment	incident fix requirements									
A33	SDLC - Application release and deployment	Prepare release plan and share (and align on) using Microsoft Excel (or equivalent) and email	2	2	A32	-2	Med	RM	Business changes	Final release plan	
A34	SDLC - Application release and deployment	Request for release using email	0.25	0.25	A31, [A33]	20	High	Dev	Final code binary	Release request	
A35	SDLC - Application release and deployment	Approve release request using email	0.25	0.25	A34	20.25	High	RM	Release request	Approved release request	
A36	SDLC - Application release and deployment	Execute release using manual scripts and CLI commands	0.5	0.5	A35	20.5	High	Ops	Approved release request	Application code (in production)	

* Following are some of the acronyms used: O/S – Operating System, IDE – Integrated Development Environment, ETA – Expected Turn Around (time), VM – Virtual Machine, CLI – Command Line Interface, ALM – Application Lifecycle Management, RM – Release Manager, GUI – Graphical User Interface

With slight changes to the nomenclature vis-à-vis the figure above on notations, we constructed the process network diagram as shown below. Further, following are the observations while the network diagram was constructed:

o To restrict the initial activity to only one (A1), we have considered "Dummy activities" emanating from the corresponding starting event E0; hence, E0 leads to E1 (through initial activity A1), E2 (through "Dummy" activity), E8 (through "Dummy" activity) and E32 (through "Dummy" activity). Downstream activities (with respect to A1) are now A2 (direct successor to A1), A3 (emanating from E2), A8 (emanating from E8) and A32 (emanating from E32) respectively. The dummy activities are denoted under "Predecessors" column within third braces ("[" and "]").

o We have used connectors (denoted by a circle and named C1, C2, et al) to connect parts of the diagram where space restrictions did not allow us to directly construct the path.

o Relative start times are enclosed in brackets beside the total time and manual time notations. Note here as an instance, that whereby A32 has been denoted as a dummy successor to A1 – even though A32 starts earlier (4 days earlier relative to A1 which starts on the 0th day) – this is due to the fact that A1 is the starting point of the primary IT process to be analyzed in this context (in this case, for a production rollout of an application), and all such other activities are done to assist in completing this primary activity, say as pre-requisite steps towards its fulfilment.

- o Criticality is denoted by "Hi" (for high), "Md" (for medium) and "Lo" (for low) respectively.

- o The additional field at end of each activity, denoted by "a", "b", "c" or "d", describes the transformation type between input and output, thereby indicating the type of input that an activity takes and the type of output that it generates. The output, unless it results in a final event, is picked up by the activity's successor(s). The notation is as follows:

  - **a** – Material to Material; example is A17 (input is configuration scripts, and output is configured VM)
  - **b** – Information to Information; example is A3 (input is non-functional requirement or NFR, and output is software requirements specification or SRS)
  - **c** – Material to Information; example is A8 (input is infrastructure configuration, and output is details in environment request form)
  - **d** – Information to Material; example is A16 (input is the environment request, and output is VM provisioned on cloud services)

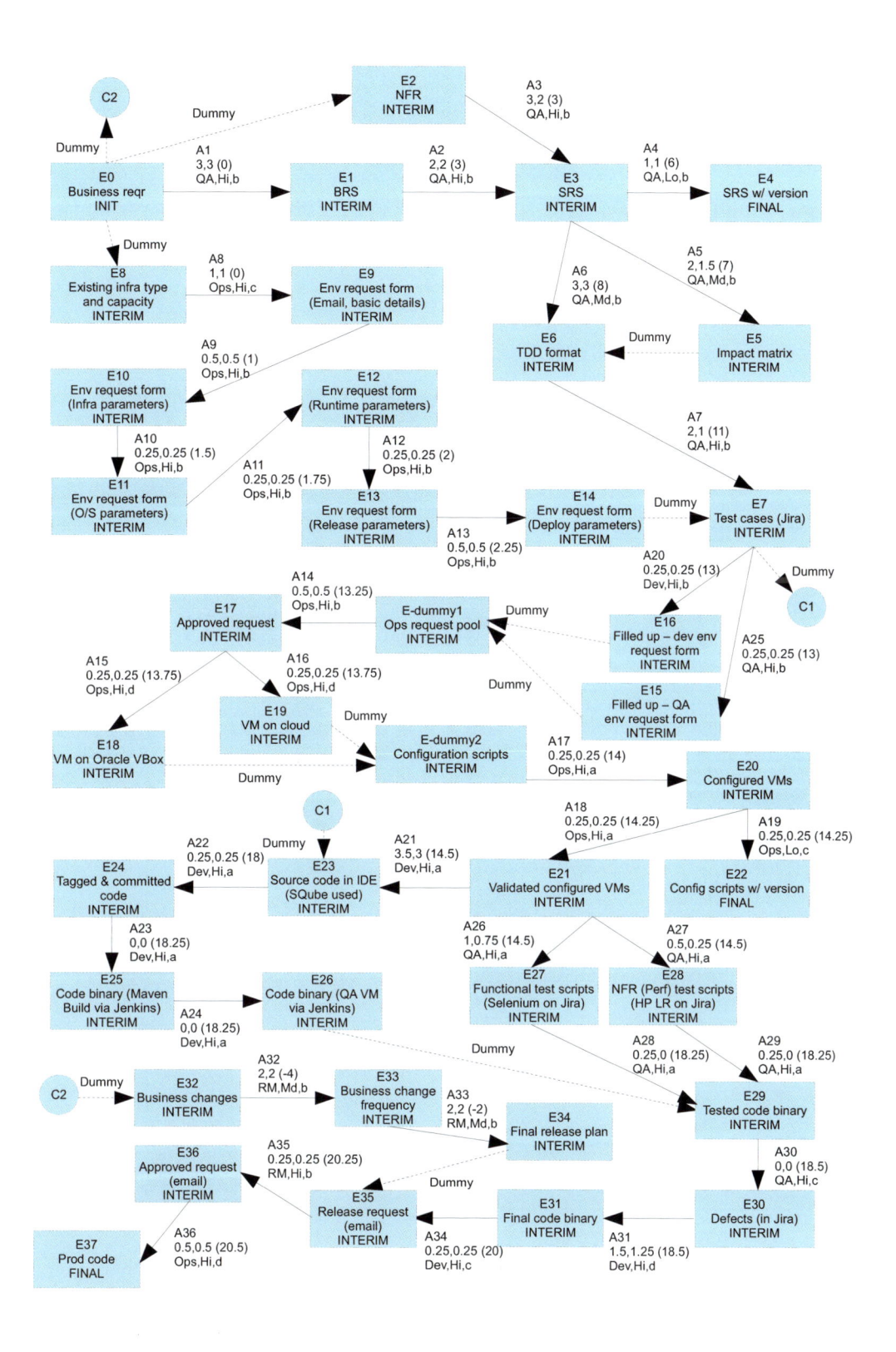

Figure 14: Example of the As-Is Process Architecture

Note: We alternatively call the above representation as "Process Architecture", hence we would use this term interchangeably with "process network diagram" or simply, "network diagram".

Traversing through the above constructed As-Is process architecture, we found out all the possible paths – from the initial activity (or, successor to the initial activity) to each of the final activity – as given in the table below. Also note that we need to consider the total cycle time (computed from start to finish) taken for every path considered, as well as factors such as final output type and average criticality over the path, that you may consider to evaluate and find out the critical path.

S#	Path	Start time	Finish time	Total cycle time	Min float	Max float	Net duration considering min float	Net duration considering max float	Final output type	Average criticality
1	A1 - A2 - A4	0	7	7	1	1	6	6	Information	Med
2	A3 - A4	3	7	4	0	0	4	4	Information	Med
3	A3 - A5/A6 - A7 - A20/A25 - A14 - A15/A16 - A17 - A19	3	14.5	11.5	2	3	9.5	8.5	Information	High
4	A3 - A5/A6 - A7 - A20/A25 - A14 - A15/A16 - A17 - A18 - A21 - A22 - A23 - A24 - A30 - A31 - A34 - A35 - A36	3	21	18	2.25	3.25	15.75	14.75	Material	High
5	A3 - A5/A6 - A7 - A20/A25 - A14 - A15/A16 - A17 - A18 - A26/A27 - A28/A29 - A30 - A31 - A34 - A35 - A36	3	21	18	4.75	6.25	13.25	11.75	Material	High
6	A1 - A2 - A5/A6 - A7 - A20/A25 - A14 - A15/A16 - A17 - A19	0	14.5	14.5	3	4	11.5	10.5	Information	High
7	A1 - A2 - A5/A6 - A7 - A20/A25 - A14 - A15/A16 - A17 - A18 - A21 - A22 - A23 - A24 - A30 - A31 - A34 - A35 - A36	0	21	21	3.25	4.25	17.75	16.75	Material	High
8	A1 - A2 - A5/A6 - A7 - A20/A25 - A14 - A15/A16 - A17 - A18 - A26/A27 - A28/A29 - A30 - A31 - A34 - A35 - A36	0	21	21	5.75	7.25	15.25	13.75	Material	High
9	A8 - A9 - A10 - A11 - A12 - A13 - A20/A25 - A14 - A15/A16 - A17 - A19	0	14.5	14.5	10.25	10.25	4.25	4.25	Information	High
10	A8 - A9 - A10 - A11 - A12 - A13 - A20/A25 - A14 - A15/A16 - A17 - A18 - A21 - A22 - A23 - A24 - A30 - A31 - A34 - A35 - A36	0	21	21	10.5	10.5	10.5	10.5	Material	High
11	A8 - A9 - A10 - A11 - A12 - A13 - A20/A25 - A14 - A15/A16 - A17 - A18 - A26/A27 - A28/A29 - A30 - A31 - A34 - A35 - A36	0	21	21	13	13.5	8	7.5	Material	High
12	A32 - A33 - A35 - A36	-4	21	25	20.25	20.25	4.75	4.75	Material	High

* Note that for the sake of simplicity we combined some of the paths that share parallel activities; however, since such set(s) of activities can have different start times and/or finish times, we have to consider the different float time(s) introduced by such activities, hence for

In the above table, we will consider combined path numbered 3 as our example to demonstrate how we have computed the numeric fields, as follows:

Path no. 3: A3 → A5/A6 → A7 → A20/A25 → A14 → A15/A16 → A17 → A19

> **Note**: Time unit considered is days. This path could be further broken up into 2^3 = 8 individual paths, given that we have considered three sets of parallel activities (two in each) – A5 and A6, A20 and A25, and A15 and A16; they have been combined for simplicity here.

Total cycle time = Finish time – Start time = 14.5 – 3 = 11.5 days

Minimum and maximum float times

For A1 (predecessor for A3): A1 finishes on 0 (relative start time) + 3 (duration) = 3rd day
      A3 starts on 3rd day itself (same as the day A1 finishes)
      Hence, there is no float time for A1 on this path

For A3: A3 finishes on 3 + 3 = 6th day
    A5 starts on 7th day, hence A5 introduces a 1 day float time for A3 ….. (a)
    A6 starts on 8th day, hence A6 introduces a 2 days float time for A3 ….. (b)

For A5: A5 finishes on 7 + 2 = 9th day
    A7 starts on 11th day, hence A7 introduces a 2 days float time for A5 ….. (c)

For A6: A6 finishes on 8 + 3 = 11th day
    A7 starts on 11th day, hence there is no float time for A6 due to A7

For A7: A7 finishes on 11 + 2 = 13th day
    Both successors on this path, A20 and A25, start on 13th day, hence no float

Computing likewise further for succeeding activities, we did not find any additional float times.

Hence, considering A5, we found from (a) and (c) above that the float time = 1 + 2 = 3 days. Similarly considering A6, we found from (b) above that the float time = 2 days. Therefore, for this combined path:

Minimum float time (introduced due to A6) = 2 days
Maximum float time (introduced due to A5) = 3 days

Net duration for the path, considering float times
Given that we are considering a combined path:

Net duration considering minimum float = 11.5 – 2 = 9.5 days
Net duration considering maximum float = 11.5 – 3 = 8.5 days

> **So, what do we consider to select the critical path – total cycle time, or net duration considering float times?**
>
> Float time indicates either or both of the following two scenarios for the given path:
>
> a. There are quite a few dependencies on activities on other paths, thereby causing frequent float time(s) between completion of one activity and start of the succeeding ones, resulting in substantial float time accumulated across the path. In such cases, we typically observe that such path is not critical (hence, have to wait so long in between for others). The last path in the table above (numbered 12) is an example of this scenario. Hence, even though the total cycle time for this path is very high (25 days) with respect to other paths, we consider float times to compute its net duration. Therefore, it is prudent to consider this net duration while selecting the critical path, as it would clearly indicate the actual duration taken by the IT specific activities only (and not the waiting times), on the path.

b. There are possible cultural and/or technological factors leading to float times rather than any dependency on other path(s). In such cases, upon completion of one activity, the team executing the successor activity may either introduce a delay due to say, completing some other intermediate operational processes (not specific to IT, however possibly redundant in terms of the given context) or resolving an intermediate frequently recurring technical issue required to execute the successor activity (though not captured as part of the given IT process). In both these cases, it is important to consider the net duration after adjustment with the float times, to understand if the path should be treated as critical based on actual IT activity-only cycle time. The path (numbered 3) considered above to demonstrate the time related computations, is such an example.

To select the critical path, in this case we considered two additional fields: (a) final output type – we considered paths that have "Material" as its final output type in its final event or state, and (b) average criticality across the path – we considered paths that have "High" criticality, of course provided the first condition above is met.

Based on the above criteria, we selected **path numbered 7 as our critical path**. The criteria based evaluation, in order of relative importance, was as follows:

o Final output type is "Material" (output being production code, as per final event E37)

o Longest net duration (considering minimum float, 17.75 days; considering maximum float, 16.75 days); this criterion closely corresponds to traditional CPM technique

o Average criticality is "High" across the path; note that this criterion may be optional for you, and you may consider other factor(s) as well to choose your critical path

Note that in case there are several paths that satisfies or closely satisfies the first two criteria above – hence, it becomes difficult for you to select the critical path – you have two options. You may either quantify criticality for each activity (say "1" for Low, "2" for Medium, "3" for High) and compute the average criticality for each given path, in order to find out the path with numerically maximum criticality, or choose any other criteria important to your context to further filter out non-critical paths and select the critical path.

So what did we do till now with the filled up questionnaire?
1. We computed the relative start times of respective activities in the questionnaire
2. Using the predecessor-successor relationships across activities, we constructed the process network diagram with boxes for events and arrows for activities connecting the respective events
3. From the process network diagram above, we tabulated all the possible paths along with their respective IT cycle times (after adjustment with float times, where applicable)
4. We applied our criterion for selecting the critical path from the list of possible paths; such criterion is primarily to find out the path with the longest IT cycle time and output type "Material"

Analyzing the Critical Path

The objective of analyzing the critical path is to optimize the path in terms of the IT cycle time. Hence, we considered each activity, both at an individual level and in relation to other activities in the path, for optimization.

The analysis was done in three steps considering each activity on the critical path:

1. Identify if the activity contributes to or generates "waste" (which we will describe below); in such cases, the objective is to eliminate or reduce the scope of the activity.

2. Evaluate if the activity, in relation to other activities within or outside the critical path, can be preponed to complete earlier, hence contribute to reduced IT cycle times across the path (in such cases, the dependent activities also need to be evaluated for any change in scope, sequence or timing). Note that typically a chain of activities belonging to the same engineering practice (as outlined in the 3rd chapter above) may together be preponed. However, you may not be able to prepone activities in case such activities have dependencies on others that belong to one or more of the other engineering practice(s). Hence, you may categorize the activities on the critical path by corresponding engineering practices for such analysis.

3. Based on the above two, evaluate if the activity may further need to be enhanced in scope; alternatively, new activities may be identified in such cases to add to the overall IT scope, say in enhancing software quality and system reliability aspects.

The Notion of "Waste"

The concept of waste comes from lean engineering principles, however for our purpose we would define it to be any outcome (of an activity) that is not relevant to run the core IT functions as expected by the organization's business or users. In that respect, all outputs that are of type "Information" contribute to waste. This is because of three reasons:

- It takes additional effort (in terms of dedicated activities) to generate such output

- The outputs are not actually consumed by the business or users of the organization, but only serve to act as aid and system of records for the IT personnel for execution of IT processes, or for later reference respectively

- All such outputs are derivable (if required), through appropriate re-engineering automation, from the core IT "material" outputs, typically for human IT personnel for later reuse or reference

In addition to the above, if any "material" output such as code, script or environment are found to be redundant without being actually used later on in the IT process in context, however have been generated by any activity, such output may also be considered as waste; unless, of course, such output may be used as part of say, an enhanced scope.

Once we have analyzed the critical path given the aforesaid guidance for each activity, we found that there can be four types of changes at the activity level that can be done to re-design the critical path:

- **Prepone** – Preponing the activity (which would also impact the dependent activities, if any) brings in higher parallelism to complete activities substantially earlier, thereby reducing IT cycle time across the path

- **Enhance or alter scope** – Increasing or changing the scope of the activity, in terms of what it does, helps in either eliminating or reducing scope of other related activities that introduce waste, or bring in other relevant paradigms for making the IT process more robust; say, in terms of higher quality and reliability

- **Eliminate** – This is applicable to activities that generate waste; however, note that under practical circumstances for most organizations that want to optimize their IT through DevOps at a given state, they may not yet want to reduce all waste; for example, you may not yet want to do away with your test cases and test results ("information" output type) as they may be used by the IT personnel in executing downstream IT activities along the path

Note that we did not typically consider postponing an activity while optimizing the path, given that such change typically would increase the IT cycle time of the path. However, there may be situations where you may want to postpone an activity, say in case the organization wants to split their IT process into more manageable buckets (which can, of course, be anti-DevOps in terms of breaking up existing teams and/or responsibilities) or drastically alter the scope of the entire IT process to introduce new paradigms.

Moreover, each of the above type of change entailed changes to either the cultural aspect, or to the technology aspect, or both; thereby impacting the associated people and technology architectures respectively. We will briefly describe the two architectures in subsequent chapters, given that they can be easily derived in their To-Be state from their respective As-Is counterparts and the To-Be process architecture itself.

Continuing with our example, following was our analysis for the critical path:

Activity	Task description	Prepone	Postpone	Eliminate	Enhance	Add	None	Reason	Change details	People change	Technology change
A1	Create (or obtain) the BRS						X	Formal BRS needs to be published to business	No change		
A2	Create the SRS from the BRS			X				Creating SRS is redundant documentation w.r.t. BRS	Eliminate A2 and extend A6		
A5	Assess impact to components						X	Can start earlier as A2 is eliminated	A5 is preponed along with A6 as per flow		
A6	For system centric requirement, apply TDD principles and templatize repeatable requirements in TDD format				X			Can start earlier as A2 is eliminated	Directly convert BRS to TDD led test cases in Jira		Jira as the ALM tool

A7	Translate into test cases via a workflow using a workflow/ rules engine and feed into Jira		X			Test cases can be directly formulated from BRS	Eliminate A7 and extend A6		
A20	Request for dev environment	X		X		Requesting environment is late	Involve Ops (with Dev) after preparing BRS to obtain environment parameters	add Ops role	
A25	Request for test/ QA environment	X		X		Requesting environment is late	Involve Ops (w/ QA) after preparing BRS to obtain environment parameters	add Ops role	
A14	Approve environment request (based on availability) through workflow mentioning ETA		X			Ops approval becomes irrelevant post A20 and A25	Eliminate A14		
A15	Spin up VM via Oracle VirtualBox directly using GUI or scripts		X			Provisioning VM and then configuring in two steps take substantial time using scripts/ GUI	Eliminate A15 and extend A17 by implementing an orchestrator running Vagrant and Chef		
A16	Spin up VM over public cloud directly		X			Provisioning VM and then configuring in two steps take substantial time using scripts/ GUI	Eliminate A16 and extend A17 by implementing an orchestrator running AWS OpsWorks and Chef		
A17	Configure environment in the VM manually (using CLI scripts and installations)			X		Two step provisioning and configuration is time consuming	Implement orchestrator and provision + configuration in one step		Orchestrator (to be decided) running Vagrant, AWS OpsWorks, Chef, test automation, using scripts from NEXUS
A18	Validate environment with dev/test team			X		Validation required for compliance	Validation automated by orchestrator		Orchestrator (tool or platform to be decided)
A21	Code application using IDE using in-line code quality check using SONARQube				X	No change in coding process required as per IT	No change		
A22	Generate tags and commit code manually in SVN				X	No change in coding process required as per IT	No change		
A23	Build (upon unit test) application using Maven through Jenkins				X	100% automated	No change		

Activity	Task description	Prepone	Postpone	Eliminate	Enhance	Add	None	Reason	Change details	People change	Technology change
A24	Promote application code to QA environment through Jenkins on success build					X		100% automated	No change		
A30	Defects recorded in ALM tool					X		100% automated	No change		
A31	Defects are resolved and closed by dev team in ALM tool (subject to test team validation)					X		No change in coding process required as per IT	No change		
A34	Request for release using email			X				No change in coding process required as per IT	Involve release manager (RM) for one step approval and place release request through ServiceNow	add Release Manager (RM) role	ServiceNow
A35	Approve release request using email			X				One step approval suffices by modifying A34	Eliminate A35 and extend A34		
A36	Execute release using manual scripts and CLI commands			X				Deployment takes significant time	Use Octopus Deploy as part of orchestrator for near-instant deployment		Orchestrator (to be decided), Octopus Deploy

Corresponding to the above changes to the critical path, we further analyzed the related activities (on paths other than the above) for associated changes, as follows:

Activity	Task description	Prepone	Postpone	Eliminate	Enhance	Add	None	Reason	Change details	People change	Technology change
A3	Identify and include NFRs as part of SRS						X	Preponed critical path	Start time preponed		
A4	Store BRS / SRS in the project document library with versioning						X	Preponed critical path	Start time preponed		
A8	Identify mode of request form (email) and basic set of parameters for the given release	X			X			Email needs modification every time for a release, and is not audit traceable	Provide template on ServiceNow, the current workflow/ ticketing tool; prepone to templatize across releases	add DevOps Engineer (DE) as a separate role	ServiceNow
A9	Incorporate parameters for infrastructure - CPU, disk space, etc.	X						Templatize across releases prior to usage by customer IT	Preponed as successor to A8	add DE role	ServiceNow

ID	Activity						Notes 1	Notes 2	Notes 3	Tool
A10	Incorporate parameters for O/S - Linux, Unix, Windows, etc.	X					Templatize across releases	Preponed as successor to A9	add DE role	ServiceNow
A11	Incorporate parameters for runtime incl. language compiler & runtime, IDE, zones, etc.	X					Templatize across releases	Preponed as successor to A10	add DE role	ServiceNow
A12	Incorporate parameters for release	X					Templatize across releases	Preponed as successor to A11	add DE role	ServiceNow
A13	Incorporate parameters for deployment	X					Templatize across releases	Preponed as successor to A12	add DE role	ServiceNow
A19	Store configuration scripts in project document library			X			Configuration scripts cannot be auto-reused	Store configuration scripts in NEXUS to be re-used by orchestrator		NEXUS
A26	Prepare functional test scripts [regression & integration] using Selenium integrated to Jira			X			Preponed critical path; test case to script conversion is manual	Start time preponed; add plug-in to convert TDD (Gherkin) to test scripts		TDD (Gherkin) to script conversion plug-in for Jira
A27	Prepare NFR test scripts [performance] using HP LR integrated to Jira			X			Preponed critical path; test case to script conversion is manual	Start time preponed; add plug-in to convert TDD (Gherkin) to test scripts		TDD (Gherkin) to script conversion plug-in for Jira
A28	Execute tests using automation tool - regression & integration					X	Preponed critical path	Start time preponed		
A29	Execute tests using automation tool - performance					X	Preponed critical path	Start time preponed		
A37	Analyze deployment orchestration requirements from business requirements and infra details			X					add DE role	
A38	Based on requirements, evaluate, select and install orchestrator tool			X					add DE role	Orchestrator
A39	Configure (and integrate) orchestrator tool based on automation requirements			X					add DE role	Orchestrator
A40	Configure NEXUS for binary repository			X					add DE role	NEXUS
A41	Migrate existing scripts from project library to NEXUS for later reuse			X					add DE role	NEXUS

Incorporating the above two tables to the As-Is process architecture yielded the To-Be process architecture, as follows:

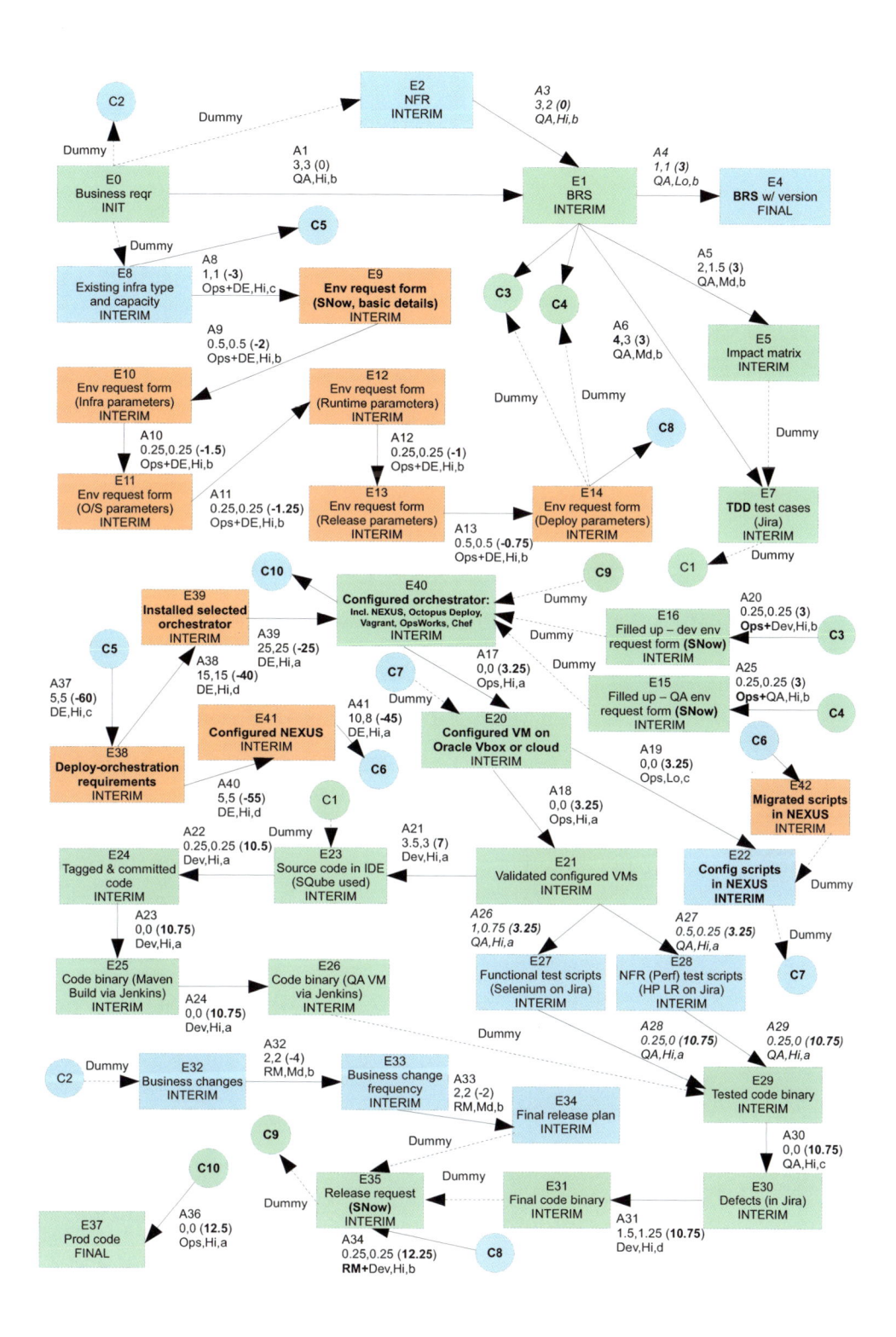

Figure 15: Example of the To-Be Process Architecture

Note that while we constructed the To-Be process network diagram, we computed the cycle times (including the total time, manual time and relative start time) for each activity. You may either choose to perform a forward pass or a backward pass computation as you construct the diagram, either progressively or retrogressively respectively.

We followed the following color conventions for the boxes representing the events, and connectors:

DevOps implementation activity	These are typically new or enhanced activities to create the underlying DevOps infrastructure in order to realize the changes in IT process
Activity on analyzed critical path (now changed)	These are the activities pertaining to the As-Is critical path, including those changed (or say, preponed), thereby re-defining the path
Activity on paths other than the critical path in context	These are the activities pertaining to the paths other than the critical path, including those changed vis-à-vis changes to the As-Is critical path

Since we have analyzed the critical path and arrived at the To-Be process architecture, we would need to find out if this is the optimal state of DevOps that can be reached, or we still have a clear critical path (based on the criteria we outlined earlier) – either the changed one itself, or another path that has now become the new critical path – that can be further optimized.

Hence, we tabulated all the paths in the To-Be process architecture to find out the total IT cycle time for each of them (note that we have combined some of the paths for convenience, where applicable, as we have done in our earlier analysis):

S#	Path	Duration	Start time	End time	Min float	Max float	Net duration considering min float	Net duration considering max float	Final output type	Average criticality	Critical path?
1	A1/A3 - A4	4	0	4	0	0	4	4	information	Medium	N

2	A1/A3 - A5 - A22 - A23 - A24 - A30 - A31 - A34 - A36	12.5	0	12.5	5.5	5.5	7	7	material	High	N
3	A1/A3 - A6 - A22 - A23 - A24 - A30 - A31 - A34 - A36	12.5	0	12.5	3.5	3.5	9	9	material	High	?
4	A1/A3 - A20/A25 - A17 - A18 - A21 - A22 - A23 - A24 - A30 - A31 - A36	12.5	0	12.5	4	4	8.5	8.5	material	High	?
5	A8 - A9 - A10 - A11 - A12 - A13 - A20/A25 - A17 - A19	3.25	0	3.25	0.25	0.25	3	3	information	High	N
6	A8 - A9 - A10 - A11 - A12 - A13 - A20/A25 - A17 - A18 - A21 - A22 - A23 - A24 - A30 - A31 - A34 - A36	12.5	0	12.5	4	4	8.5	8.5	material	High	?
7	A8 - A9 - A10 - A11 - A12 - A13 - A20/A25 - A17 - A18 - A26/A27 - A28/A29 - A30 - A31 - A34 - A36	12.5	0	12.5	6.25	6.75	6.25	5.75	material	High	N
8	A32 - A33 - A36	16.5	-4	12.5	12.5	12.5	4	4	material	High	N

Note that in the above table, we have not considered the activities that correspond to DevOps implementation, as such stories do not contribute to the day-to-day IT process in context.

From the above table, we see that paths 3, 4 and 6 contend in terms of total IT cycle time; they have the same cycle time (12.5 days) if we do not consider the float times, however are very near to each other (path 3 has 9 days, paths 4 and 6 have 8.5 days) if float times are considered. Even though we could have considered path 3 as the critical path for further optimization, we stopped at this point given that the difference between the cycle times between path 3 and the other two paths (4 and 6) to be significantly small (9 – 8.5 = 0.5 days).

Hence, we considered our final To-Be process architecture to be the one given in the figure above.

Further note: Even though paths 2 and 7 have the same cycle time (12.5 days) as paths 3, 4 or 6 without considering float times, they have quite lower cycle times (7 days, and 6.25 days [with min. float] / 5.75 days [with max. float], respectively) while considering the respective float times; hence we do not consider them as competing paths. Similarly, even though path 8 has the highest cycle time (16.5 days) without considering float time, it drastically reduces to 4 days if we consider float time, hence is not considered as a competing path as well.

Deriving the Target IT Process

Based on the example To-Be process architecture as derived in the previous chapter, the target IT process can be tabulated to activity-wise detailed view of the process. Further, the new, modified or eliminated activities (if you want to retain them in the table for later reference) may also be suitably color coded.

Note that the DevOps implementation activities may be tabulated separately to provide a clean view of the core IT life cycle process. This is because, the DevOps implementation activities are typically one-time – to create the DevOps based automation infrastructure – that together enables establishing the changed IT process.

Stories for the Target IT Process

Going back to the example in previous chapter, we derived the following as the target IT process with associated details:

S#	Epic	Story	Total time	Manual time	Predecessor	Relative start time	Criticality	Role/ team	Input	Output	Automation tool
A1	SDLC - Requirements analysis	Create (or obtain) the BRS	3	3	-	0	High	QA	Business requirement	BRS	
A2	SDLC - Requirements analysis	Create the SRS from the BRS									
A3	SDLC - Requirements analysis	Identify and include NFRs as part of SRS	3	2	A2, A3	0	High	QA	NFR	SRS	
A4	SDLC - Requirements analysis	Store BRS / SRS in the project document library with versioning	1	1	A2, A3	3	Low	QA	SRS	SRS with version	
A20	SDLC - Coding	Request for dev environment through ServiceNow	0.25	0.25	A3	3	High	Dev, Ops	BRS	Filled up dev environment request form	ServiceNow
A25	SDLC - Testing	Request for test/ QA environment through ServiceNow	0.25	0.25	A3	3	High	QA, Ops	BRS	Filled up QA environment request form	ServiceNow

A5	SDLC - Requirements analysis	Assess impact to components	2	1.5	A2, A3	3	Med	QA	SRS	Impact matrix	
A6	SDLC - Requirements analysis	For system centric requirement, apply TDD principles and templatize repeatable requirements in TDD format	4	3	A1	3	Med	QA	BRS	TDD format	
A7	SDLC - Requirements analysis	Translate into test cases via a workflow using a workflow/ rules engine and feed into Jira									
A14	SDLC - Environment provisioning	Approve environment request (based on availability) through workflow mentioning ETA									
A15	SDLC - Environment provisioning	Spin up VM via Oracle VirtualBox directly using GUI or scripts									
A16	SDLC - Environment provisioning	Spin up VM over public cloud directly									
A17	SDLC - Environment provisioning	Spin up and configure VM either on Oracle VirtualBox or on-cloud (say, AWS)	0	0	A39	3.25	High	Ops	Orchestrator template	Environment configured VMs	Vagrant, Chef, AWS OpsWorks
A18	SDLC - Environment provisioning	Validate environment with dev/test team	0	0	A17	3.25	High	Ops	Environment configured VMs	Validated configured VMs	Orchestrator
A19	SDLC - Environment provisioning	Store configuration scripts in NEXUS	0	0	A17	3.25	Low	Ops	Environment configured VMs	Configuration scripts with version	NEXUS
A21	SDLC - Coding	Code application using IDE using in-line code quality check using SONARQube	3.5	3	A18	7	High	Dev	Validated configured VMs	Quality checked source code in IDE	SonarQube
A22	SDLC - Coding	Generate tags and commit code manually in Subversion	0.25	0.25	A21	10.5	High	Dev	Quality checked source code in IDE	Tagged and committed code	
A23	SDLC - Coding	Build (upon unit test) application using Maven	0	0	A22	10.75	High	Dev	Tagged and committed code	Code binary	Maven, Jenkins

101

		through Jenkins								
A24	SDLC - Coding	Promote application code to QA environment through Jenkins on success build	0	0	A23	10.75	High	Dev	Code binary	QA released code binary	Jenkins
A26	SDLC - Testing	Prepare functional test scripts [regression & integration] using Selenium integrated to Jira with automated TDD to test script conversion plug-in	0.5	0.25	A18	3.25	High	QA	Validated configured VMs	Functional test scripts	Jira, plug-in for TDD (Gherkin) to test scripts
A27	SDLC - Testing	Prepare NFR test scripts [performance] using HP LoadRunner integrated to Jira with automated TDD to test script conversion plug-in	0.25	0	A18	3.25	High	QA	Validated configured VMs	NFR (performance) test scripts	Jira, plug-in for TDD (Gherkin) to test scripts
A28	SDLC - Testing	Execute tests using automation tool - regression & integration	0.25	0	A26	10.75	High	QA	Functional test scripts	Functional tested code binary	Selenium
A29	SDLC - Testing	Execute tests using automation tool - performance	0.25	0	A27	10.75	High	QA	NFR (performance) test scripts	Performance tested code binary	HP LoadRunner
A30	SDLC - Testing	Defects recorded in ALM tool	0	0	A29	10.75	High	QA	Tested code binary	Defects	Selenium, Jira
A31	SDLC - Testing	Defects are resolved and closed by dev team in ALM tool (subject to test team validation)	1.5	1.25	A30	10.75	High	Dev	Defects	Final code binary	
A32	SDLC - Application release and deployment	Identify business change or incident fix requirements	2	2	-	-4	Med	RM	Business requirement	Business changes	
A33	SDLC - Application release and deployment	Prepare release plan and share (and align on) using Microsoft Excel (or equivalent) and email	2	2	A32	-2	Med	RM	Business changes	Final release plan	

A34	SDLC - Application release and deployment	Place release request through ServiceNow with same step approval by release manager	0.25	0.25	A13, [A31], [A33]	12.25	High	Dev, RM	Release request	Approved release request	ServiceNow
A35	SDLC - Application release and deployment	Approve release request using email									
A36	SDLC - Application release and deployment	Execute release using scripts configured in Octopus Deploy	0	0	A39	12.5	High	Ops	Approved release request	Application code (in production)	Octopus Deploy

Note that we have used the following color conventions, both in the above table and the one below (listing out the DevOps implementation stories):

DevOps implementation activity (indicated only in first column)	Activity modified or changed	Activity eliminated	New activity added	Activity preponed

Note that more than one color convention may be applicable for an activity. Hence for convenience, if an activity is both preponed and modified, we only indicated the color convention for it being modified. However, in the table below, we have indicated the stories being DevOps implementation stories by using the appropriate color convention in the first column only; whereas the next few columns used color convention to indicate if the activity is preponed or newly added.

DevOps Implementation Stories

Here, note that the relative start time for the given activities are all in negative, thereby indicating that these activities need to be completed prior to the actual main stream IT life cycle process (as outlined in the above table). Moreover, there are no specific automation tools that are specified for implementing such DevOps infrastructure, given that this is typically expected to be executed once. Further, we have introduced the "DevOps Engineer" as a separate role to execute the implementation activities; however, based on whether there is a specific group (say, Dev or Ops-infra) who has the primary propensity to adopt DevOps, such existing role(s) may also execute the activities instead of introducing a new role altogether.

S#	Epic	Story	Total time	Manual time	Predecessor	Relative start time	Criticality	Role/ team	Input	Output	Automation tool
A8	SDLC - Environment provisioning	Identify mode of request form (ServiceNow) and basic set of parameters for templatization across releases	1	1	-	-3	High	Ops, DE*	Existing infrastructure capacity	Basic environment Request form	
A9	SDLC - Environment provisioning	Incorporate parameters for infrastructure - CPU, disk space, etc.	0.5	0.5	A8	-2	High	Ops, DE	Basic environment request form	Environment request form (+ infra parameters)	
A10	SDLC - Environment provisioning	Incorporate parameters for O/S - Linux, Unix, Windows, etc.	0.25	0.25	A9	-1.5	High	Ops, DE	Environment request form (+ infra parameters)	Environment request form (+ O/S parameters)	
A11	SDLC - Environment provisioning	Incorporate parameters for runtime incl. language compiler & runtime, IDE, zones, etc.	0.25	0.25	A10	-1.25	High	Ops, DE	Environment request form (+ O/S parameters)	Environment request form (+ runtime parameters)	
A12	SDLC - Environment provisioning	Incorporate parameters for release	0.25	0.25	A11	-1	High	Ops, DE	Environment request form (+ runtime parameters)	Environment request form (+ release parameters)	
A13	SDLC - Environment provisioning	Incorporate parameters for deployment	0.5	0.5	A12	-0.75	High	Ops, DE	Environment request form (+ release parameters)	Environment request form (+ deploy parameters)	
A37	DevOps Setup - Orchestration	Analyze orchestration requirements including tool specific integration required	5	5	-	-60	High	DE	Existing infrastructure capacity	Orchestration requirement	
A38	DevOps Setup - Orchestration	Evaluate, select and install orchestrator	15	15	A37	-40	High	DE	Orchestration requirement	Installed orchestrator	
A39	DevOps Setup - Orchestration	Configure orchestrator	25	25	A38	-25	High	DE	Installed orchestrator	Configured orchestrator	
A40	DevOps Setup - Orchestration	Install, integrate (to orchestrator) and configure NEXUS	5	5	A37	-55	High	DE	Orchestration requirement	Installed and configured NEXUS	
A41	DevOps Setup - Orchestration	Migrate existing binaries from project library to NEXUS	10	8	A40	-45	High	DE	Installed and configured NEXUS	Migrated scripts to NEXUS	

* DE – DevOps Engineer

You may want to derive an implementation plan for the above stories on DevOps implementation, and a corresponding support plan for the implementation. Such plan would typically cover the stories with estimates – we recommend Agile estimation – based on a specific implementation team profile (and velocity).

Also note that as outlined in the next chapter, your timelines may be impacted due to the cultural aspects of the team. Hence, such plan would need adjustments based on the people pattern analysis, if done for the assessment in context.

Quantifying People Architecture

To understand how to derive and use the people aspect for DevOps assessment, you may go back to the chapter on "Defining the Cultural Aspect" for a quick recap of our culture model. Based on our understanding and using a very simple example of activities and related interactions across the roles, we first draw the processes mapped to people roles in the team, to analyze the respective propensities:

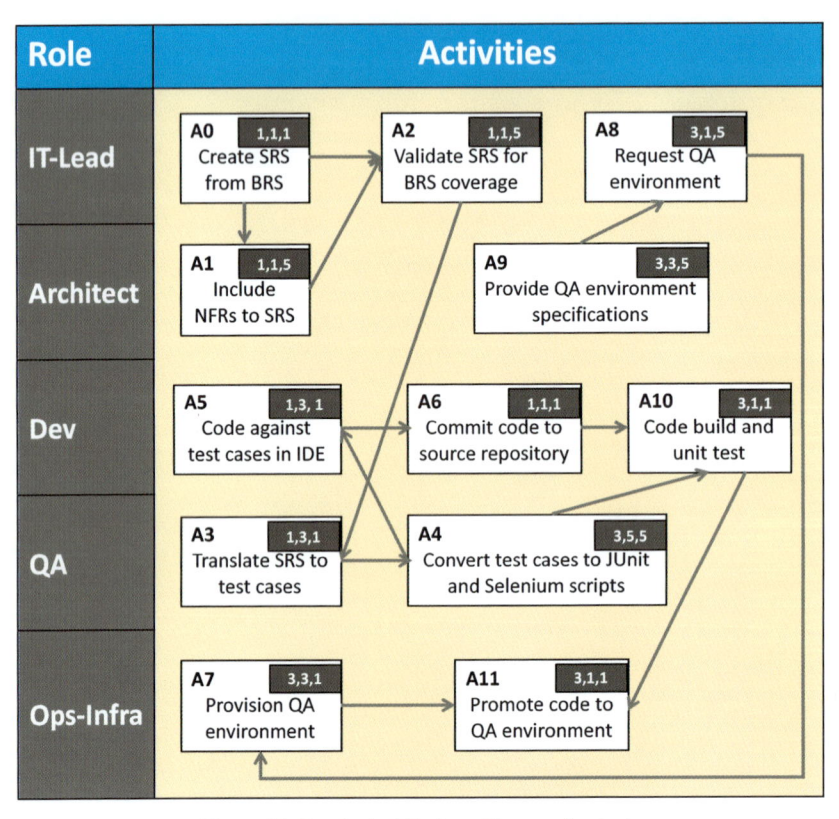

Role	Activities
IT-Lead	**A0** (1,1,1) Create SRS from BRS — **A2** (1,1,5) Validate SRS for BRS coverage — **A8** (3,1,5) Request QA environment
Architect	**A1** (1,1,5) Include NFRs to SRS — **A9** (3,3,5) Provide QA environment specifications
Dev	**A5** (1,3,1) Code against test cases in IDE — **A6** (1,1,1) Commit code to source repository — **A10** (3,1,1) Code build and unit test
QA	**A3** (1,3,1) Translate SRS to test cases — **A4** (3,5,5) Convert test cases to JUnit and Selenium scripts
Ops-Infra	**A7** (3,3,1) Provision QA environment — **A11** (3,1,1) Promote code to QA environment

Figure 16: People Architecture Diagram for As-Is

Propensities are represented in X,Y,Z format as follows:

X = practice propensity, Y = technology use propensity, Z = collaboration propensity

Here, the activities are drawn in boxes against the respective roles; we have simplified the notation by stating the activity number and description only. The activities are connected to each other, either within the same role or to activities of a different role based on the respective predecessor-successor relationships. Following is the scoring mechanism we defined for the respective propensities as per our cultural model, as follows:

Practice propensity:

We used the following scoring criteria for the activities with respect to practice propensity:

- 1 if the activity has no automation (total time taken by activity = manual time taken)
- 3 if the activity has been automated partially
- 4 if the activity is primarily or fully automated (manual time taken ~ 0)
- 5 if the activity is fully automated, and uses intelligent agent, say incorporating a rule engine or machine learning algorithms to control and/or monitor the associated workflow

Note that we have not used a value of "2" for practice propensity. We did this to factor in the wider disparity between manual effort and automation at even a minimum level. This is a major cultural shift for any team. We found this approach to be accurately reflecting this cultural shift from a propensity perspective for the majority of teams.

Technology use (or, usage) propensity:

We used the following scoring criteria for the activities with respect to technology use propensity:

- 1 if the activity is executed manually; or uses any software, technology or tool that provides documentation, graphical and limited action-recording facilities (such as a spreadsheet software's macro facility) to product the output directly
- 3 if the activity uses any software, technology or tool using which the IT team can change the underlying configurations to control the software's behavior and/or associated workflow, using a textual or graphical user interface; which in turn, tunes the underlying rules or algorithms to produce the output
- 5 if the activity uses any software, technology or tool that executes code or scripts – that can be accessed and changed by the IT team or role executing the activity – for controlling the software's behavior and/or the associated workflow

We typically look at realizing (and generating) all the core entities in **IT as Code** to be a relatively mature state of DevOps, for example, requirement-as-code; code-to-generate-application-code, infrastructure-as-code, test-as-code, deploy-as-code, security-as-code, et al; given that realizing the entities as code, incorporating appropriate rules or learning algorithms, is the most optimal and fastest method for an IT process execution

Note that we have not used the values of "2" and "4" as the above values sufficiently categorize the propensity levels for technology use. This approach has two advantages; it provisions for disparity between the states of documentation-led versus configuration-led versus coding-led technology usage, and also scales our scoring mechanism within a value of 1 to 5.

Collaboration propensity:

We used the following scoring criteria for the activities – either manual or using automation – with respect to collaboration propensity:

- **1** if the activity requires a given role to work in a silo, for example, developer writing code or a tester executing test cases
- **3 or 5** if the activity requires individuals in a given role to work as a group; this typically are activities such as peer review and validation; design and creation of forms, templates and blueprints (such as software requirements specification including both functional and non-functional requirements, environment request forms, developer checklists, test plans, et al); consolidation or merging, and splitting of code or environments; request for environments, code or information in either electronic or non-electronic format (say, documents, reports, et al)
    - **3** if the activity's output becomes a direct input to, or impacts the execution of, the successor activity for the same role
    - **5** if the activity's output becomes a direct input to, or impacts the execution of, the successor activity for a different role; note that for multiple successors, this score applies when at least one successor activity has a different role

The next step is to compute the respective average scores for each role, as follows:

Role	Activities	Practice propensity	Technology use propensity	Collaboration propensity
IT-Lead	A0 (1,1,1) Create SRS from BRS → A2 (1,1,5) Validate SRS for BRS coverage → A8 (3,1,5) Request QA environment	(1+1+3)/3 = 1.7	(1+1+1)/3 = 1.0	(1+5+5)/3 = 3.7
Architect	A1 (1,1,5) Include NFRs to SRS; A9 (3,3,5) Provide QA environment specifications	(1+3)/2 = 2.0	(1+3)/2 = 2.0	(5+5)/2 = 5.0
Dev	A5 (1,3,1) Code against test cases in IDE → A6 (1,1,1) Commit code to source repository → A10 (3,1,1) Code build and unit test	(1+1+3)/3 = 1.7	(3+1+1)/3 = 1.7	(1+1+1)/3 = 1.0
QA	A3 (1,3,1) Translate SRS to test cases → A4 (3,5,5) Convert test cases to JUnit and Selenium scripts	(1+3)/2 = 2.0	(3+5)/2 = 4.0	(1+5)/2 = 3.0
Ops-Infra	A7 (3,3,1) Provision QA environment → A11 (3,1,1) Promote code to QA environment	(3+3)/2 = 3.0	(3+1)/2 = 2.0	(1+1)/2 = 1.0

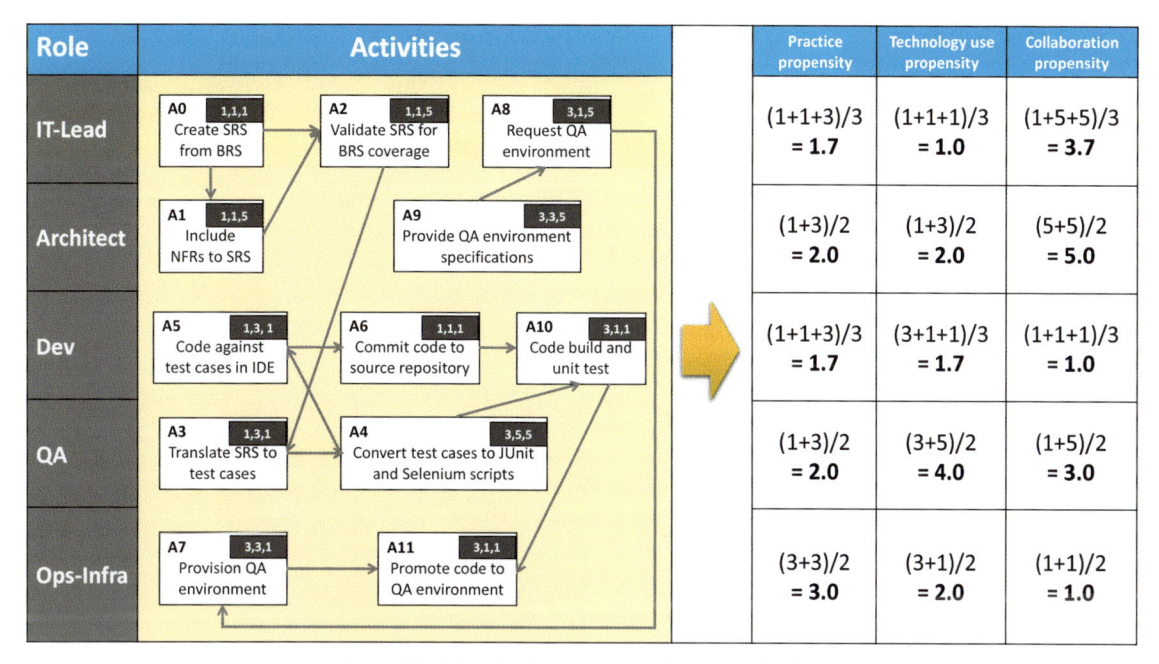

Figure 17: Role-wise People Propensity Scores for As-Is

In the above computations, we considered an accuracy of up to one decimal place. Further note that the above people architecture is not a complete one, but a partial representation we are giving as an example.

Following gives a brief description of how we arrived at the scores for each of the roles' activities:

a. **IT Lead**: Creating the SRS from the BRS is completely manual, hence X = 1; the SRS is created using say a spreadsheet software without any rule configurations, hence Y = 1; the document creation itself did not require any collaboration, hence Z = 1. For the next two activities, since they are too done manually, X = 1 and Y = 1 for both of them respectively. However, validating the SRS required inter-role collaboration with the Architect, as well as provided input to the QA's activity in creating test cases, hence Z = 5. Similarly, requesting for QA environment required inter-role collaboration, hence Z = 5.

b. **Architect**: Including NFRs in the SRS was a manual activity without any specific tool configuration, hence X = 1 and Y = 1. However, including NFRs into the SRS was a direct input to the IT Lead's SRS validation activity, hence Z = 5. For providing QA environment specifications, the Architect employed a design tool to partially automate the process, hence X = 3. Further, the tool provided configuration options for making changes to the specification based on specific business requirements, hence Y = 3. Lastly, the activity resulted in a direct input to the QA environment request for the IT Lead, hence Z = 5.

c. **Dev**: Coding and committing the code were manual activities, though using tools; hence X = 1 for both of them respectively. The tool (IDE for coding) provided several configurations to manage coding environment, check code syntax, et al; hence for the coding activity, Y = 3. However, committing the code was straight-forward standardized (for all developers) through the IDE, hence Y = 1. Code build and test activity was automated partially, hence X = 3. However the process itself was standardized (as for all developers), hence Y = 1; and required no collaboration, hence Z = 1.

d. **QA**: Translating SRS to test cases was a manual activity, hence X = 1. The tool for conversion, however could be configured for specifying test case conversion rules (though automatic conversion did not happen), hence Y = 3. There was no specific collaboration required as SRS was already available, hence Z = 1. Conversion of test cases to test scripts in JUnit and Selenium was partially automated through assisted code generation and checking through the tools, hence X = 3. Apart from the assisted coding aspects, the tool provided full-fledged test scripting facility for the test cases, hence Y = 5. Further, the coded test scripts directly impacted the coding and build-test activities of the developer.

e. **Ops-Infra**: Provisioning the QA environment was partially automated using the request from IT Lead, hence X = 3; the provisioning tool provided configuration changes, hence Y = 3. However, no specific collaboration was further needed, hence Z = 1. For promoting the packaged code from development to QA environment, the workflow was already automated using a continuous integration server, hence X = 3; however, since the process was standardized for all such pipelines without provision to change configurations, Y = 1. And since no specific collaboration was required for the activity, Z = 1.

Next, we found out the average propensities across the roles. Following are the values:

Practice propensity, $X = 2.08$

Technology use propensity, $Y = 2.14$

Collaboration propensity, $Z = 2.74$

For the sake of simplicity, we would construe the practice and technology use propensities to be relatively "Low", and the collaboration propensity to be "High". Based on the people pattern as described in the chapter "Defining the Cultural Aspect", the given scenario maps to the following:

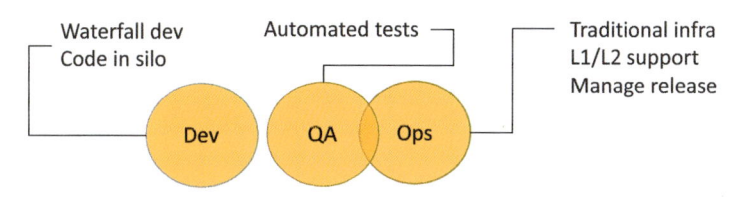

Figure 18: People pattern for Low-Low-High Propensity Combination

Here, Dev still works in a silo whereas QA takes the first step towards automation and collaboration. Ops takes up managing releases so that disparity in expectations between Dev and Ops reduces; Ops would not blame Dev for "bad code" as they now own the release. For similar reason vice versa, all environment requests are done through standardized request templates released by Ops. QA automation further ensures test driven development (TDD); this is the only avenue for automation.

Elaborating on the people architecture for the above pattern, we obtained the following:

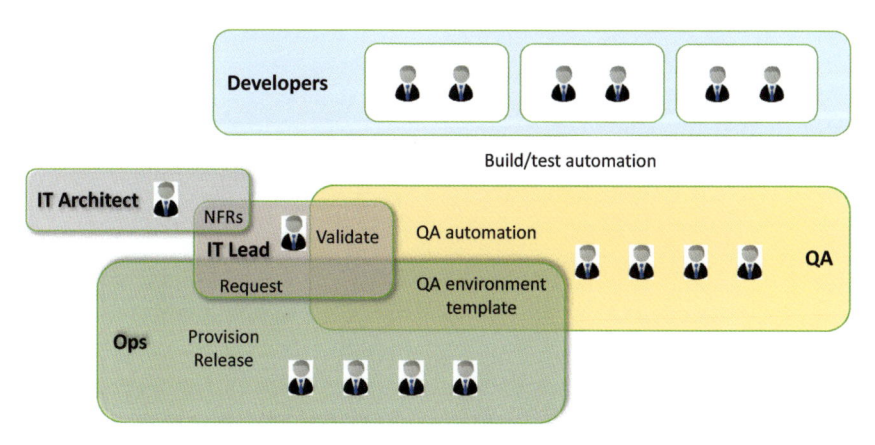

Figure 19: Simplified As-is People Architecture

We would repeat the above exercise for the To-Be people architecture. Once we have the role-wise average propensities of the To-Be architecture, we can find out the variation of the values vis-à-vis those of the As-Is architecture as found above. The higher the variation, the higher would be the impact in bringing any change to the people aspect on that specific propensity. This is because a higher variation would mean significant cultural shift for the specific role (or, team). We would reasonably expect that the respective propensities would not decrease – if not increase – in the To-Be architecture with respect to the As-Is architecture.

While we arrive at the To-Be architecture (through process optimization as outlined in the previous chapters), there can be two basic impacts to the respective propensities as given below. However note that actual optimization of the process would dictate how the To-Be detailed people architecture would exactly look like.

a. **Practice propensity goes from "Low" to "High"** – The two groups that exhibit lowest practice propensities are IT Lead and Dev. Appropriate process optimization should entail engineering task automation for SRS validation (for IT Lead), and incorporating application architecture change to support faster code changes (for Dev). From Ops perspective, a coded release pipeline may be established to better manage the release dependencies. Following may be the possible To-Be people pattern:

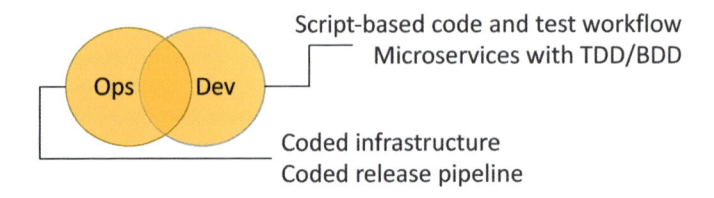

Figure 20: To-Be People Pattern - Option (a)

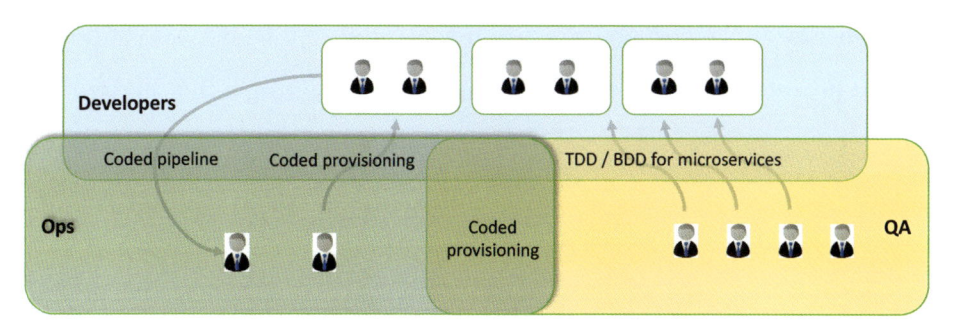

Figure 21: Simplified People Architecture for Option (a)

b. **Technology use propensity goes from "Low to "High"** – The two groups that exhibit lowest technology use propensities are still the IT Lead and Dev. Process optimization should look for leveraging technologies that support text parsing and specification generation (for IT lead), and code metrics with feedback loops to suggest changes, auto-resolution for change commit conflicts, et al (for Dev). QA may establish higher test automation, say for NFRs. Ops may look at a configurable release pipeline with an integrated monitoring tool to better manage release dependencies. Following may be the possible To-Be people pattern:

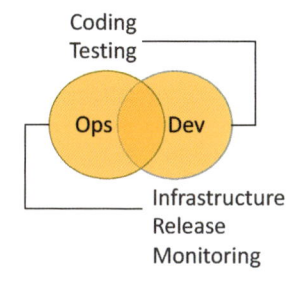

Figure 22: To-Be People Pattern - Option (b)

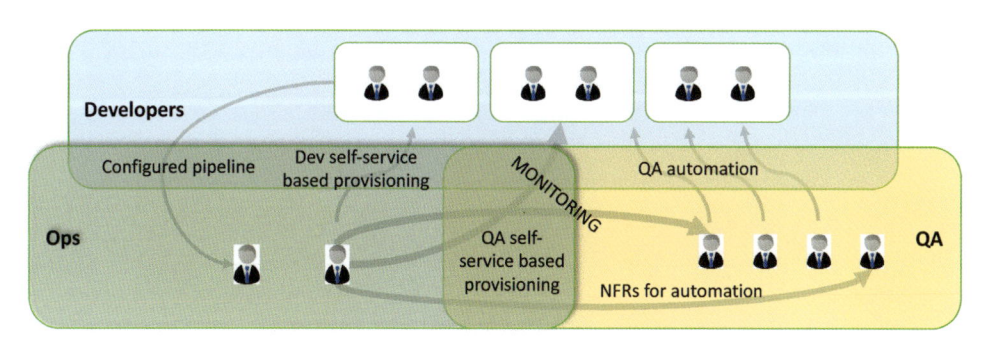

Figure 23: Simplified People Architecture for Option (b)

You may combine the above two options for a highly optimized To-Be state or bring in drastic changes to the process (say, introducing containers, introducing cloud in case the current infrastructure is on-premise, et al), however high disparity between As-Is and To-Be propensities may also result in longer DevOps implementation and adoption times (hence, longer IT cycle times than what is estimated) for the IT team.

Hence, thereby we compute the cost for the DevOps implementation and adoption times from people perspective. Two rules of thumb from our experience in conducting multiple assessments are as follows:

a. With respect to implementation time, the actual timeline varies with respect to the process-based estimates (as computed in the previous chapter) due to the mentoring aspect for people who would be utilizing the new (or changed) technology or incorporating a given practice, rather than the new (or changes made to the) technology or the practice itself. This variation is 10%, 15% or 20% over and above the process-based estimates, based on how many of the three propensities respectively are substantially changing (substantial change is typically 10% or more).

b. With respect to the adoption time or actual IT cycle time in the To-Be state (post implementation period), whichever is the highest among the percentage variations of respective propensities, is to be factored in as additional cycle time over and above the process analyzed timeline; this is valid for the first time the new or changed IT process is executed. However, note that the first time variation is not more than 50% of the process analyzed timeline. The variation decreases with further cycle runs; it is typically the mean of the percentage propensity variations for the second run, and thereafter it somewhat follows the curve below till it merges with the process analyzed timeline.

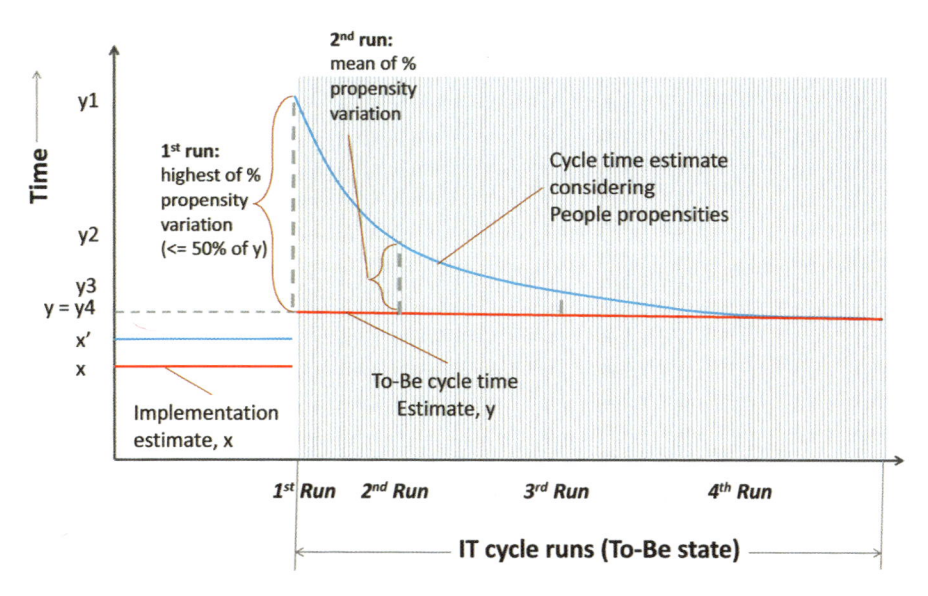

Figure 24: Variations to time estimates due to People Propensities

To illustrate the costs on timelines, we consider the following two examples:

a. In the first scenario, say the average propensities across the roles from As-Is to To-Be states change as follows:

Propensity	Value (As-Is)	Value (To-Be)	% Variation	Impact on implementation time	Impact on adoption time
Practice	2.08	2.78	34%	10% as only the practice propensity has substantially changed	34%; practice propensity has highest variation
Technology use	2.14	2.20	3%		
Collaboration	2.74	2.74	0%		

Hence, if the process-based estimate for implementation time is say, 20 days, the actual implementation time becomes 20 x (1 + 10%) = 22 days

If the process analyzed timeline for the To-Be IT cycle is 25 days, the actual adoption time (hence, the IT cycle time) for the first time the IT cycle is executed, is 25 x (1 + 34%) = 33.5 days. Later for the second cycle run, considering the integer mean of the percentage propensity variations, (34% + 3% + 0%) / 3 = 12%, the adoption or new cycle time comes down to, 25 x (1 + 12%) = 28 days. Thereafter, it further reduces till it merges with the process analyzed timeline in steady state (typically by the 3rd or 4th cycle run).

b. Following are the average propensities across the roles from As-Is to To-Be states:

Propensity	Value (As-Is)	Value (To-Be)	% Variation	Impact on implementation time	Impact on adoption time
Practice	2.08	2.24	8%	15% as technology use and collaboration propensities have substantially changed	50%; technology use propensity has highest variation, however we consider 50% variation as maximum
Technology use	2.14	3.42	60%		
Collaboration	2.74	3.11	14%		

Hence, if the process-based estimate for implementation time is say, 30 days, the actual implementation time becomes 30 x (1 + 15%) = 34.5 days

If the process analyzed timeline for the To-Be IT cycle is 20 days, the actual adoption time (hence, the IT cycle time) for the first time the IT cycle is executed, is 20 x (1 + 50%) = 30 days. Later, considering the integer mean, (8% + 50% + 14%) / 3 = 24%, the adoption or new cycle time comes down to, 20 x (1 + 24%) ~ 25 days. Note that we have considered 50% for technology use propensity, instead of 60%, to compute the mean.

Given the above, the second scenario of To-Be architecture entails a higher impact of culture on the envisaged change. Note the higher impact on the corresponding implementation time and the IT cycle time post-implementation, at least for the first two cycle runs.

While you use the rules of thumb above

Note that while the aforesaid rules of thumb are based on our observations across a number of assessments done for various organizations (and tallying them later on how accurate were the computations during actual execution), the actual results can still vary – either for DevOps implementation or for the new IT cycle time – with respect to the computations we illustrated. Hence, the thumb rules are to be treated only as guidelines to help you predict the impact of culture during an assessment.

Further, note that there are environmental or one-off factors such as delays in software or manpower procurements, team member unavailability, security incidents, network failure due to service providers, et al, which are not considered for the assessment.

Articulating Technology Flow

By tabulating the To-Be process architecture diagram, similar to the example given as in earlier figure above, you can easily identify the technology and tools that would form part of the revised IT process. Note that for any changes to – including addition, configuration or removal of, a tool – a corresponding implementation activity for DevOps needs to be present as part of the process network diagram (for example, as represented by Orange boxes in the earlier figure above).

Given that the relevant technology and tools have already been considered as constraints while constructing the As-Is and To-Be process network diagram, we would simply provide an example of such an architecture and its corresponding tabulation here. Selection of tooling is based on the existing tool licenses of the organization in context, and the organization's plans for tool procurements based on available IT budget and specific feature-wise fitment of such tools to the To-Be IT process.

Following is an example of technology architecture as derived from the process architecture, either in context of As-Is or To-Be. Note that this does not conform to any formal technology architecture representations, however suffices to indicate how the relevant technologies and tools work together as part of the respective IT process. This is because the approach to creating this architecture diagram is process centric. Based on your or your organization's rigor in using suitable terminology, you may rather term it as the "process view of technology landscape" for the given DevOps assessment.

In the diagram below, we had separately pointed out the tools (technologies in case you want to bring out development stack specific details such as Java, .NET, C#, PostgreSQL, et al) for Dev/QA and Ops, in addition to common tools that are used by both teams and/or IT leads and architects.

Note: Tool names provided are representational only, and are without explicit mention of corresponding registered vendor names owning the tool(s)

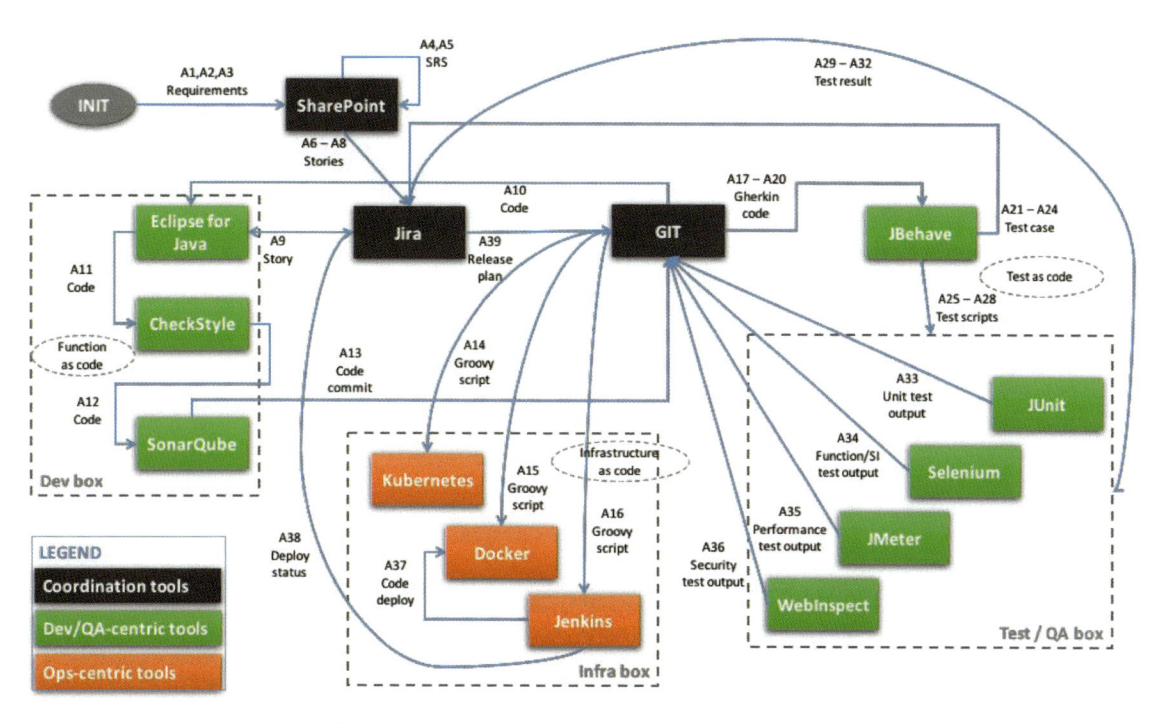

Figure 25: Technology/ Tools architecture representation

The corresponding tabulation may be provided as follows:

Tool name	Technology supported	Owning role	Activity mapping	Change type
SharePoint	API based integrations	IT Lead	A1 – A5	Configuration
Jira	API based integrations	IT Lead	A6 – A8, A21 – A24, A29 – A32, A38	Configuration
GIT	API based integrations	IT Lead	A13, A33 – A36, A39	Configuration
Eclipse for Java	Java/ JEE	Dev	A9, A10	Code
CheckStyle	Java/ JEE	Dev	A11	Configuration
SonarQube	API based integrations for multiple language compilers/ IDEs	Dev	A12	Configuration
JBehave	Java/ JEE	QA	A17 – A20	Code
JUnit	Java/ JEE	QA	A25	Code

119

Selenium	Java/ JEE	QA	A26	Code
JMeter	Java/ JEE	QA	A27	Code/ Configuration
WebInspect	Java/ JEE web applications	QA	A28	Code/ Configuration
Jenkins	API based integrations	Ops	A16	Code (pipeline)/ Configuration (using plug-ins)
Docker	UNIX/ LINUX, Cloud services	Ops	A15, A37	Code
Kubernetes	UNIX/ LINUX, Cloud services	Ops	A14	Code/ Configuration

In addition to the aforesaid view, you may also want to add the technology architectures (both As-Is and To-Be) – say, layered infrastructure architecture, et al – as per formal architecture definitions using standard architecture frameworks. An alternative way to get around this (in case you do not want to include such formal representations in your DevOps assessment) is to collaborate with specific application development teams or Ops teams to map the DevOps based architecture as represented here, to the respective formal architectures provided by such teams. We typically follow or recommend The Open Group's TOGAF® framework for such architecture views, where applicable.

Deriving the Key Metrics

Given that a metrics-driven DevOps implementation and IT execution is the most effective way to ensure success of such implementation, we recommend to have in mind a metrics framework to follow for your organization's DevOps initiative at the assessment stage itself. We have seen several assessments that do not address metrics adequately, and leave any decisions on this aspect for the due diligence or execution phase during downstream implementation. In such cases, the metrics decided upon become quite constrained; being primarily based on the technology/ tools' choices that get finalized instead of the IT process itself.

Metrics should be decided based on the process architecture optimization that has been evaluated as part of the assessment, irrespective of the technology/ tools' choices that can come later. This is because it is the depth and breadth of metrics selected that should determine the success or failure of the IT process itself. This would enable taking control of the process at the right time, and take corrective actions accordingly, in case something goes out of compliance with respect to expected or target values. Hence, the choice of metrics should have an influence on such technology/ tools' choices, rather than the other way round.

Further, as the organization matures gradually on its DevOps journey, the metrics would still exist (and get added on) irrespective of new technology and tools that may be introduced, and older tools having expired with or without replacements based on the context.

For the purpose of DevOps, we use the following metrics structure. However, based on your context, you may want to bring quality or cost as your high priority metrics. In such case, the assessment itself would need to be guided by such parameter whereas for us, time (reducing IT cycle time) has been the primary parameter. Further note that cost may be construed as a derived parameter arising out of the other two; typically say, reducing IT cycle time or improving quality – notwithstanding other associated factors such as manpower costs and capital costs locked in technology investments, etc. – may result in reducing related costs.

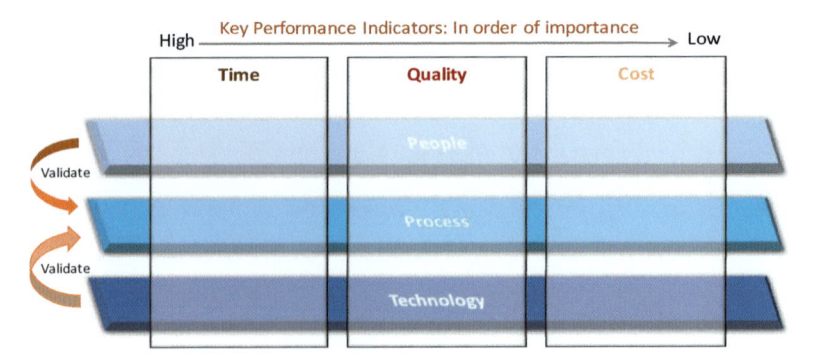

Figure 26: Metrics structure for DevOps

The metrics structure shown is a matrix across key performance indicators (KPIs; Time, Quality and Cost) and the three DevOps dimensions (People, Process and Technology).

Note that the key performance indicators are arranged in order of importance. Metrics with respect to time (here, IT cycle time) is the primary indicator for achieving a given state of DevOps, followed by quality and lastly, cost. Also note that the metrics pertaining to process are of significance; both people and technology metrics should corroborate – in fact, should be validated against – one or more of the process metrics.

Given the above, the choice of metrics that need to be considered for a given target scenario of DevOps would need to be primarily derived from the To-Be process architecture.

Following sections expand on specific metrics across each of the dimensions, starting with process metrics. Note that certain metrics indicated in **bold** are key metrics for DevOps that are typically relevant for most of the cases that we have seen. We have however not covered general IT metrics that may or may not be specific to DevOps, for example, % SLA (Service Level Agreement) compliance, number of team cross-trainings in Agile and/or DevOps, or defect density for a specific QA environment; we understand that you as an informed reader would be the best judge to select such metrics for your IT considerations.

Process metrics

Following is the representative list of process metrics:

No.	Metrics	KPI	Description and intent
1	% increase in production release frequency	Time	Release frequency is the number of releases in a given period of time Intent is to increase release frequency aligned to changing requirements from business
2	% decrease in lead time to change (till production rollout)	Time	Lead time to change is the time taken from requirements to production release Intent is to reduce the IT cycle time for development life cycle
3	% decrease in Mean Time To Repair (MTTR)	Time	MTTR is the average time taken to resolve an incident (through suitable workaround without resorting to any code fix) in production Intent is to reduce MTTR
4	% increase in Mean Time Between Failures (MTBF)	Time	MTBF is the average time taken for specific application failure in production Intent is to increase MTBF
5	% time taken for a specific practice with respect to total IT cycle time	Time	Practice would include: environment provisioning, requirement capture and analysis, design, code, test, build and release, incident capture and analysis, incident resolution Intent is to analyze which practice is taking significant time, based on which the process can further be optimized
6	% manual time taken vis-à-vis the total IT cycle time	Time	Alternatively, % automation time may also be considered as the metric Intent is to analyze the extent of automation adopted across the process
7	Change success ratio (ratio of pre-production defects	Quality	Ratio of number of defects in prior to production rollout, to number of defects in production;

	to production defects)		analyzes how well the test processes during SDLC work in capturing defects Intent is to maximize defect capture (and resolution) in pre-production prior to rollout, as production defects are more critical, complex (say, for want to proper traceability) and expensive to fix
8	% activities that are generating "Waste"	Quality	"Waste" is as described earlier, including outcomes classified as "Information"; the metric may be categorized further by criticality of activities Intent is to analyze extent of non-value adding activities with respect to IT deliverables
9	% traceability of issues (defects or incidents)	Quality	Traceability to code, database or infrastructure (including environment); may be categorized further by functional issues or non-functional issues such as performance and security Intent is to analyze the effectiveness of the process in incorporating feedback loops for issue resolution
10	% incidents resolved (or changes executed) without manual approval workflows	Quality	The metric is for issues arising due to production runs or changes requested; may be further categorized by issues or requests pertaining to code, database or infrastructure/ environment Intent is to analyze the extent of manual touch points (alternatively, automation) during issue resolution or fixes, or during change request workflows
11	% rework effort	Cost	Rework effort including iterative activities due to recurring defect fixes/ re-fixes, environment re-configurations, change or service request workflow corrections, et al Intent is to analyze effort-based costs incurred during process execution for rework

12	% decrease in application (or infrastructure) downtime during application deployments or production fixes	Cost	Time may be in say, minutes, hours or days; as relevant with respect to the context of application usage in production; it is assumed that the time can be directly translated to business costs Intent is to analyze costs – direct and indirect (including opportunity cost) – incurred due to process delays impacting say, end customer experience in accessing the given application

People metrics

Following is the representative list of people metrics:

No.	Metrics	KPI	Description and intent	Impact on process
1	% manual time spent (role-wise)	Time	The metric need to be evaluated for each role based on total time spent by the role across the process Intent is to find out if there is a decrease in manual effort (hence, possible increase in automation for the role) in To-Be state vis-à-vis the As-Is state	Reduce role-wise IT cycle times possibly due to higher automation across the process; higher automation may also imply higher quality and reliability, and less rework effort across roles
2	% increase in team velocity (each for Dev and Ops)	Time	Agile metric categorized by Dev and Ops Intent is to find out if there is an increase in respective team velocities in To-Be state vis-à-vis the As-Is state	Expected to reduce IT cycle times due to improvement in efficiency of Dev and Ops teams respectively

3	% non-coding effort of Dev team	Quality	Based on time spent by Dev team in doing non-coding activities typical of Ops tasks Intent is to find out if there is a decrease in such effort for Dev in To-Be state vis-à-vis the As-Is state	Expected to free up more time for Dev in doing actual coding (functional) work across the IT process, thereby resulting in better utilization of Dev
4	% coding effort of Ops team	Time	Based on time spent by Ops team in shifting over to coding approaches for Ops activities (for example, preparing infrastructure as code, or release pipeline as code) Intent is to find out if there is an increase in such effort for Ops in To-Be state vis-à-vis the As-Is state	Transforming the Ops team into executing coding based activities; accelerate Ops thereby reducing IT cycle time, increase predictability of Ops, and easily extend Ops to scale say, to support new deployments
5	Ratio of collaboration points across the process (None : Intra-role : Inter-role)	Time	Collaboration can be as follows: a. None b. Within same role (Intra-role) c. Across different roles (Inter-role) Intent is to find out if there is a shift from 'a' to 'b' or 'c' (as above), or from 'b' to 'c'	Higher collaboration can result in faster activity execution, however may increase dependency across subsequent activities thereby putting constraints on executing activities in parallel across roles
6	% change in propensity scores from As-Is state to To-	Cost	Propensities are as defined in previous chapters on handling cultural aspects of DevOps	While extent of increase in maturity level for a given propensity can result in

	Be state (each for Practice, Technology use, Collaboration)		Intent is to analyze if there is a shift from lower maturity to higher maturity for each of the propensities; for example, documentation-oriented to coding-oriented technology use propensity	higher DevOps implementation and adoption times, it may also result in faster IT cycle time in the long term as the teams' behavior adjusts to such maturity
7	% DevOps-specific members (DevOps consultants, architects, mentors and engineers)	Cost	The metric is based on total IT team size comprising of DevOps-specific members and the rest of the IT team roles (Dev, QA, Ops, et al) Intent is to analyze the extent of separately maintaining DevOps-specific members, as opposed to the IT team imbibing and adopting DevOps	Provides insight to IT cycle time in implementing (and supporting) DevOps led automation – hence, IT-for-IT effort – versus effort and cycle time in executing actual IT-for-end users activities

Technology metrics

Following is the representative list of technology metrics. Note that there are two types of technology metrics:

A. Metrics pertaining to cycle time and quality of say, the application or software that is subject to the DevOps processes (and related infrastructure) to undergo change(s), based on the impact of underlying technologies used to establish such processes (and infrastructure)

B. Metrics pertaining to the operating time and reliability of technologies themselves that are used to establish or build the DevOps processes (and related infrastructure)

We denote the corresponding metrics in the table below as "Type A" and "Type B" based on the above.

No.	Metrics	KPI	Description and intent	Impact on process
1	% application build failure (Type A)	Quality	The metric need to be evaluated by causes such as functional (application code) or database failures. Intent is to establish automated monitoring and tracking of the metrics using corresponding build/ test tools	Reduce iterations in rework, and thereby increase build success (hence developer throughput) resulting in reduced IT cycle time and better software quality
2	% application release failure for code/ database issues (Type A)	Quality	The metric is to find out failures due to coding and testing issues in pre-prod environment(s) or during production rollout. Intent is to establish automated monitoring and tracking of the metrics using corresponding release tools	Reduce iterations in rework typically caused by code/ database configuration issues pertaining to specific pre-production environment(s), thereby reducing IT cycle time
3	% test automation in-sprint; functional including regression, non-functional (Type A)	Time	The metric is to find out (a) extent of test automation, (b) extent of Dev-QA collaboration. Test automation in-sprint (coding and testing in same sprint) reduces rework enabling test-driven coding as a practice, and leverage test automation technologies	Expected to reduce IT cycle time by enabling paradigms such as test driven development (TDD) or behavior driven development (BDD) early-on during the development cycle

4	% production incidents due to application/ database issues (Type A)	Quality	The metric is to find out issues that crept out of application or database post production release and defects' closure. The intent is to increase the effectiveness of the prior change cycle (required to resolve the incident) in capturing and resolving issues	Higher number of incidents due to application and/or database issues would mean higher IT cycle time for change (code-test) cycles for incident fixes
5	**Average time taken to provision (and configure) a pre-production environment (Type B)**	Time	The metric is to find out agility in terms of provisioning an environment, say the development environment itself, specific QA, or staging environment. The intent is to have the least possible time to provision any given pre-production environment	Less the time taken to provision environments, less the overall IT cycle time for the given process
6	Average time taken to prepare test bed and/or execute a test data refresh for a given environment (Type B)	Time	The metric is to find out agility in supporting QA function for DevOps, as test data has significant impact for multiple-stack release dependencies. The intent is to have the least possible time for having a test bed with/without test data refresh	Less the time taken to prepare test beds (with correct test data requiring no re-work), less the overall IT cycle time for the given process, especially for multiple stacks using the same test data sets
7	Average time taken to trace back	Time	The metric is to find out the level of traceability from issue to requirements, for	Faster the traceability pointing to requirements

	production incident to requirements (Type B)		production incidents; impact is on issue identification and resolution times The intent is to have the least possible time with correct traceability established with related automation	accurately, faster would be the issue identification (and resolution) time; hence, less the overall IT cycle time
8	% production incidents due to infrastructure and non-functional factors (Type B)	Quality	The metric is to find out issues that crept out of infrastructure and with respect to non-functional factors such as performance (say, in terms of availability, scalability and reliability) and security, post production release and defects' closure The intent is to increase the effectiveness of the Ops (and security) team in capturing and resolving issues	Higher number of incidents due to infrastructure and non-functional factors would require higher Ops focus with respect to the IT process stream
9	% incidents auto-resolved in production (Type B)	Time	The metric is to find out extent of automation in terms of resolving incidents, either as rule-based or using adaptive/ intelligent mechanisms The intent is to increase the level of automation to realize self-healing systems	Higher the percentage of auto-resolved incidents, lower the IT cycle time – both due to automation, and elimination of change workflow tollgates – resulting in lower IT process cycle time

| 10 | **% utilization of provisioned environments Type B)** | Cost | The metric is to find out utilization of environments required to build, test, deploy and host applications. The intent is to increase the utilization of the environments leveraging suitable automation for say, necessary load balancing across environments; for example, load balancing across container nodes over a cluster | Higher the % utilization, lower the cost across the IT process; it would also indicate the effectiveness (and impact) of underlying automation on the process in terms of optimal provisioning and de-provisioning of environments |

Based on the To-Be architecture across people, process and technology, the target values for some of the aforesaid metrics can be derived. For example, the IT cycle time optimization done on the process architecture itself would provide the target estimate for "lead time to change" metric.

Cross-metrics Mapping

Based on the above lists, following gives a mapping view of people and technology metrics respectively to the process metrics. Note that for each of the people and technology metrics, not all possible mappings are depicted (in order to have better readability), however only the primary mappings are given.

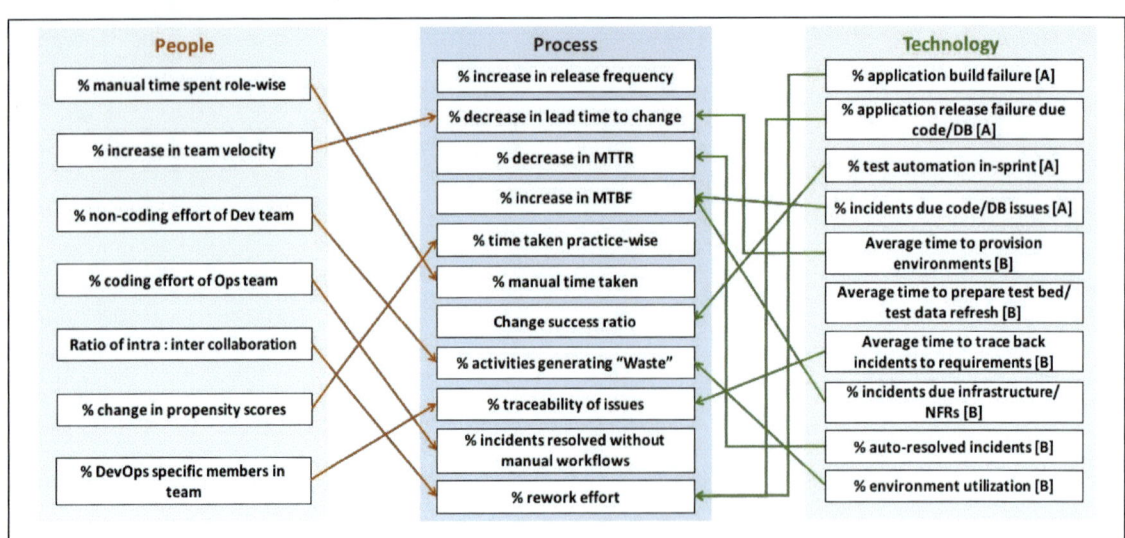

People	Process	Technology
% manual time spent role-wise	% increase in release frequency	% application build failure [A]
% increase in team velocity	% decrease in lead time to change	% application release failure due code/DB [A]
% non-coding effort of Dev team	% decrease in MTTR	% test automation in-sprint [A]
	% increase in MTBF	% incidents due code/DB issues [A]
	% time taken practice-wise	Average time to provision environments [B]
% coding effort of Ops team	% manual time taken	Average time to prepare test bed/ test data refresh [B]
	Change success ratio	
Ratio of intra : inter collaboration	% activities generating "Waste"	Average time to trace back incidents to requirements [B]
% change in propensity scores	% traceability of issues	% incidents due infrastructure/ NFRs [B]
	% incidents resolved without manual workflows	% auto-resolved incidents [B]
% DevOps specific members in team	% rework effort	% environment utilization [B]

Figure 27: Mapping to Process Metrics

The above approach would enable you to evaluate what should be the typical people and technology metrics connected to the process metrics that you may consider for a specific DevOps assessment.

How To: The Steps to Consulting

Consulting itself is a topic that warrants a separate book altogether. However, this chapter is to serve as a refresher on the steps that you should keep in mind while working as an IT consultant for an organization, with specific focus on DevOps requirements. While every consultant has all the required weapons – templates, artefacts, checklists, nice looking tablets or laptops, a shining suitcase and a trendy corporate outfit in the wardrobe – such lists vary from person to person, and from organization to organization.

For any DevOps assessment, we typically recommend having at least two consultants. One is the DevOps process consultant who specializes in understanding people behavior in context of the overall organizational culture, the IT processes and the organization's management perspectives. The other is a technical architect and hence, have a sound understanding of technologies and tools and how they map to respective architectural frameworks.

DevOps assessments may be broadly scoped into three categories, each of them further dealing with either the development life cycle, or the production cycle post application(s) rollout:

a. **Assessment for a single application portfolio, or say two to three similar portfolios** – This may typically involve the two consultants as outlined above.

b. **Assessment for an application platform or a set of portfolios that follow disparate processes** – This may typically involve a team of consultants; while the process consultants can work in parallel across several portfolios to analyze process dependencies, the architects can pick up one or a few similar portfolio(s) at a time, for analysis.

c. **Enterprise IT assessment** covering all (or, the primary) departments in the organization consuming IT services – This also involves a team of consultants; two to three consultants forming a sub-team (with a mix of process consultants and technical architects) may work on one or a few similar portfolio(s); with multiple such sub-teams working on the other portfolios. This would also require a governance team – or say, executing a "Scrum of Scrums" – to provide directions for the assessment so that it is completed on-time and as per the expectations set, consolidate the outcomes, and resolve dependencies and impediments, if any.

Nevertheless, following is our recommended list of not-to-forget items for a DevOps consulting assignment:

a. The questionnaires (on your laptop, of course) – Both the Pre-Assessment Questionnaire, and the Detailed Questionnaire

b. Papers, pens, markers and duster for taking down notes and white-boarding; for DevOps, this is essential for capturing tacit details on people dynamics, say across Dev and Ops teams; that may impact understanding of the nature of team's activities in terms of collaboration, and how automation tools are leveraged by such teams

c. Secondary research data (or, directly obtained if possible) on the organization with regard to the following:
    - A view of the organization structure, possibly with a list of changes since the last few days, months or years in the organization, and senior management profiles; if the assessment is for a specific portfolio, the structure of such portfolio and management profiles of the portfolio personnel is preferred
    - Report(s) on previous IT assessment(s) done, if any
    - Existing IT vision, focus areas (say, tool standardization, cloud or container adoption strategy, IT security, et al), roadmap or architecture documents

d. List of the following stakeholders, possibly with corresponding meeting schedules:

Category	Stakeholder Roles
Business	o Leadership or management for department(s) in context – may include CxO (executive, finance, marketing, et al), managing director, presidents, executive vice presidents, vice presidents, directors, department heads (marketing, finance, administration, human resources, et al), general manager, assistants to management functions o On-the-floor business owners, release owners and supervisors (say, people who directly use the underlying applications and IT services in context)
IT	o CTO, CIO, CDO (for Technology, Information and/or Digital respectively) o Head of Dev and/or QA; developers, testers o Head of Ops across infrastructure management, release management, IT services and support; system administrators and operations personnel, application maintenance and support teams o IT Security Head, IT security teams (say, for application security, data security, infrastructure and network security) o IT Reliability Head, Reliability engineering team o Artificial Intelligence (AI) led operations team, with related maintenance and support team o IT Procurement Head, procurement team
Others	o Vendor teams and contractors; both IT and non-IT (or, business)

	o Third party personnel and system integrators who work on interfacing third party systems and artefacts, to the organization's business processes

Once you ensure that the above points are taken care of, following are the steps that you need to follow and establish in the organization during the assessment:

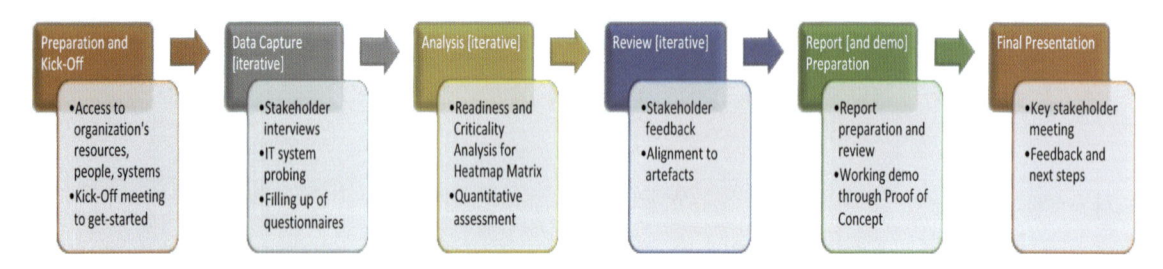

Preparation and Kick-Off
- Access to organization's resources, people, systems
- Kick-Off meeting to get-started

Data Capture [iterative]
- Stakeholder interviews
- IT system probing
- Filling up of questionnaires

Analysis [iterative]
- Readiness and Criticality Analysis for Heatmap Matrix
- Quantitative assessment

Review [iterative]
- Stakeholder feedback
- Alignment to artefacts

Report [and demo] Preparation
- Report preparation and review
- Working demo through Proof of Concept

Final Presentation
- Key stakeholder meeting
- Feedback and next steps

Figure 28: Steps for Consulting

a. An initial kick-off meeting with the interest-group head with his/her few key members need to be executed. The interest-group is the group that sponsors and initiates the DevOps assessment.

b. A formal get-started meeting to get all stakeholders – definitely with presence from both Dev and Ops teams – into a single room to provide them an outline of the assessment, is a must. Further, expectations should be set on participation and support required, say with respect to access to the premises, infrastructure, IT systems and people in the organization within the constraints of security and other administrative policies.

c. During the data capture phase, such exercises should be done through pre-scheduled meetings as far as possible. Given that this phase typically takes the longest time and effort due to validation required for the collected data – requiring you to go back to the stakeholders for corrections and filling up of missing data – the phase should be as structured as possible. It is a good practice to consolidate all queries or doubts after the first round of data collection, before going back to any stakeholder.

d. Analysis should be done in a neutral environment without presence of the organization's employees, vendors or other people. This is to eliminate the risk of having any bias or errors due to distractions, et al, during the actual study based on the collected data. This is extremely important as DevOps is a people-first philosophy.

e. While the outcomes – target architectures, DevOps stories, metrics – are being derived, it may require multiple validations with the documents, artefacts and diagrams already provided by the organization prior to start of the assessment or later during the data collection or the analysis phase.

f. It may be required to go back to any of the stakeholders in the organization during the analysis phase itself, say for data integrity, adequacy or consistency requirements of the collected data. Such discussions should be restricted to the collected data, without yet divulging any information – as far as possible – on the analysis itself.

g. There may be multiple reviews of the assessment outcomes required with the stakeholders. We typically start with the interest-group head with a few key members of his/her team, followed by other groups – possibly including both Dev and Ops – once the interest-group has more or less mutually agreed to the outcomes.

h. Outcomes may be revalidated, re-analyzed and feedback solicited during such review meetings. With sufficient access to people and IT systems, on-the-floor developers, testers or operations personnel may be approached on specific points in the outcomes.

i. Relevant stakeholders from the senior management may only be brought in during the review phase if the outcomes envisage a direct impact on organization-level objectives to adopt DevOps; for example, the CIO may be looking at driving cost efficiencies through DevOps adoption. In that case, the CIO or senior members associated with the CIO's office may need to be provided with outcomes having data points on cost impact.

j. It is recommended to have a working demonstration of the target software setup – say, the DevOps pipeline hosting sample application(s) and/or database(s) in context – created as a proof of concept, to accompany the assessment report during the final presentation.

k. Before the final presentation, all the key stakeholders from Dev and Ops teams should be aligned on the assessment outcomes. The final presentation should typically have all the stakeholders who were present in the get-started meeting as covered in point (b) above.

l. The final presentation should be concluded with a set of next steps – typically on plans for downstream implementation – and feedback which can later be used to enrich the questionnaires and methodology for assessment.

Assessment Report Outline

Following is a sample outline of an Assessment Report (text in **bold** indicate key items as featured in the description that may not be apparent from the section name):

S#	Section Name	Brief Description
0	Executive Summary	A summary of the assessment exercise, along with a **section-wise outline** of the report, and the key outcome(s) typically with the most important metrics for senior management or key stakeholder(s)
1	Organization Profile and the Assessment Objectives	Describes the organization and its prerogatives that led to the DevOps assessment, thereby outlining the objectives; a briefing of the **organizational structure** in context of assessment may also be articulated
2	Assessment Approach and Methodology	A brief outline of the methodology including methods used for selection of portfolio(s) for DevOps assessment, and the detailed assessment methodologies using quantitative methods

3	Portfolio(s) Selection for Assessment *[this is optional, and only applies to cases where the assessment scope itself needs to be defined]*	The DevOps Readiness report(s) of portfolios, followed by business criticality versus DevOps readiness analysis – portfolio heatmap(s) and the derived **heatmap matrix**; observations, such as business' priorities on portfolio(s) requiring DevOps adoption, cloud strategy planned, et al, may also be articulated
4	As-Is (or, Baseline) State Analysis	The detailed filled up questionnaires with the derived People, Process and Technology Architectures
5	Critical Path Identification and Analysis Notes	The critical path identified in the process network diagram for optimization, along with observations from the diagram; for example, the cycle time taken by the critical path, gaps identified along the path, et al
6	To-Be (or, Target) State Analysis	The revised critical path with target People, Process and Technology Architectures; observations including specific data points or metrics such as the revised IT cycle time may also be articulated, along with the **table of revised process activities** mapped to people-roles and technologies
7	What is Changing from As-Is (or, Baseline) to To-Be (or, Target) State	This is to articulate the list of stories in the revised IT life cycle or process, color coded as preponed, eliminated, enhanced or newly added; along with people-role and technology impact, and rationale to "why" the change and "what" has changed

		May also articulate the **key metrics** on IT release cycle times (or support timelines, in case of DevOps in post-production scenario) along with **estimates of target values** vis-à-vis baseline (say, existing) values, thereby illustrating the improvements envisaged
8	DevOps Roadmap	DevOps implementation stories with suggested **team structure, timelines** for implementation, specific **training and mentoring plans** for people in the organization who would adopt DevOps practices, et al; **Risks, assumptions and dependencies** of the assessment study may also be articulated here
9	Conclusion and Next Steps	A brief outline of suggested next steps and **key benefits** of target state vis-à-vis the baseline state, in terms of business and IT value streams

Assessment report structure and content may vary from organization to organization, and based on the methodology followed. Further, there may be a greater emphasis on certain aspects for a specific assessment which may hence, demand separate section(s) for such aspects. For example, an organization trying to focus more on the people or culture change, may want to have a separate section in the report dedicated to cultural aspects outlining the current people structures, target structures, risks of such change and enablers of such change.

Cases in DevOps Assessment

As organizations strive to get their people, process and technologies aligned to achieve business goals – while IT remains the backbone to improve, sustain and adapt – they either go top-down, whereby the management direction results in certain changes to the three aforesaid dimensions at various levels; or, go bottom-up, whereby changes to the operational levels are tried and tested first, followed by adoption by the management and propagation across the enterprise. Both the approaches can work together at different points in time for an organization, based on factors such as business cycles, types of market, competitive pressures, et al.

While we did assessments across organizations globally – starting from medium-sized businesses to large multinationals – we found that organizations which focus on Agility as a primary objective tend to adapt faster to changing market and regulatory conditions, provide better and highly consistent customer experience, and stay ahead of the competition.

Here, we present three case studies to cover DevOps assessments done at three different levels; one of them starting with understanding the "Big Picture" first, another trying to define its DevOps roadmap for a specific business platform, and yet another who focused on a specific application portfolio as a greenfield project, hence without any As-is state or baseline to apparently start with.

Enterprise Governance for a Large Insurance Organization

The organization is an independent body working closely with the government in insurance products and services, targeted to and supporting a specific set of communities. It is one of the largest institutional investors in the world, with substantial investments across the major capital markets to raise funds for the insurance business.

From a business layer perspective, it is divided into front office (customer systems), middle office (primarily handling two aspects: markets and investments, and enterprise governance) and back office as the business entities. For the enterprise governance portfolio, the organization has multiple application stacks that spread across legacy systems (primarily mainframe and AS/400) to distributed (customer facing systems primarily on java/J2EE, AngularJS, .NET, et al). The backbone consists of databases (Oracle, and MS SQL Server with SSRS) and TIBCO for integration and analytics across infrastructure and data layers; apart from the underlying infrastructure itself which is primarily on-premise.

The organization started with identifying inefficiencies internally in the enterprise governance portfolio – as it would have a medium impact to daily operations with respect to business criticality, and also would be apparently easy to hop onto the DevOps journey by creating necessary pipelines for Java/J2EE. However, conducting proofs of concept to take them to the portfolio level iteratively resulted in incremental cost overheads over time, without any visible return on such investments. This was why the organization reached out for an overarching assessment approach to embark on their transformation journey for DevOps.

As consultants, we broke down the problem of assessing the organization's IT into three parts, gradually engaging their IT managers and team leads in phases:

a. We first drew out a heatmap of eleven portfolios, at application stack level, for the enterprise governance portfolio. The heatmap helped us in pin pointing the need for in-depth assessment on DevOps for two of the portfolios – regulatory compliance and vendor management. From a business criticality perspective, the aforesaid portfolios were impacted due to being unable to adjust to frequently changing regulatory compliance needs, and frequent integration issues with vendor systems resulting in high vendor dissatisfaction. From readiness perspective, since both the systems are on .NET with MS SQL Server and Oracle, we found that standard pipelines from technology perspective for these stacks could suffice with minor configuration changes to start with.

b. As we discussed with the various stakeholders in the organization, we found a cultural problem – the vendor systems' management follows a separate path from the customer systems' management – in terms of setting up DevOps teams and infrastructure. Whereas there is already quite a mature adoption of DevOps in the customer systems portfolio –

and the pipelines could be easily brought in on an enterprise "bus" – there were significant differences in how the people and IT systems worked; more so as the senior management was new to the organization as a result of an inorganic takeover of the portfolio. Hence, we got the senior leadership of the vendor systems into a workshop to draw out a high level process architecture of the As-is state. The assessment of the state at this level was sufficient to bring out the high level gaps with respect to achieving a target state of DevOps. In this case, vendor experience was defined by a set of metrics that were found to influence the metrics on IT agility. As next step, we got into an in-depth assessment of the portfolio.

c. We used our quantitative framework for the deeper assessment across all the three dimensions – people, process and technology. While the analysis of the people (or, culture) pointed to Dev-without-Ops Agile practices, the analysis of process included manual workflows for infrastructure provisioning, lack of adequate test management and test data management practices, and no integrated process for the software development life cycle in terms of monitoring, tracking and governance. A low utilization of procured DevOps tools – without the Dev sufficiently aligned to Ops – was another reason. While we brought out the gaps and assessed the target state, we also found out the detailed stories that can be built on top of the DevOps practices in customer systems portfolio; this was to enable a higher level of collaboration between the customer system and vendor system IT teams. The average IT cycle time for the selected portfolios at this stage was envisaged to reduce from **30 days (baseline) to 18 days (target state)**.

The downstream implementation based on the target architectures and stories identified, along with establishing the key metrics to track progress of the transformation, resulted in more than forty percent faster response to changes in vendor system integrations, faster infrastructure turnaround for developers (read, Dev-with-Ops Agile Scrums) and significantly reduced failure rates in data transmission problems from and to vendor systems. A higher collaboration between the two portfolios was enabled at the leadership level, extending the DevOps pipelines across an enterprise "bus" with enhanced data security and pipeline reliability.

A similar assessment for the compliance portfolio was done, and the pipeline with necessary configuration changes were also implemented downstream as part of the enterprise "bus" so created. Further, the enterprise architecture itself was enhanced to accommodate multiple DevOps pipelines, thereby bringing in higher system resilience in terms of security and reliability.

Digital Platform for a Global Media and Information Firm

The organization is a multinational mass media and information services firm. It caters to small and large businesses across media, legal, government and financial companies by working as the database backbone through supplying relevant data on time. It negotiates with corresponding institutions, apart from its own research and reporters, that provide such data for aggregation, analysis and presentation in multiple formats.

Given the legacy of the organization in providing such data through traditional media, the customer started their journey in leveraging digital channels for faster, more accurate and multi-channel distribution of data. Its digital transformation programs necessitated specific assessments to be done from an IT agility, quality and security standpoints for the digital divisions. However, due to significant inorganic growth across its divisions, there were people dynamics that resulted in a relatively slower pace in driving the initiatives.

This was the reason for which the organization called upon for consultants to have a third eye view of the IT estate and its people, and to bring out data-point based outcomes to resolve any conflicting perspectives.

We as consultants started small, with one digital application platform that facilitated bringing in data from third party institutions for data analysis, management and multi-format presentation. The platform consisted of four technology stacks; Adobe Experience Manager (AEM) for digital asset and content management, SFDC (SalesForce Dot Com; CRM platform on cloud) for managing institutions and customers, Enterprise Services Integration (ESI) as the organization's own enterprise IT "bus" for interfacing systems, and Informatica for data transformation and management. The system has numerous inbound and outbound applications it integrates with.

We analyzed the respective application portfolios under the platform, including the dependencies existing across the applications that brought in the additional challenge on integrity, especially during releases; developers, along with release operations team, spent sleepless nights during releases to make the deployments right.

We found out that the impact on cycle times was due to the following:

a. Substantial time taken to provision environments (due to manual provisioning workflows) and environment refresh (due to manual validation and loading of data, resulting in issues of data integrity; hence, requiring repetitive manual checks)

b. Manual testing for unit tests, regression tests and smoke tests; resulting in low test coverage and high change failures once code has moved to production; no automation on non-functional tests resulting in issues of system performance during data analysis, and security vulnerabilities; a post-facto test practice where code development and testing existed as segregated functions

c. Significant manual effort in release coordination workflows between Dev and Ops, due to complex release dependencies; no automation on release pipeline existed

d. Manual deployment to higher pre-production and production environments; resulted in discrepancies across environments (hence, high failure rates during tests), and delays in deployments; thereby having high impact on the customer experience

During our data capture and analysis phase, we additionally found out a specific cultural problem whereby, the Dev wanted to have a self-service pipeline to manage releases, whereas the Ops team wanted to have a coded pipeline for fine-grained control and better scalability for new deployment workflows. Hence, the Dev's definition of the "Golden Image" for the technology architecture and that of the Ops, had significant differences.

While arriving at the target state, the other constraint we had was that, the platform is largely proprietary, hence we would not be able to propose changes easily from a code and data engineering perspective. However, we went ahead with addressing the Ops problems in build and deploy, and environment engineering respectively, and then doing a shift-left in integrating quality engineering practices to the pipeline. For the cultural problem highlighted above, we selected the Ops-driven path for DevOps, given significant investment being already made in corresponding technologies. Further, a self-service paradigm required significant training investment for Dev, which would have delayed the execution of the transformation programs.

As the outcome of the assessment, we defined an Ops-driven path for realizing DevOps from people and technology perspectives. Towards such approach, we formulated a Unified Deployment Model for build to deploy cycles. We further identified the key metrics for the initiative that estimated a **thirty percent reduction in the IT cycle times**, forty percent less developer involvement in non-coding activities resulting in significant improvement to quality (functional, performance, data security and data integrity) of the change, and a thirty percent effort saving for Ops in managing environments and releases.

We provided a coded pipeline-based approach to be built on a Puppet based ecosystem, given the corresponding investments already being made by the organization; this was envisaged to result in a **forty percent reduction in environment provisioning and refresh times**. We further provided an option for future consideration – once the Dev comes up to a significant maturity in adopting (and managing) better application architectures – having provision of a self-service approach for Dev using standard deployment tools; for the standard deployment pipelines without significant release dependencies to be handled.

Post actual implementation downstream of the proposed target architecture, we found that the first time the IT cycle is executed, the overall release time from requirements capture to rollout was reduced by twenty percent (instead of the thirty percent we estimated). This was due to the higher DevOps adoption time taken by Dev team in relation to Ops. It took a few more IT cycles to be executed, before realizing the target state of thirty percent release cycle time reduction, along with the other key metrics reaching their estimated target values respectively.

Integration and BI Portfolio for a Large Insurance Company

The organization is a large subsidiary of its parent group which is a global insurance and risk management firm. It itself was a leading risk and reinsurance provider which was acquired by the parent firm for its capabilities in reinsurance services.

The inorganic growth of the parent firm has historically created disparate IT systems to support its businesses, thereby posing significant challenges in services consolidation across people, process and technology. Hence, the organization planned to adopt DevOps across the enterprise in order to seamlessly consolidate its systems, from an execution perspective, to its parent firm's IT systems across the three aforesaid dimensions; starting with the greenfield projects that provide integration services across the systems. It selected its interfaces built on APIGEE backed by PostgreSQL databases, and its business intelligence reporting suite on Microsoft platform for its next generation development using DevOps principles. An additional objective was adoption of Microsoft Azure cloud services for reducing its total cost of infrastructure ownership.

We started the assessment by first drawing out the DevOps Readiness report to find out the high level focus areas. Thereafter we applied our detailed assessment framework for analysis of the current state. The overall release time from requirements analysis to production rollout for any changes using the traditional software development life cycle for similar stack came to **5.2 weeks**. However, this included on-premise development cycle with manual processes for environment provisioning, testing and deployment. Further, there was quite low adoption of Agile across projects, without any Ops participation in the Agile Scrums.

Our target state analysis envisaged the following:

a. Better Agile adoption, with Agile Scrum teams that included Ops team that managed environments and releases

b. Test-first paradigm using test driven development and significant test automation across both functional and non-functional tests

c. An integrated application life cycle management approach for release tracking in real-time across developers, testers and Ops team

d. Containerized deployment on Azure cloud using Azure Kubernetes Services (AKS) for high scalability, effective management of container clusters, and supporting integrated release pipelines using Visual Studio Team Services (VSTS) – currently known as "Azure DevOps"

e. Nine key metrics to be established for the release pipeline

With the aforesaid changes proposed for the target state, the overall release time was envisaged to come down to **2.1 weeks (60% faster cycle time)**, apart from significant improvements to quality of the software, infrastructure manageability and better management of release dependencies across systems, especially given the disparate IT landscape.

The downstream implementation of the DevOps pipeline on Azure cloud, along with relevant people mentoring on Agile practices to close the associated gaps, and establishing the key metrics; corroborated the estimates on the metrics target values envisaged during the assessment phase.

Assessment Recap Step-by-Step

We provide here all the steps of assessment as discussed in the earlier chapters, as a quick reference. Note that where indicated, certain steps may not be applicable for a specific assessment scenario; you may skip such steps in context of the assessment, and use what is applicable. Further, figures provided in this chapter are part or excerpt of complete figures given in earlier chapters, hence are for representational purposes only. You may go back to the earlier chapters to refer to the complete figures, if required.

Following are the summarized steps towards our DevOps assessment approach:

1. First identify the layer where the assessment has to be done in context of the organization – application, data, or technology

   (*Note that this step is optional in case the portfolio(s) for assessment has already been decided upon*)

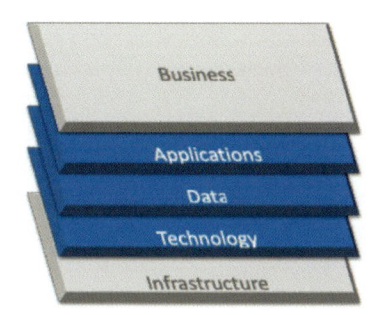

   ![Layered diagram showing Business, Applications, Data, Technology, Infrastructure]

2. Identify the portfolios which may be evaluated for need of assessment

   (*Note that this step is optional in case the portfolio(s) for assessment has already been decided upon*)

3. We start with a pre-assessment for the identified portfolio(s), as a pre-cursor to the actual detailed assessment

4. Obtain the business criticality for each portfolio; based on business's need to go the DevOps way for each portfolio, **say, as a score from 1 to 5**

   (*Note that this step is optional in case the portfolio for assessment has already been decided upon*)

5. Based on the pre-assessment (as in step 3), compute the DevOps Readiness Score for each portfolio(s) by using dimension-wise (Culture, Process, People, Metrics) weighted average of parameters, to create the Portfolio Heatmap based on the scores

   (*Note that this step is optional in case the portfolio for assessment has already been decided upon*)

	Central Customer Portal	Financial Reporting	Enterprise Functions	Enterprise Data Management
Technology Stack	React JS, Java/J2EE, Oracle, MS SQL Server	Angular, MVC, C#, Oracle, MS SQL Server	Angular, MVC, MS.NET, Oracle	Informatica, .NET, MS SQL Server, Oracle, OBIEE, Cognos
Culture	1	3	1	3
Process	3	3	3	3
Tech	1	3	1	3
Metrics	3	4	4	3
DevOps Readiness Score	17.7	30.8	18.5	33.8

6. Create a portfolio heatmap matrix (difficult or easy for IT to implement DevOps, versus critical or non-critical for business to adopt DevOps); to decide and prioritize which portfolio(s) to be taken up for assessment

(Note that this step is optional in case the portfolio for assessment has already been decided upon)

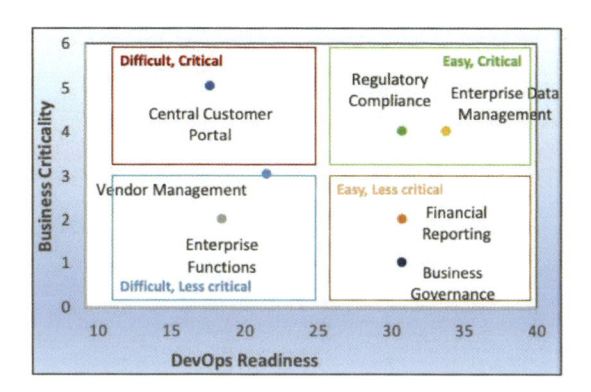

Difficult, Critical
- Central Customer Portal

Easy, Critical
- Regulatory Compliance
- Enterprise Data Management

Difficult, Less critical
- Vendor Management
- Enterprise Functions

Easy, Less critical
- Financial Reporting
- Business Governance

(Axes: Business Criticality vs DevOps Readiness)

7. For a given portfolio, get the detailed questionnaire filled up; you may need to identify and talk to relevant people in the organization, at strategic or leadership, tactical, and operational levels

S#	Epic	Story	Total time	Manual time	Predecessor	Predecessor	Predecessor	Predecessor	Criticality	Role / Team	Input	Output	Automation tool

8. Compute the relative start time for each story (or activity)

S#	Epic	Story	Total time	Manual time	Predecessor	Relative start time	Criticality	Role/team	Input	Output	Automation tool
A1	SDLC - Requirements analysis	Create (or obtain) the BRS	3	3	-	0	High	QA	Business requirement	BRS	
A2	SDLC - Requirements analysis	Create the SRS from the BRS	2	2	A1	3	High	QA	BRS	SRS	

9. Construct the As-Is process network diagram using the relative start time and duration for each activity

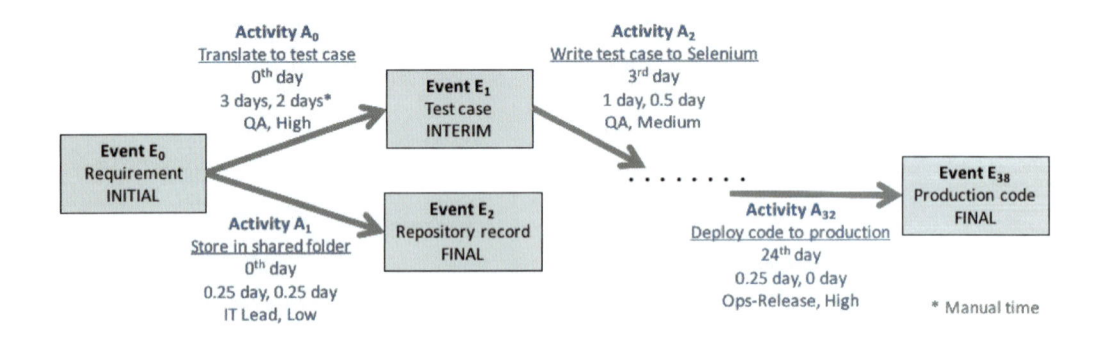

Activity A₀
Translate to test case
0ᵗʰ day
3 days, 2 days*
QA, High

Event E₁
Test case
INTERIM

Activity A₂
Write test case to Selenium
3ʳᵈ day
1 day, 0.5 day
QA, Medium

Event E₀
Requirement
INITIAL

Activity A₁
Store in shared folder
0ᵗʰ day
0.25 day, 0.25 day
IT Lead, Low

Event E₂
Repository record
FINAL

Activity A₃₂
Deploy code to production
24ᵗʰ day
0.25 day, 0 day
Ops-Release, High

Event E₃₈
Production code
FINAL

* Manual time

10. Tabulate all the possible paths in the As-Is network diagram

S#	Path	Start time	Finish time	Total cycle time	Min float	Max float	Net duration considering min float	Net duration considering max float	Final output type	Average criticality
1	A1 - A2 - A4	0	7	7	1	1	6	6	Information	Med
2	A3 - A4	3	7	4	0	0	4	4	Information	Med
3	A3 - A5/A6 - A7 - A20/A25 - A14 - A15/A16 - A17 - A19	3	14.5	11.5	2	3	9.5	8.5	Information	High

11. Evaluate the paths and find out the critical path

```
[Final outcome as "Material"?] → [Longest path duration?] → [High average criticality?]
```

12. Optimize the critical path activities based on the principle of reducing IT cycle time

Activity	Task description	Prepone	Postpone	Eliminate	Enhance	Add	None	Reason	Change details	People change	Technology change
A1	Create (or obtain) the BRS						X	Formal BRS needs to be published to business	No change		
A2	Create the SRS from the BRS			X				Creating SRS is redundant documentation w.r.t. BRS	Eliminate A2 and extend A6		

13. Optimize activities other than those on the critical path, based on changes planned for the critical path

Activity	Task description	Prepone	Postpone	Eliminate	Enhance	Add	None	Reason	Change details	People change	Technology change
A8	Identify mode of request form (email) and basic set of parameters for the given release	X			X			Email needs modification every time for a release, and is not audit traceable	Provide template on ServiceNow,; prepone to templatize across releases	add DevOps Engineer (DE) as a separate role	ServiceNow

14. Construct the To-Be process network diagram based on the changed paths

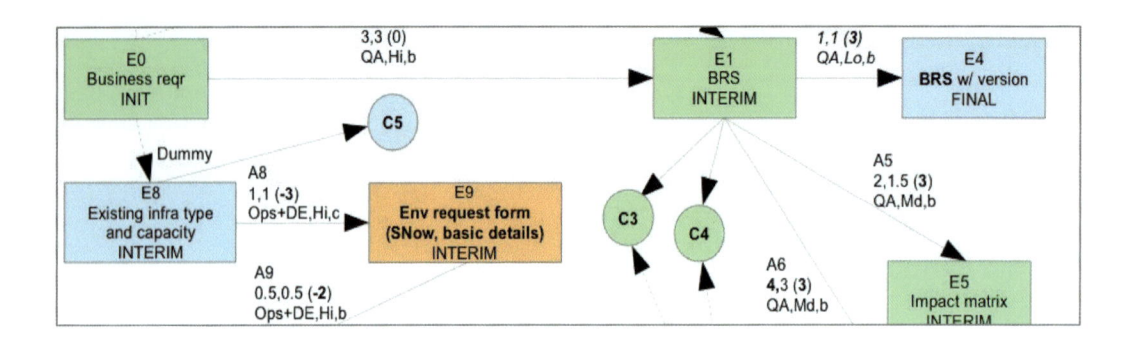

15. Tabulate the To-Be IT life cycle based on the To-Be network diagram

S#	Epic	Story	Total time	Manual time	Predecessor	Relative start time	Criticality	Role/ team	Input	Output	Automation tool
A1	SDLC - Requirements analysis	Create (or obtain) the BRS	3	3	-	0	High	QA	Business requirement	BRS	
A2	SDLC - Requirements analysis	Create the SRS from the BRS									
A3	SDLC - Requirements analysis	Identify and include NFRs as part of SRS	3	2	A2	0	High	QA	NFR	SRS	
A20	SDLC - Coding	Request for dev environment through ServiceNow	0.25	0.25	A3	3	High	Dev, Ops	BRS	Filled up dev environment request form	ServiceNow

16. Tabulate separately the DevOps implementation stories

S#	Epic	Story	Total time	Manual time	Predecessor	Relative start time	Criticality	Role/ team	Input	Output	Automation tool
A8	SDLC - Environment provisioning	Identify mode of request form (ServiceNow) and basic set of parameters for templatization across releases	1	1	-	-3	High	Ops, DE*	Existing infrastructure capacity	Basic environment Request form	
A9	SDLC - Environment provisioning	Incorporate parameters for infrastructure - CPU, disk space, etc.	0.5	0.5	A8	-2	High	Ops, DE	Basic environment request form	Environment request form (+ infra parameters)	

17. Factor in the people aspect (propensities) for estimation of implementation and DevOps adoption (target IT cycle time) times; you may also identify the applicable people pattern and expand on the people architecture based on the pattern, at this stage

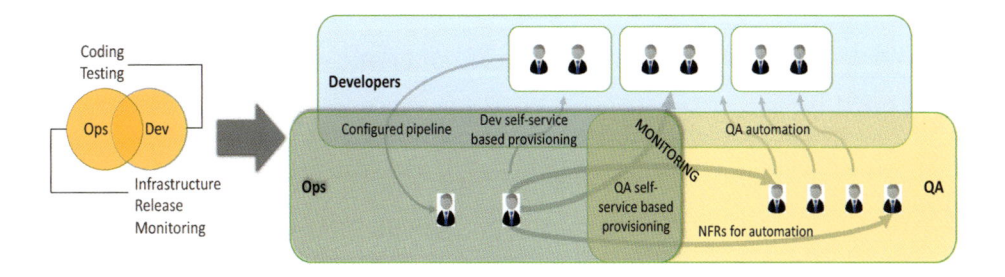

18. Construct the process view of technology landscape; additionally you may create a table to map the activities or stories in the target IT process to corresponding people roles and technologies or tools, if applicable

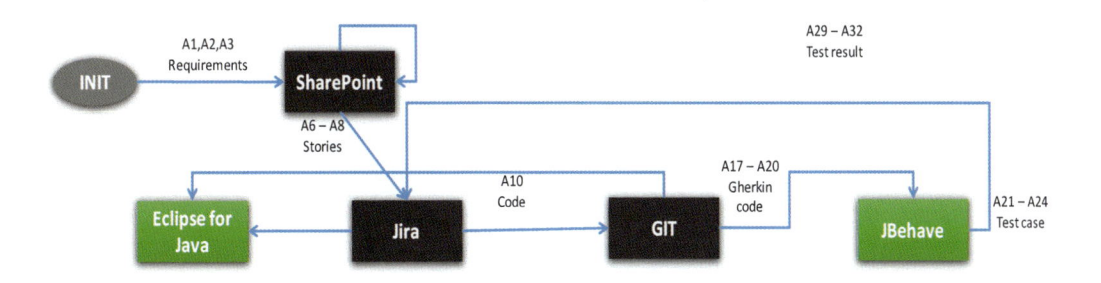

19. Finalize the list of key metrics

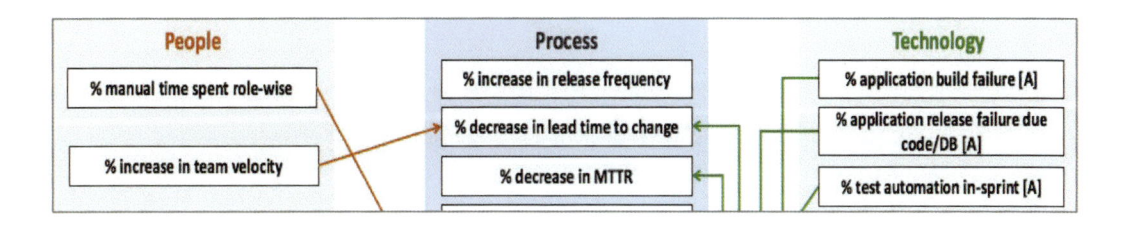

And all that is left to do is to take the above outcomes to actual implementation!

Select Focus Areas for IT Assessments

While the assessment methodology can be applied to a variety of IT engagements ranging across application development, maintenance and enhancement; database and data migration or conversion; application portfolio rationalization exercises; IT monitoring and service management including production support; service desk support, et al, there are specific focus areas that we typically see coming up for consideration during IT assessments in general. We present here a collection of such focus areas to demonstrate how they impact IT assessments, or how they can be assessed as part of the larger assessment scenarios.

For each of the given focus areas, a brief description is given along with what is its impact or relevance to DevOps assessment. This is followed by a list of questions that either conforms to our pre-assessment approach (to gauge overall requirements) or in a story format (and at times, related questions) that can be used for the detailed assessment using quantitative methods. Where possible, relevant metrics are also mentioned.

Chaos Engineering

Chaos Engineering is an offshoot of reliability engineering that provides personnel managing the IT systems – ranging from developers and testers to infrastructure and support personnel – an opportunity to assess IT system reliability, typically on an on-going basis, with an objective to identify and fix failures in the system before such failures result in substantial business impact.

The engineering practice entails injecting inputs to the IT system in a planned manner that cause specific failures (called "Chaos Tests"), and observing how the system – or more specifically, a given IT service – responds to the tests. The system is expected to handle failures in a graceful manner; for any deviation, it may need to be re-designed at application, data, technology or infrastructure layer; to handle such failures. Unlike traditional quality tests, chaos tests are (a) targeted to run in production thereby having real-time impact to business users, hence exposing real world failure scenarios, and (b) discover unknown errors that could not be anticipated earlier.

Once the tests are successfully carried out – typically manually – over an IT system in a controlled manner, the chaos tests can be automated (and included) in the DevOps pipeline(s). Such an approach leads to the state of "Continuous Chaos", through which failures can be injected and system response analyzed on a continuous basis for every pipeline cycle run. Based on the observations, the system design can later be improved to handle such failures.

The ability for the IT system (or service in context) to withstand a chaos test and recover to a desired state or behavior is defined as Resilience of the system or service. This becomes the basic parameter to analyze reliability of the system or service.

Scenarios for a single chaos test

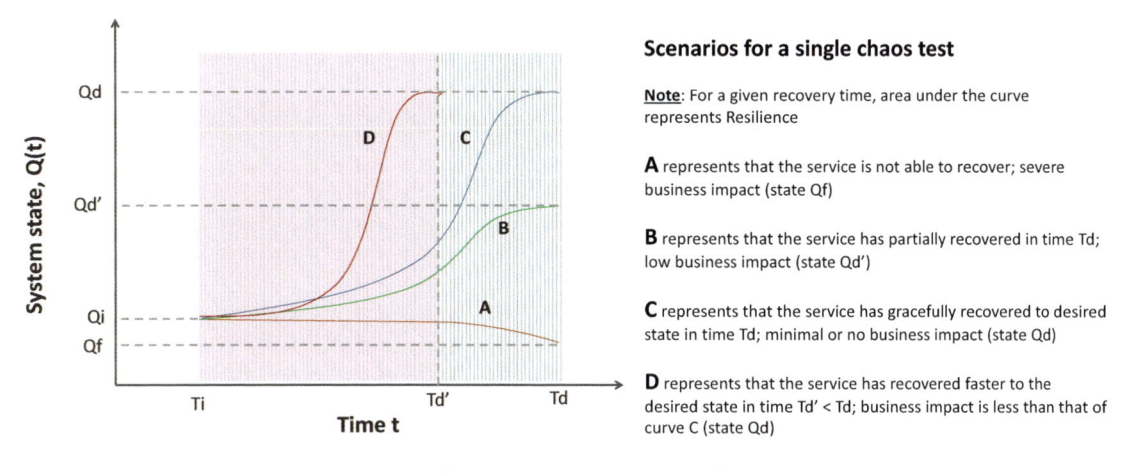

Note: For a given recovery time, area under the curve represents Resilience

A represents that the service is not able to recover; severe business impact (state Qf)

B represents that the service has partially recovered in time Td; low business impact (state Qd')

C represents that the service has gracefully recovered to desired state in time Td; minimal or no business impact (state Qd)

D represents that the service has recovered faster to the desired state in time Td' < Td; business impact is less than that of curve C (state Qd)

Figure 29: Possible Resilience curve variations for Chaos Test

In the above figure, Qi is the state where say, the IT service is subjected to the chaos test at time Ti. This would result in an immediate reduction in quality or performance of the service Q(t), where t is time. Say, the service restores to the desired state, Qd in time Td. Hence, the time to recover Ti is given as:

$$Tr = Td - Ti$$

The objective is to, (a) design the service such that it achieves the state of Qd gracefully, and (b) minimize the recovery time Tr; respectively for all the chaos tests that are engineered into the pipeline. From an IT assessment perspective, there are two requirements with respect to chaos engineering:

a. Is the organization – and its IT system or services – ready for chaos engineering? If not, what are the pre-requisites?

b. Do the current activities or stories in the As-Is state include chaos engineering aspects (if present, what is the impact on IT cycles)? If not, what should be the chaos engineering aspects included in the To-Be state?

We cover the two aforesaid requirements for chaos engineering assessment as below.

Readiness for Chaos Engineering

To assess if the organization's IT is ready for chaos engineering, following are the typical questions that may be included during the pre-assessment stage (some of them may overlap with questions already discussed in earlier chapters), or during the initial data gathering stage.

Category	Question	Response Inference
Process: Need to adopt	Have you faced business impact/ complaint/ escalation due to one or more of the following occurrences (along with numbers) in production? a. Infrastructure failure (typically due to factors such as increased load, communication latency, network latency and partition issues, certificate expiry, system	Yes – There is a strong need to adopt chaos engineering practices No – Either the organization has not assessed impact due to such failures, or there is already a set of chaos tests established and executed on the pipeline

		clock issues, transactional data deluge, et al) b. State transmission errors c. Race situations resulting in deadlocks and system hog due to say application, data or infrastructure integrity issues d. Dynamic code injection resulting in failures, typically due to vulnerability issues e. Failure or unreliable inter-service communication or data queues f. Functional code failures say, cyclic dependencies resulting in infinite loops g. Deployment failures due to pipeline issues h. Failures due to containerized IT services (for say, inter-container partition failures, packet loss, container dependency injection causing failures, et al)	
Metrics: Need to adopt		What is the number and periodicity and/or pattern of transactions initiated per unit time?	Based on the nature of organization's business, following may be the cases that warrant adopting chaos engineering practices: a. Sudden fall in number of transactions (that typically retain a given range over time)

		b. A change in periodicity or shape of curve over time that suggests change of system user behavior
Process: Need to adopt	Are chaos tests planned to be executed in non-production or production environment(s)?	Chaos engineering is to make production systems more resilient; hence nearer the production environment, the better.
Process: Need to adopt	Are any chaos tests executed currently? If yes, at what frequency?	Yes, manually at times – Execution may be unplanned and ad-hoc, without an established controlled mechanism

Yes, at regular frequency – Execution may be established as part of DevOps pipeline

No – Need to analyze IT architecture for failure points to start with |
| Technology: Pre-requisite to adopt | Do you have continuous monitoring and related dashboard established in non-production and production environments? | Yes – Chaos tests can be introduced

No – Necessary to observe chaos test outcomes; need to track related metrics and monitoring mechanisms |
| Process: Pre-requisite to adopt | Are failure domains defined and mapped to IT failures in your organization? | Yes – Chaos tests may be introduced

No – Necessary to define business failures and map to corresponding IT scenarios |

Culture: Pre-requisite to adopt	Do you have a chaos engineering team in place? If yes, does the team provide organization-level direction, or cater to project specific requirements?	Yes – Chaos engineering may be established
		No – People with relevant skillsets need to be developed or recruited to start with

Activities or Stories on Chaos Engineering for Detailed Assessment

Readiness for chaos engineering, as discussed above, involves questions that either bring out the need to adopt such practices or indicate what should be the ground work required as pre-requisites to adopt the practices.

As such needs or readiness are observed and analyzed, the fine grained step is to identify the activities or stories that either are present (in case chaos engineering has been established to a certain extent, if not mature) or are to be designed to the target state (in case there is a strong need to adopt and pre-requisites are being met, at least partially). Following is a list of such stories along with indicative technologies relevant to respective story execution. Note that a chaos engineer (role) needs to establish and execute the stories.

Category	Story description
Application	Randomly kill a critical application instance or O/S process
Application	Randomly terminate multiple application instances in a given portfolio
Application	Runtime data injection randomly causing functions to throw exceptions
Application	Dynamic code insertion to cause failures in specific instruction processing
Data	Randomly stop a database for I/O calls to fail; check for existence and performance, if available, of a secondary fallback database and/or a rollback mechanism to handle corrupted changes
Data	Randomly block access to a storage system with multiple databases

Data	Inject changes to calls (from applications) causing deadlock in I/O operations
Technology	Remove event traces to recreate a production issue
Technology	Simulate maximum capacity of concurrent users reached, for log-in systems
Technology	Randomly kill a container or container cluster (on-premise or on-cloud)
Infrastructure	Stop a set of virtual servers to simulate failure of an entire region or data center
Infrastructure	Increase the turnaround time or latency of a server or a group of servers
Infrastructure	Forcing the system clock to a different time setting for out-of-sync condition
Infrastructure	Randomly increase the load on a server, a server cluster or a network

Following is an indicative list of metrics (for a continuous chaos setup) that can be established and measured with respect to chaos engineering analysis:

Metrics	Significance
Number of errors over a period of time	Process metrics for say, application errors; impacts online customer experience
CPU utilization before and after errors are detected (additionally, average CPU utilization)	Technology metrics; severity of errors for IT, hence IT costs
Latency in server or application response times	Process or technology metrics; delays impacting customer experience
Number of successful (or, failed) application logins per unit time	Process or technology metrics; impacts customer experience
Number of transactions that failed (say, due to choked queue) per unit time	Process metrics; revenue loss and customer flight
Recovery time in resolving database deadlocks, over a period of time	Technology metrics; customer experience, revenue loss

Application downtime by portfolio	Process or technology metrics; online customer experience
Batch runs failed for applications over a period of time by regions/ lines of business	Process metrics; revenue loss, security risk to customer data

AIOps: DevOps driven by AI

Artificial Intelligence (AI) refers to automation that enables machines use natural human language, form or comprehend abstractions and concepts, solve problems that are traditionally reserved for humans, and improve decisioning capabilities through learning. While automation is the common theme between AI and DevOps, AI improves upon the extent of automation to endow cognitive and human-like capabilities.

Before discussing AIOps as a derived concept from AI and DevOps – which is also the topic of discussion here – it is important to understand the fundamental difference between DevOps-driven-AI and AI-driven-DevOps.

DevOps-driven-AI represents AI application development – as a project, functional solution or product – using a traditional DevOps pipeline for orchestration of the development life cycle. Such a pipeline may incorporate automation tools such as IDEs and testing tools specific to AI-based applications. AI-driven-DevOps represents a software engineering discipline whereby the DevOps pipeline itself has AI capabilities – ability to learn from previously executed tasks and workflows, predict say deployment outcomes and execute suitable actions – hence providing higher resilience to failures and intelligent automation requiring little or no human intervention. This paradigm, hence, is the current notion of AIOps (and related engineering practices).

A specific extension to AIOps is ChatOps whereby conversational capabilities may be endowed for understanding of IT scenarios by the intelligent agent from say a human user. The agent may then execute corresponding IT tasks using suitable validations and failover mechanisms. ChatOps is however, more popularly used in business process automation today rather than IT process automation.

Following are the overarching questions for AIOps that may be included at the pre-assessment stage:

Overarching Questions for AIOps
1. What are the roles equivalent to the AI-based automated tasks? What is the extent of automation by each such role?
2. What IT operations functions are covered/ planned to be covered by AIOps?
3. What are the AI algorithms shortlisted, if any, as part of adopting AIOps? Do they include conversational agents and/or machine learning capabilities?
4. Is a time and cost analysis done/ planned to be done for AIOps?
5. Is ChatOps (or other forms of AIOps) established for business process automation? If yes, can such capabilities be extended for IT process automation?

Following are the example stories mapped to relevant areas in AI that may be included to assess AIOps adoption (or gaps if the organization is planning to adopt AIOps) as part of the assessment questionnaire:

Story	AI area in context
Large volume of log data is subject to automated analysis and decisioning in real time or at machine determined intervals	Neural networks
DevOps infrastructure is automatically configured based on automated demand analysis with respect to business	Evolutionary computing
DevOps pipeline automatically detects (and/or mitigates) security threats, say fraud transactions or malware vulnerabilities, using visual data characteristics	Computer vision
Perform repetitive orchestration tasks on DevOps pipeline with limited rule based algorithms	Robotic automation

Generate insights from analytics drawing inputs using a combination of AI methods, say visual, pattern-based and mathematical derivation	Expert systems
The agent analyzes IT cycle times of parallel activity streams in a DevOps pipeline by learning from past data in form of logs and data stores, to find out the critical path for IT delivery, to optimize	Machine learning
The dialog agent (capable of human speech processing) executes machine translation of a voice command to a set of DevOps tasks (say provisioning an environment, or configuring a deployment tool's parameters) in form of command/ code/ script	Speech processing
The dialog agent converses with the human agent to understand and actuate a set of DevOps tasks say, as scripts	Natural language processing

The last two stories are examples of ChatOps capabilities applied to IT process automation.

Time and Cost Analysis for AI based Automation

Though time and cost analysis can be done for any level of automation, such an analysis is of specific interest for organizations embracing AIOps. This is because, AI entails a very high degree of automation, rather bringing in human-like characteristics to machine behavior, with respect to traditional passive automation. Hence, the need for business justification through cost analysis is a criteria to adopt AI based automation, as such automation seeks to build roles equivalent to say, an existing human worker.

Following is the cost analysis for assessing the need for AIOps adoption:

Say,   T = Average time taken for a single IT cycle execution without AI

        T' = Average time taken for the single IT cycle execution after incorporating AI

Hence, (T – T') = Time saved due to AI based automation

    C = Average operations cost for a single IT cycle execution without AI

    C' = Average operations cost for the single IT cycle execution after incorporating AI

Hence, (C – C') = Cost saved due to AI based automation

Note that here, operations cost c, where c ⊇ {C, C', ...}, is a function of time (t), operations personnel cost (p) and infrastructure utilization cost (i); hence, c = f(t, p, i)

For the organization to realize the cost benefit of AIOps, we need to first find out the number of IT cycle runs after incorporating AI based automation that will recover the cost of development of the AI based automation itself.

Say, C_0 = cost of development of the AI tasks for automation
Hence, number of cycles N, to break-even prior to realizing any benefit is computed as follows:

$$N = \frac{C_0}{(C - C')}$$

Hence, if the IT cycle is for release of a specific application that say, undergoes M production releases per day, **it would take N/M days to break-even the cost incurred**.

Further, the **total time saved (T_0)** till the break-even point is reached, would be:

$$T_0 = N \times (T - T')$$

The two aforesaid metrics are important in terms of cost analysis; they represent the time taken to break-even the costs incurred, and time saved by the IT cycles in such time respectively, after implementation of AIOps. Beyond the break-even point, the IT process in context is envisaged to provide cost benefit (or rather, return on investment) due to adoption of AIOps in the IT life cycle.

Security Engineering

Security is an integral part of any IT delivery and management process. Without IT security verification and validation mechanisms, release of software may not only be risky and detrimental for the released software itself, but also for the environment and other hosted software and data integrated to operate with it. Such software would be left vulnerable to the world to exploit, with deep impact in turn to the entire connected IT ecosystem of the organization.

IT security is construed as a set of policies and rules that prevents unauthorized access to enterprise-wide IT systems and assets such as computers, network and data. It is targeted towards building trust across the IT value chain by maintaining the integrity and confidentiality of sensitive information, thereby blocking access to "low trust zones" such as say, expert hackers.

From an IT delivery standpoint, security typically impacts the following DevOps engineering practices:

1. Code and Data Engineering
    a. Application code security
    b. Data security

2. Environment Engineering
    a. Operating system security
    b. Application server security
    c. Database security
    d. Third party component/ software security
    e. Network security
    f. Web server security
    g. Proxy server security
    h. Firewall security
    i. Container security

Given that the typically practice is to treat security as a post-facto phenomenon whereby say, application code security checks are done after the application coding has already happened (and committed), this practice needs to be shifted left whereby security checks or tests become part of the application coding activity itself. Hence, from a DevOps assessment perspective, it is important at a broad level to evaluate two aspects, with the intent given in braces:

a. What is the IT cycle time impact (and cost) for security tests across the IT value chain? (manual post-facto tests take substantial time, hence a loss of focus)

b. Is continuous security through suitable automation being considered or established? (automated continuous test substantially reduce the time to detect potential security failures and fix them across the IT life cycle)

While the above broad questions may be suitable at the pre-assessment stage, following are the stories that may be considered during the detailed assessment:

Story	Stage of IT Process
Security testing or monitoring tool is integrated with / partially integrated with / works standalone with respect to the continued integration server	Establish (technology)
Security testing or monitoring tool provides APIs for all or leading tool integrations / does not provide adequate APIs for integration to the pipeline	Establish (technology)
Organization's personnel integrates the security tool to the pipeline / does not have necessary skills, hence needs mentoring for integrating to the pipeline / requires third-party personnel to integrate to the pipeline	Establish (people)
Security tools used or planned for use are certified by accredited IT security body and benchmarked / but not benchmarked	Establish

Security test plans are manually prepared / Security test scripts are coded into an automation tool integrated with say, the developer IDE	Execute
Security tests are executed in the QA environment after the developer build-and-test post the code commit / Security tests are executed during the developer code development	Execute
Security tests are executed using fully or primarily manual workflows / partially manual workflows with certain automation / fully or primarily automated	Execute
Security scans and related monitoring is done at specific intervals by dedicated security team / Security scans and monitoring is executed on a continuous basis using monitoring tool	Execute
Security tests include – application code testing, database testing, et al (as covered above under security impact on DevOps engineering practices)	Execute
Security tests are conducted by all IT personnel (Dev, Ops teams) before every check-in, commit or release / before specific pre-planned check-in, commit or release only / (not done)	Execute
Security engineer or team participates in Scrum meeting or retrospectives every time / partially / (does not participate)	Execute
Security tests are manually executed and validated through sample runs by a security tool that works in parallel over the pipeline (say, only for some tests) / not validated with any automated tests	Execute
Patches are manually applied to security tool at intervals / automatically applied at intervals / automatically applied on a continuous basis	Execute
Security tests and monitoring requirements are coded as part of the pipeline	Execute

DataOps: DevOps for Data

DataOps is a set of engineering practices that can be used to ensure the integrity, reliability, consistency, availability, scalability, concurrency, interoperability, portability and security of data for any business, application and technology needs; while streamlining the entire IT value chain across the data layer by optimizing the IT cycle time.

In general, data is described through associated metadata, which is an abstract representation of data itself. However, the intent and context of the metadata is more powerful in scope, usage and analysis than the raw data itself. This can further be abstracted through meta-metadata, and so on (generalized as $meta^N$-data). The concept of metadata is the foundation on which any operations on data may be executed.

Note that data types may typically be character (related to text) or binary (related to numeric formats); relational or non-relational; structured or unstructured; bounded or unbounded.

A Brief Note on Big Data Applications

Big data is a term that describes large volumes of data obtained typically from multiple sources – both structured, semi-structured and unstructured – that impacts an organization on a day-to-day basis. It has the potential to be mined for information and used in machine learning projects and other advanced analytics applications providing predictive or behavioral analytics. Hence we can consider Big Data to be the data oriented towards analytics.

Big Data deals with complex datasets which is different from traditional data processing applications. It deals with the stochastic side of data and provides insights and visualizations which enable people to take intelligent decisions.

The general characteristics of Big Data are:

- High Volume
- High Variety (different types of data)

- High Velocity (Data moves at a very high speed, for instance, streaming data)
- High Veracity (The quality of data needs to be high for accurate analysis)

From the perspective of the above characteristics, following are the non-functional considerations with a brief implication for each, as applied to Big Data systems (or, applications handling Big Data) that are relevant to a DevOps assessment:

a. Sensors and Networks – The essence is to understand how to filter the right data required for analytics, and handle say, missing, incorrect or redundant data

b. Processing Capability and Data needs – Big Data requires parallel processing infrastructure that are highly scalable; further, creation of data lakes (large data repository of an organization in natural or raw formats, aggregated from multiple sources) demand immense computing power over large distributed infrastructures ensuring high reliability and security of data

c. Data Model and Compute Memory – Big Data requires efficient data models and fast processing capabilities (say, leveraging in-memory grid computing)

d. Content and its Correlation Characteristics – Data manipulated should incorporate learning algorithms, et al, that can efficiently find out correlation of data with different confidence levels; rules may need to be dynamically changed based on business environment scenarios

e. Sharing of Information and Collaboration – Big Data led analytics need to be percolated and shared across all levels in the organization, with appropriate security controls while enabling collaborated workflows

f. Personalization – The plethora of data (and types of data) warrant mass personalization across levels in the organization for the resulting analytics to be meaningful to consumers of the data

Hence, quite a few of the questions provided below on DataOps also applies to Big Data applications from two perspectives; storing Big Data, and manipulating and processing Big Data for analytics.

Coming back to the discussion on DataOps with respect to the aforementioned data types and using the paradigm of meta^N-data, following are the examples of data related workflows (that can be interpreted as stories):

a. Maintain infrastructure to store the data; the data store encompasses and represents the data topology
b. Define, control, manipulate and visualize the data as required by business
c. Provide data access to any authorized party in a secure manner
d. Fulfil the non-functional requirements around the data
e. Test data against functional requirements
f. Move the data between different data stores in conjunction with say, application code

For a complete coverage of implications of such workflows on realizing DataOps, we represent here the overarching questions relevant at the pre-assessment stage, followed by the practice categorized by respective engineering practices.

Overarching Questions for DataOps
1. Is there a specific team that focuses on DataOps or data related software engineering practices?
2. What IT operations functions are covered or planned to be covered by DataOps?
3. Is DataOps considered for continuous data and/or database changes, or for one-time IT processes such as data migration?
4. What is the source(s) of data for drawing out data related requirements? How is the source(s) determined? What is the granularity of data considered (may be defined by the level of meta^N-data defined in the organization)?

5. What are the technologies used or planned to be used for data operations? What are the scope and data type(s) supported for each? (Example of such tools would be build tools for data)
6. What is the typical frequency of data and/or database change build, release and deploy?

Requirements Engineering for Data

Here, the meta^N-data operations take place. Following are the relevant stories with suitable options, where applicable, for the detailed assessment:

Story
Data and/or database change requirements are provided by business / created by business and IT (with Dev, QA, Data Admin and/or Ops involvement) collaboration
Data and/or database change requirements are linked to non-data related requirements
Data specific non-functional requirements are provided by architect / architect and one or more of the following IT roles: Dev, QA, Data Admin, Ops
Test cases for data specific requirements are created manually / using automation tool with test scripts formulated
Data specific functional requirements are tested manually (may include the methods) / using automation tools (may include tool details)
Data specific non-functional requirements are tested manually (may include the methods) / using automation tools (may include tool details)
Data Admin tasks are included as part of data specific requirements
Data specific infrastructure requirements are provided by architect / architect and Data Admin and/or Ops
Test cases for data specific infrastructure requirements are created manually / using automation tool with test scripts formulated
Data specific infrastructure requirements are tested manually (may include the methods) / using automation tools (may include tool details)

Data specific security requirements are provided by architect / architect and Data Admin and/or Ops
Test cases for data specific security requirements are created manually / using automation tool with test scripts formulated
Data specific security requirements are tested manually (may include the methods) / using automation tools (may include tool details)

Data Engineering

Scope of this practice is to write the code against the test cases, obtained through requirements engineering, relevant to data modeling and data operations. Following are the relevant stories with suitable options, where applicable, for the detailed assessment:

Story
Data models are created (and maintained) manually / using automated workflows, however manually / using automated workflows and automation tools
Data definition is done manually / using automation tools by business, architect, Data Admin and/or DataOps team
Data control is done manually / using automation tools by architect, Data Admin and/or DataOps team
Data manipulation is done manually / using automation tools by architect, Data Admin and/or DataOps team
Database scripts and data feeds are maintained manually / using automation workflows and/or tools, by architect, Data Admin and/or DataOps team
Database scripts and data feeds are stored in informal data repository / in formal data repository or store that partially / fully provides data management capabilities such as archival, versioning, access control and security, et al

Quality Engineering

Scope of this practice is to execute the relevant tests to ensure data quality, reliability, integrity, security, et al. Following are the relevant stories with suitable options, where applicable, for the detailed assessment:

Story
Data quality tests are executed manually / using automation tool with test scripts
Data script quality tests are executed manually / using automation tool on continuous basis / at pre-determined intervals
Quality gates for data are defined for data components across the IT process manually / using workflow automation modeling tool
Data governance is defined across IT process manually / using formal dashboards (incorporating reports and analytics) / using formal dashboards with automated feed from integrated data operations tool(s)
Unit tests for data are executed manually / using automation tool with test scripts
Data script unit tests are executed manually / using automation tool on continuous basis / at pre-determined intervals
Functional (including integration) tests for data are executed manually / using automation tool with test scripts
Regression tests for data are executed manually / using automation tool with test scripts
One or more the following test data management operations are executed manually / using automation tool(s) aimed at preserving sanctity of data in face of change: o   Test data reservation o   Test data versioning and archival o   Test bed/ environment provisioning and scaling o   Test data masking (and privacy related operations) o   Test data redundancy management o   Test data backup and restore o   Test data security – access control, scanning, quarantine

Build and Release (and Deployment) Engineering

Scope of this practice is to build and package the scripts and data and/or database schemas, and deploy and release to target environment. Following are the relevant stories with suitable options, where applicable, for the detailed assessment:

Story
Build scripts are executed manually / using automation tool as a standalone activity / using automation tool integrated to a defined DevOps pipeline
Release scripts are executed manually / using automation tool as a standalone activity / using automation tool integrated to a defined DevOps pipeline
Deployment scripts are executed manually / using automation tool as a standalone activity / using automation tool integrated to a defined DevOps pipeline
Build, release and/or deploy reports are generated manually / using automation tool / using automation tool with data operations tool(s) integration
Build, release and/or deploy analytics are derived manually / using automation tool / using automation tool integrated to analytics tool or incorporating analytics capabilities
Data or database errors are captured and analyzed manually / using automation tool / using data reporting and analytics

The intent for the assessment for this practice is to find out if and how changes to database deployment artefacts – database scripts, database packages, DDL statements, stored procedures, database triggers, et al – move through a DevOps pipeline for automated and seamless operations, as relevant to (and integrated with) the associated application code changes.

Environment Engineering

Scope of this practice is to manage environments as relevant to data and/or database changes. Following are the relevant stories with suitable options, where applicable, for the detailed assessment:

Story
Capacity for data to be provisioned for an application is determined by architect, Data Admin, DataOps team and/or Ops team (say, infrastructure team)
Data is provisioned for an application using manual workflows / using automated workflows
Data integrity – for data maintained across different environments for the same application – is ensured manually / using automation tool and/or through automated workflows
Data replication is executed manually / using automated workflows and/or with automation tool
Data replication is executed at pre-determined intervals based on test batches for say, a set of releases / on-demand whenever one or more application(s) need to be tested
Replicated data lying unused for more than thirty days (as an example, whereby release cycle time is of ten days) may be removed or archived
Data is refresh is executed manually / using automated workflows and/or with automation tool
Data refresh is done every ten days on selected or all test beds (as an example, assuming an average release cycle time of ten days)
Data store administration is executed manually / using automated workflows and/or with automation tool
Data store, relational or non-relational, is administered for production grade setup at pre-determined intervals / on-demand / on continuous basis, to address one or more of the following: o   Data store access and security o   Data store refresh o   Data store quality and integrity administration o   Data store backup and restore o   Data store updates and patches o   Data store life cycle administration using versioning and archival

VMs and/or containers for databases are created using manual service / automated tool integrated to say, a hypervisor (typically, on-premise) / automated tool integrated with cloud management services (on cloud)
Persistent / non-persistent volumes are configured as part of the VMs or containers using manual services / automated services on-premise or on-cloud
Environment engineering is integrated partially / fully as part of the DevOps pipeline (if partial, you may find out what percentage or scope is outside the pipeline)

A Brief Note on Data Migration

Note that for assessments specific to data migration initiatives, specific automation tools can be used to analyze the database (typically rule-based), generate data models and schemas, provide related ETL (Extract – Transformation – Load) facilities, ensure data quality and detect and/or fix errors and data redundancies, and provide automated configurable change management workflow capabilities. For effective utilization of such capabilities as part of the DevOps pipeline, corresponding stories for data migration – that may have been already covered in the above tables – need to be included as part of the assessment.

Branching and Merging Strategy

Given that this and subsequent sections are discussions on specific strategies based on given processes or technologies – rather than engineering practices – we would briefly explain how each of the strategies is important with respect to DevOps and the overarching questions for the associated approaches; based on which you may derive the stories for your detailed assessment.

Branching and merging strategy execution is relevant, and typically gets covered as part of, code (and data) engineering practice. However, implications of the strategy lies in all the other practices. Given that how the code being developed is managed or planned to be managed, the rest of the practices need to accommodate the changes accordingly. For example, tests and releases planned, and environments to be provisioned will be different for a branching and merging strategy at story-level, vis-à-vis that for the strategy at the release-level.

A developer coding alone is a completely different situation then many developers working together. Every developer adds a given number of lines of text [code or data] into the source code repository system. This line of code is written against a set of test code that describes the feature or a part of the feature. This may be defined as a "Minimal Viable Product" (MVP). Terms such as Critically Viable Product or, Optimally Viable Product may also be in use; the difference is in how the organization defines the granularity of the features developed.

If multiple developers are working on the same feature, then the developer work streams needs to be integrated into a common code, which eventually may be deployed in production. Hence, how quickly the code is merged into a single production ready codebase assumes relevance.

There are several branching and merging strategies and the choice depends on the analysis of the same in the context of the organization.

Strategy	Relevant DevOps Question
Trunk Based Development [No Branching]: all the developers work on the same branch.	1. How many developers are there in the project? 2. Do the developers work as a team or they mostly work alone on their own code branches? 3. Are only a few developers taking the entire feature code till production? 4. Is the team planning to use the feature toggle facility?
Release Branching: The release is contained within a branch; when a team starts working on a new release, a branch is created and all the	1. Is the team following a mix of Agile and Waterfall in their development process? 2. How many people are working on the same branch ? 3. How are the conflicts managed at the check-in and checkout stages?

work done until the next release is stored in this branch.	4. How long is the release cycle? [If the release cycle is too long, release branching may be very problematic] 5. How long is the testing cycle? 6. Is the release process manual or automated? 7. How are the code for different features in the same release integrated? Is there any automation for the same?
Feature Branching: This strategy combines the feature toggle facility and collects all the code for feature in the same code store, and then merges the same back with the master branch.	1. How are the stories mapped to the features ? 2. Are the developers of the stories checking the code into one feature branch only ? 3. How are the new stories added to the feature ? Does this mean that a story is tagged to multiple features? 4. How frequent is the release needed ? 5. Is the team ready for continuous delivery? 6. Is the team okay for small incremental releases ? 7. Are all the stories subscribe to the philosophy of MVP?
Story or Task Branching: This strategy connects the user story changes to the code; it is the lowest level of branching and each issue is resolved in its own branch. (Note that every branch is typically connected with a single user story id)	1. How well is the Agile methodology followed ? 2. Are the requirements broken down into fine grained user stories? 3. Are the stories individually releasable? 4. Is the enterprise ready for continuous deployment? 5. Is there any restriction on the number of deployments in production?
Manual code review and merging strategy: This strategy uses manual means to do code review and testing before moving to the master branch; the master branch is the main	1. What is the level of human error that is induced by improper manual merging and review ? 2. Has the team been impacted by any cascading impact due to improper manual review and code merge ?

branch from where production build happens.	3. Were there any known issues of build, release or deployment which have their root cause in manual merging? 4. Has the team considered any automated reviewing and merging strategy? What are the problems perceived in automated review and merging?
Minimal Continuous integration: Uses a build orchestration tool such as Jenkins or GitLab Runner to compile and test the source code; this is done through a series of quality gates which requires no human intervention. The code review is automatic and if the tests do not pass - the code is not tagged to the master - hence, the code does not reach production. The problem with this strategy is that it is difficult to manage different types of testing, particularly if the testing cycle is long. Also, this strategy is not good at handling large feedback cycles. If there are different types of testing – for instance, performance or security – this method may not be suitable.	1. Is a process of central build followed ? (Central build can also be looked at as integration builds, implying build of all the components within one build cycle) 2. How many types of testing automation are used in the pipeline? 3. How long are the testing cycles for each type of testing? (If the testing cycle is too long then this method may not be suitable) 4. How long are the feedback cycles? (Long feedback cycles indicate that a production event is possibly taking a lot of time to reach the developer) 5. What is the extent of manual testing? (Strategy may not be right if there is substantial manual testing) 6. How frequently code is being checked into the master? 7. Does every code check results in a build ? 8. How robust is the build pipeline? (If there are too many build requests coming from a large development team, the build pipeline needs to be scalable) 9. What is the team size? (This strategy may not be suitable for relatively large teams)

Continuous Integration Pipeline with Quality Gates: This strategy leverages the principles of integration branching. Integration branching refers to mapping the branches with the stages of the DevOps pipeline. This stages can be the quality gates, automated code review and automated merging. Once all the gates are cleared, the code in the branch is merged into the master for production builds. This strategy takes care of long testing cycles - as the long running tasks can reside in separate branches, and can be integrated at any given point of time with the master; provided all the quality gates are cleared.	1. Are the teams co-located or distributed? 2. Are there multiple vendor development teams in the same project? 3. Is the development team and maintenance team different? 4. What is the frequency of commits to the master? 5. Are the testing cycles relatively long? What are the respective durations? 6. Does the team practice (or plan to practice) automated reviews? 7. Does the team practice (or plan to practice) automated merging? 8. How are the branches mapped to the MVPs?

Based on our experience in assessing branching and merging strategies, we observe that the leading practice is to go for **story branching** with automated reviews and merges from the quality gates within the continuous integration pipeline. Of course, there is a need to assess suitability based on the baseline state, and the desired target state of the IT life cycle.

There are two key benefits in creating a branching and merging strategy for an enterprise engaged in development activities:

a. Having a defined strategy allows for integration of rapid changes while still enforcing mechanisms to ensure quality, thereby removing the apparently conflicting notions of achieving faster IT cycle times versus implementing quality gates as checkpoints

b. Separating changes into small, discrete units can help encourage testing changes in isolation, thereby increasing the odds of identifying defects earlier in the software development life cycle

Teams should adopt the best-fitting branching and merging strategy, and rely on existing resources and plug-ins from their build orchestration tools. Over time, the team can iteratively add quality gates and adopt smaller-scoped branches, reducing release sizes and cycle times to bring features to production faster.

Container Strategy and DevOps

DevOps is, at times, considered synonymous with the concept of a container. The container technology in a nutshell is a method to package an application so that it can be run, along with its dependencies, isolated from another process. This means that the entire application infrastructure is available as a code to the developer. This enables the developer to check-in the infrastructure code in the same way as the application code is being dealt with. The infrastructure code can be written in text format, compiled and then executed.

This essentially means that the focus of containerization is to move towards a NoOps state where no involvement is needed from the operations team to release a software. The container instances run typically run on a container platform that may provide additional container management capabilities.

To explain it in a better way, let us take an example of Docker as compared to how traditional java (or, C++, et al) development is done.

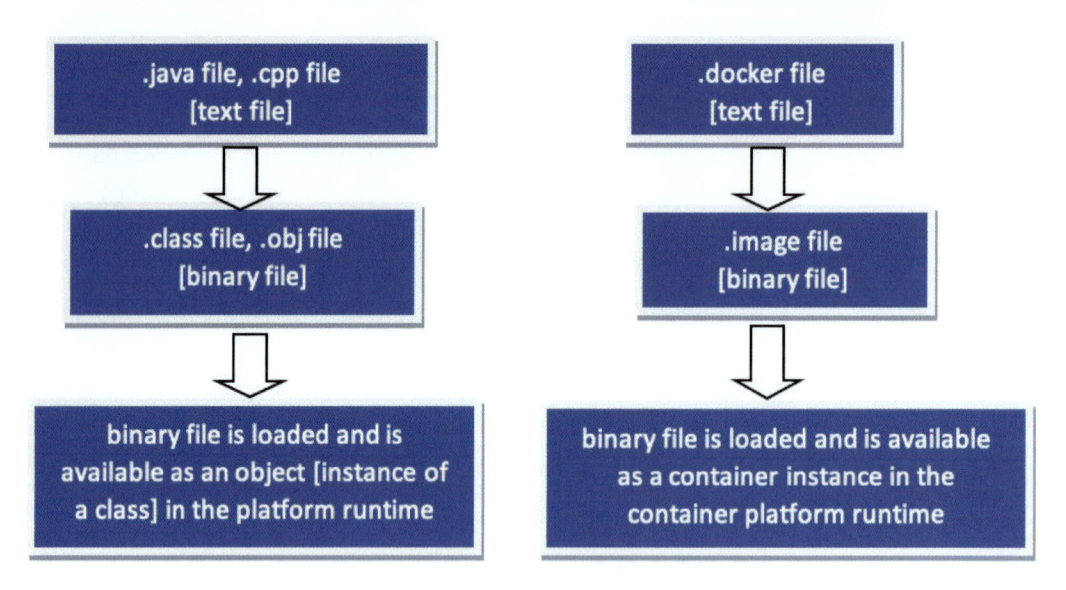

```
.java file, .cpp file              .docker file
    [text file]                     [text file]
         ⇩                               ⇩
.class file, .obj file              .image file
    [binary file]                   [binary file]
         ⇩                               ⇩
binary file is loaded and is      binary file is loaded and is available
available as an object [instance of   as a container instance in the
a class] in the platform runtime      container platform runtime
```

Figure 30: Traditional versus Container based Deployment Approach

In the case of Docker, the developer – also at times termed as the "full stack engineer" - adds the infrastructure needs of the application as code and checks in the same to the source code repository. When the build is triggered the infrastructure is built automatically along the process.

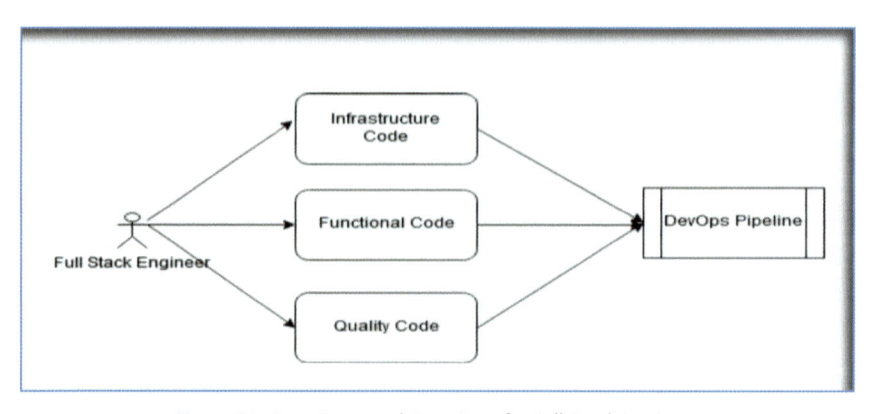

Figure 31: Containers and Function of a Full Stack Engineer

The container itself can be viewed as an implementation of a complete set of code ("Image file") that represents an application hosted along with its related dependencies on a layered infrastructure; typically consisting of an application server, a runtime, an O/S, and with necessary hardware abstraction layer.

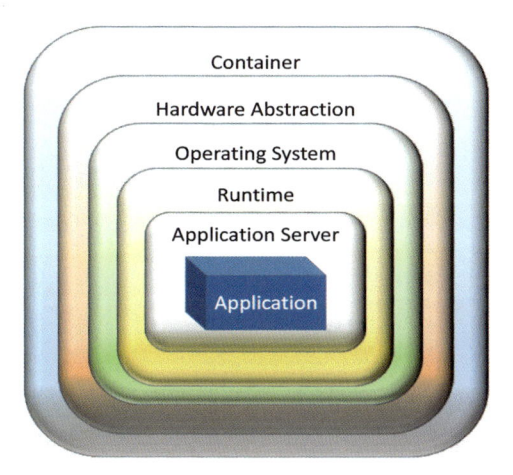

Figure 32: Visualization of a Container

Hence the impact of container technology on DevOps is substantial. However it is worth mentioning that moving to containers has its own impact on people and process. Since the infrastructure is now available as code, the control shifts more towards a developer oriented IT process, and people with less coding skills needs to focus on the functional side of IT; given that with DevOps everything is seen as code and automation. Hence, there is an impact on the existing workforce when container technology is introduced in the enterprise.

Container technology impacts the entire operations process in a big way as it introduces Agile operations from a Developer perspective. The Developer will no longer be dependent on the Ops team for infrastructure needs; they can simply code the infrastructure on their own, including networking requirements. There is a significant impact on the IT cycle time if container technology or container platform is used. This is because there is no specific need of a fixed environment - the environment itself has become immutable. It can be recreated on the hardware as many number of times as needed via the container platform runtime.

Container technology is closely based on the concept of VMs. Almost all the applications which does not use container technology definitely are hosted on VM(s). The VM provisioning exercise can be done manually, though there is scope of full automation. The fully automated VM can behave closely like a container - but a container is more lightweight and is immutable. VM is not necessarily immutable. Hence, migration to container technology essentially means that the VM technology is assuming less relevance in the face of DevOps needs.

The initial set of questions that needs to be asked, say at pre-assessment stage, are as follows:

1. What is the readiness of the people in terms of accepting container technology? Has the team obtained adequate training on container technology?
2. How is the application environment currently hosted?
3. How is VM Technology used in the current state?
4. What is the O/S that is being used by the applications? Are there any custom O/S?
5. What are the types of application runtime? (For example, java runtime, Windows runtime, et al); Are there any custom application runtime(s)?
6. Is the current build, release and deployment automated ? (It is important to note at the time of writing this book, container technology is construed to be at a higher state of technology maturity, and hence assumes that a given degree of build, release and deployment automation is already in place as part of continuous integration pipeline)

The questions that need to be discussed during the assessment are (you may derive the corresponding stories for the assessment accordingly):

1. What is time needed to provision a non-production environment?
2. What is the time needed to provision a production environment?
3. What is the method to test the correctness of the provisioned environment?
4. What is the method to achieve scalability in the current state ? (The container platform typically provides clustering, orchestration and failover support capabilities)
5. Are the Ops team and the Dev team belong to the same vendor, or different vendors?
6. How is security managed? (Container security is of paramount importance and hence, the current security capabilities need to be evaluated)
7. What are the current server hardening and tempering mechanisms?
8. What is the current network architecture?
9. What is the current level of protocol support needed? (For example, http, ftp, et al)
10. What is the current level of port privileges? (For example, port 22, 8080, et al)
11. What is the current build process? (The current application build process will significantly influence the container build process)

12. Where is the application binary stored? (The container binaries or image repository needs to be identified. Many enterprises have their own private container repository separate from the application repository, however there are also instances where the repository for container images and application binaries is the same)
13. What is the current release and deployment process? (The current release and deployment process will significantly influence the container based processes)
14. How is the current infrastructure monitored?
15. How are production level events captured?
16. How are they propagated to the development team?
17. In case of a server failure, what and how are the remedial actions taken?
18. In case of an O/S failure, what and how are the remedial actions taken?
19. In case of an application server failure, what and how are the remedial actions taken?

There are various ways to implement container in the release and deployment process. The following are the two commonly found ways:

a. Application and container are built separately, and an automated release and deployment process is used to push the application to the container.

b. The application and container are built together in the same branch (say, a story branch) and taken as a whole to production. This state is at a higher technological maturity as the application and infrastructure follows through the same process together and container moves along with the application itself. The container and what is contained in it (the application and its dependencies, and the layered infrastructure) is seen as one.

Cloud Strategy and DevOps

Cloud technologies have taken DevOps to the mainstream of IT. If we look at the history of IT development with the advent of containers and application release automation, there was more focus to a lowering of the Total Cost of Ownership (TCO), specifically as applied to hardware infrastructure. The most costly hardware became obsolete in a few years, the rate of obsolescence being very high.

The operations team slowly started to understand that it is costlier to maintain hardware, including servers, on their own; than to have someone else manage the same. They outsourced the same to some vendor. However that only aggravated the problem because of vendor lock-in. Some of the vendors started charging exorbitantly and hence, essentially turned up to be another problem to be solved.

The cloud providers had a different proposition; they guaranteed a few core services:

- Infrastructure services
- Platform services
- Software services

All the backend framework, hardware and network backbone are taken care of by the cloud provider. The user simply gets an Application Programming Interface (API), a Command Line Interface (CLI) and/or an User Interface (UI) for whatever to use the services. Entire VMs can be created on cloud; these VMs being termed differently by different cloud providers. Amazon calls them as EC2 instances while Microsoft calls them as Azure Resource Manager (ARM); essentially all of them provide the three main categories of services.

All cloud providers leverage the use of container technology at different scales. There is a private cloud option available for organizations as well, who does not want to move to a public cloud. In such a case, the cloud platform is configured within the data center of such organization.

Serverless Computing

The idea of Serverless computing is becoming more relevant with the maturity of immutable infrastructure and container services. The principle of Serverless computing is to establish an execution model in which the cloud provider runs the server and dynamically manages the allocation of machine resources. Pricing is based on the actual amount of resources consumed by an application, rather than on pre-purchased units of capacity.

Serverless computing can simplify the process of deploying code into production. Scaling, capacity planning and maintenance operations may be hidden from the developer or operator using suitable abstraction layers. Serverless code can be used in conjunction with code deployed in traditional styles such as microservices. Alternatively, applications can be written to support purely Serverless state and use no provisioned servers at all for execution.

Cloud Bursting

Cloud Bursting is an application deployment model wherein the cloud platform can span between private (where is application is originally hosted, and executes) and public environments seamlessly. Whenever there is a "spike" or a peak demand for the application execution, the additional load is transferred to a public compute resource whereby additional application instances can run on the public cloud. Thus, the organization only has to pay for the additional compute resources when the public cloud is leveraged. We observe that cloud bursting may be used for applications that need to support high workloads and encounter execution "spikes" – typically high performance – but are not particularly critical for the organization.

One has to be cognizant of the fact that any service has a cost, so improper choice of services can lead to a cost overhead. Storage cost is a continuous cost and has to be accrued at all times (which are due to say, database volumes consumed), however the cost of the instances is on a pay per use model. However, cloud storage cost is typically cheaper than the cost of data storage in the data center.

The relevant questions for cloud computing for the pre-assessment stage are as follows:

1. For a potential move to cloud adoption, has it been assessed which customer facing, middleware and back office workloads need to move to the cloud, and why?

2. Is there appropriate sponsorship available for a cloud assessment and migration work? (Putting up a cloud strategy needs a strong senior management commitment due to substantial degree of the organizational change envisaged)
3. What is the current release process? (To understand fitment to cloud in the target state)
4. What is the current release frequency? (To understand the expectation from cloud adoption with respect to speed of IT delivery)
5. Is container technology used?
6. Will the data reside inside the data center or on cloud? [There are organizations who prefer to keep the data in their local data centers rather than on cloud, or more specifically public cloud]
7. What type of applications are targeted to be hosted on cloud?
8. Are there any Commercial-Off-The-Shelf (COTS) or legacy tool that also needs to be hosted on cloud?
9. Is data security considered for cloud?
10. Is there any political or geographical constraints for data storage? (Given the regulatory constraints for data, for example, the UK Data Protection Act)
11. Is there a cloud adoption and a cloud governance model established at the enterprise level, with the governance team or stakeholders identified?

The above questions typically lay the foundation for a cloud migration assessment. Given that moving to a cloud platform entails a significant change in the organizational culture and the speed that can be potentially achieved (and improved) in managing IT changes in the target state, assessment for cloud is typically done for putting up a cloud migration strategy.

Cloud Migration Assessment from a DevOps Perspective

With the advent of NoOps and serverless computing, the developers have been significantly empowered with the capability to manage infrastructure themselves; such practices are termed as "Developer Self-service".

The detailed questions for cloud migration from a DevOps perspective are as follows. You may derive the corresponding stories for assessment accordingly:

1. Has the relevant stakeholders been identified, notified and aligned for the cloud migration?
2. What are the platform runtimes that is needed in the current state? (The current platform runtimes needs to be supported by the cloud infrastructure)
3. What is the current release process ?
4. What is the up-time requirement or availability expected for the application(s) in production?
5. What is the data transfer need for the application(s)?
6. What is the scalability required and the peak transaction rate(s) of the application(s)?
7. Has application containerization been considered? (The platform may typically provide container services, however vanilla container orchestration engines are also available)
8. What is the current development model; is the development approach bi-modal or hybrid?
9. Is continuous integration and continuous delivery/ deployment practiced?
10. What are the container services required? (The cost of service must be given due consideration, else the cloud operations costs may shoot up uncontrollably)
11. How is image management going to be done?
12. How is the application going to be deployed in the container images?
13. How is the Virtual Private Cloud (VPC) going to be designed?
14. What are the Intellectual Property (IP) security restrictions that needs to be established for cloud operations to be secure?
15. In case the enterprise decides to go for a different cloud provider, is there any automation available for moving the compute resource contents from one provider to the other?
16. What are the O/S supported by the cloud provider?
17. What is the cloud security model that is mandated at the enterprise level?
18. How is the end point security established for cloud systems?
19. Is there any specific choice of container technology orchestration needs?
20. What are the different cloud services being considered to be used vis-a-vis vanilla installation?

21. How will authentication and authorization done from a cloud environment to a local network, and vice-versa?
22. What are the cloud service providers Service Level Agreements (SLAs) that best meet the organization's needs?
23. Determine if the cloud infrastructure or any of its components complies to a single-tenant or fully multi-tenant architecture?
24. What is the available network segmentation?
25. What are the functions that are preferred to be automated?
26. What are the Business Continuity (BC) and Disaster Recovery (DR) provisions?
27. Where are the DR locations and the security measures available at these locations?
28. Does the cloud provider offer managed recovery; either automated or manual?
29. Will the cloud service provider allow the flexibility to add controls specific to the enterprise?
30. Who will exercise the rights to order additional services for the organization?
31. What is the risk management plan of the cloud service provider?
32. What is the governance structure that the cloud service provider recommends?
33. What are the compliance requirements that the cloud service provider meet?
34. Who will be responsible for moving workloads on the new cloud platform?
35. Who will perform the migration – will it be vendor driven or internally driven by the organization?
36. What are the changed orders for the migration process?
37. Is the cloud service provider capable of providing a detailed Statement-Of-Work (SoW) in advance?
38. What is the success rate of the cloud provider meeting the contractual requirements of cloud migration projects?
39. What are the conditions under which the organization can terminate the contract with a cloud provider?
40. Is there any resiliency (or, reliability) report available for the cloud platform?
41. How does automated recovery happen on the cloud platform?
42. Is there a cloud risk management strategy available for the organization?
43. Can the interdependent applications be moved in bundles to the cloud platform to avoid unnecessary outages?

44. What is the state of application(s) that needs to be moved to cloud; is it part of a Greenfield project or a Brownfield project ?
45. Is Lift-and-Shift the initial method to host applications on cloud, or the applications need to be re-architected or factored to make them cloud ready?
46. Will the vendors be involved in the migration, or it will be done solely by the employees within the organization?
47. Is the billing model, including payment terms, of the Cloud service provider clearly understood?
48. Will the DevOps tools and DevOps APIs be provided by the cloud provider, or will they be created in-house or provided as a vendor developed framework?
49. Is there a view of the steady state DevOps metrics, including cost related metrics?

DevOps for Legacy Modernization

Legacy modernization is an approach to reduce the total cost of ownership by replacing or refactoring old technologies (hence, the term "Legacy") to newer ones for better support and maintenance. Technologies such as those related to mainframe systems may be relatively old, but at the end of the day they are capable of providing huge computing power suitable for large enterprises and have stood the test of time. The O/S of mainframe and midrange systems (IBM Z-series and i-series) have also evolved in the face of embracing new technologies and IT paradigms.

All the concepts of DevOps is now applicable to mainframes as well as any old technologies like client-server based systems, even extending to COTS products. The core objective is to be able to process legacy system code through the DevOps pipeline, especially where the corresponding application is accessed across heterogeneous infrastructure including legacy systems. With the advent of container technology, the runtime can be created as needed using infrastructure as code.

However, the problem with large scale monolithic systems like mainframe itself that, a virtual mainframe environment cannot be easily replicated from an existing one. This is an extremely difficult task to run mainframe O/S on a lower end hardware platform. Virtualization of the O/S is also very difficult, given how mainframe O/S has been designed.

However with recent advances like the advent of IBM LinuxOne, DevOps on mainframe is a sure possibility. It may be noted that a state of DevOps can be achieved on mainframe even without LinuxOne. There are a plethora of tools that can help in achieving CI/CD for mainframe applications.

Hence from a DevOps assessment perspective, legacy application modernization in the context of mainframe systems require the following overarching questions to be asked at the pre-assessment stage:

1. How are build and unit tests conducted for applications in mainframe?
2. Which and how are the functional and non-functional tests conducted for applications in mainframe?
3. How is the code quality checked for applications in mainframe? Are there integrations to the IDE or a separate tool is run? How is technical debt for code determined?
4. How are releases done (and managed) for applications in mainframe? What are the environments available; QA, staging, et al?
5. How are applications monitored in mainframe?
6. How is requirement engineering currently happening in the mainframe world?
7. What are the other systems interfacing with the mainframe, and how? In this context, which applications are hosted in each of such systems, including mainframe, that need to have execution capabilities across one or more of the interfacing systems?
8. How are Logical Partitions (LPARs) managed in the mainframe? What is the strategy behind which LPARs to be created and made available to IT teams?

Following may be the questions relevant to the detailed assessment (you may derive the stories accordingly for the assessment):

1. How is Agile currently practiced by team(s) working in mainframe projects?
2. Which Requirement Engineering tool is used? (For example; Jira, IBM Rational Team Concert or RTC, et al)
3. Is a test driven development approach followed?
4. What are the automation tools used for the respective IT activities, as covered in the aforesaid questions for the pre-assessment stage?
5. How are the requirements traced back to code for applications in mainframe?
6. How is code managed for development in mainframe?
7. What is the branching and merging strategy used in mainframe?
8. Is an automated code review and/or automated code merge process established?
9. Can the mainframe code be compiled outside mainframe ? (This question can help identify whether the CI/CD platform can reside within the mainframe environment or outside the mainframe environment; both the approaches need to be evaluated in detail with the right stakeholders from Dev and Ops teams)
10. Is the build tool modern enough to be integrated with a CI server? (If not; there are quite a few modern mainframe oriented build tools out of which a suitable one may be selected based on requirements, cost, support structure and ease of use)
11. What is the CI server used for mainframe application code? (If no such CI server is available; default is Jenkins, however there are many products from leading vendors such as IBM, CA, Microfocus who have tools for the same suited for mainframe)
12. Are there any deployment failures? If yes, how is the root cause identified?
13. What is the current Mean-Time-To-Repair (MTTR) and Mean-Time-Between-Failures (MTBF) for applications in mainframe production environment?
14. What is the current deployment automation tool that is used by the enterprise outside mainframe technology? (Need to evaluate if the current CD tool for non-mainframe environments can be leveraged for mainframe deployments as well. For example, many organization having IBM as their infrastructure vendor may already have IBM UrbanCode that is suited for both mainframe and non-mainframe environments)
15. What are the available LPARs for IT teams to use? How are they provisioned, and who does it? Does LPAR management happen in a demilitarized zone? (Need to evaluate which LPARs may become redundant in case the organization plans to integrate non-mainframe systems to the mainframe for say, applications that need to be executed on both)

16. Are LPARs in mainframe mapped or, planned to be mapped, to equivalent environments in non-mainframe infrastructure on which the DevOps pipeline is planned to be implemented?

Tools for Mainframe DevOps

Given that DevOps on mainframe is an emerging (and yet to rationalize) area in spite of mainframe being a legacy system, we are specifically covering a sample of mainframe DevOps tools here, albeit the consolidated tools list available in one of the subsequent chapters.

Requirement Engineering	Jira, IBM RTC, Caliber [Microfocus], Collabnet VersionOne [Compuware], CA Endevour
Code and Data Engineering	IBM Rational Developer for Z-series (RDZ), ISPW
Quality Engineering	IBM, CA, Compuware, Microfocus are the primary vendors having quality engineering tools in the mainframe space; this may be subject to change based on the market)
CI Server (Build Engineering)	Jenkins
CD Server (Release and Deployment Engineering)	IBM UrbanCode, XL Deploy, ChangeMan
Monitoring	IBM, CA, BMC are the primary vendors having respective monitoring tools; this may be subject to change based on the market

It is also to be noted that there may be quite a few customizations required for an end to end DevOps solution in mainframe. The aforesaid questions are expected to bring up such insights on customization required, as well.

A Brief Note for DevOps on COTS and Other Legacy Systems

There are many other legacy systems, including COTS products, that were otherwise believed to be traditionally unsuitable for applying DevOps practices. With the advent of new DevOps technologies and tools, old client server applications in say, Visual Basic, FoxPro, et al; as well as COTS packages such as SAP, Oracle Apps, et al; can also be subject to DevOps practices.

The only consideration is how the COTS vendor company is exposing suitable APIs or integration hooks such that the COTS configuration and runtimes can be controlled by a DevOps pipeline.

Containerization may not be specifically needed in all scenarios, however consideration for containers may be taken up as a primary discussion point with the organization. Note that for containerization there may be a need for application re-factoring, if required to a different technology stack, that may break down large monolithic application modules into say, smaller more manageable services.

Extending DevOps to Business

DevOps as a phenomenon in IT has its roots in identifying two teams – Dev, the team that owns, builds and manages the core outcomes serving the IT team's customers; and Ops, the team that provisions systems to enable the Dev team deliver the outcomes or value to business – and bringing in a set of practices that help in Dev and Ops to function together collaboratively to achieve a common objective. The objective typically is to achieve high IT agility consistently, thereby creating value for the business. Here, being consistent every time is to ensure high quality, system reliability, security and performance of the outcomes in context.

As organizations strive for high agility in delivery of value to its consumers (and internally, value to its employees and shareholders), we define the objective of its business functions – delivering such value – as trying to achieve high business agility, thereby leading to enterprise agility. We define the enterprise as the overarching entity for business and IT to function together towards achieving a definite vision. In this context, the enterprise may not only be a profit making company, but also a non-profit institution, a social welfare body or a government establishment as well.

> **Enterprise Agility = Business Agility + IT Agility**

Given the above, we may construe Business to be the "Dev" team for the enterprise, and IT to be the "Ops" team for the enterprise.

Agility as the Rationalized Objective of Enterprise IT

The enterprise consists of various moving parts that work in unison in order to contribute to the overall objective of the enterprise. Depending on the type and nature of business, the core objective may vary widely; say, margin in case of a profit-making firm, social welfare index for a non-governmental organization, or percentage of planned strategic investments implemented for a government organization. For IT as part of the enterprise, rationalizing such varied objectives through the "moving parts" or business functions results in one measure; **cycle time as a measure of enterprise agility**. This is important from DevOps perspective, as every such business function for the enterprise needs to constantly adapt to the demands of the other business functions that draw their inputs from the former.

For example, take the case of a mobile phone manufacturer striving to imbibe DevOps practices for enhanced customer experience. Dynamic changes in consumer demand with respect to features in its smartphone line-up and availability on online retail channels, require a series of near real-time changes in allocating working capital requirements through finance; to its inbound logistics in terms of procuring new parts; in inducting personnel with new competencies through human resource management (HRM); to design, build and test processes on the assembly line; to its outbound logistics in terms of reaching out to digital distribution channels; to its advertising processes; to customer service for supporting new features; and subsequently, delivery of value to the end consumer. As the value moves from one business function to the next (or in parallel), the underlying IT systems need to ensure high agility with respect to delivery of the value from one business function to the next.

Defining the Enterprise Value Chain

For effectively assessing the enterprise from a DevOps perspective, we define the enterprise value chain as a set of functions in a logical flow – comprising of both sequential and parallel streams – that lead to the rationalized objective of high IT agility. There are two parallel streams in the value chain; one, the core operations of the business or the "line functions", and other, the "staff functions" that provide necessary support to the line functions. There are several sequential components that may be defined within the parallel streams, leading to the concept of "chain" that delivers value at each step. **Value at any step is defined as the benefit accrued at the given step vis-à-vis the cost incurred till the given step of the value chain.**

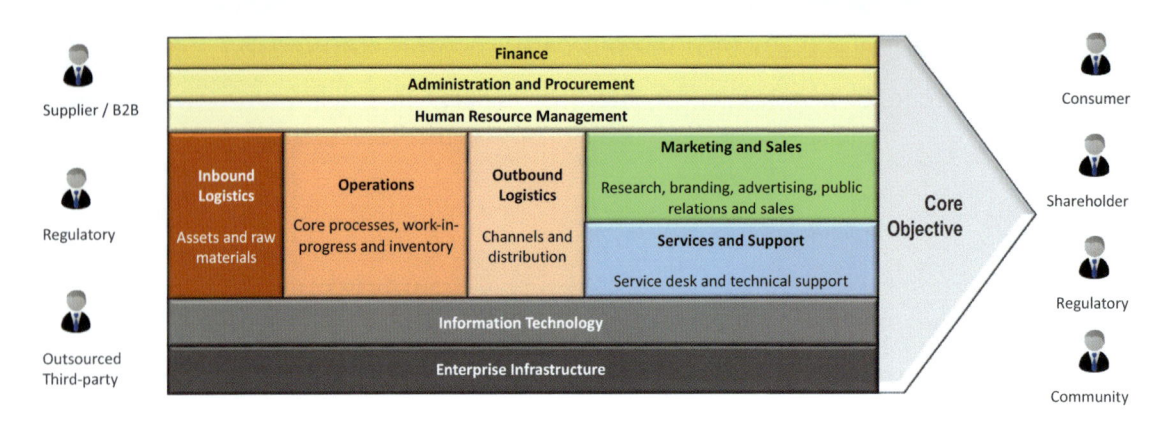

Figure 33: Enterprise Value Chain

The typical flow of value starts with the necessary backbone in place, comprising of enterprise infrastructure and IT. The staff functions work in parallel to allocate working capital and track revenue (Finance), provision non-manpower resources (Administration and Procurement), and provision, train and manage manpower (HRM). Each of these functions provide necessary inputs to the line functions.

From a line function perspective, note that we have indicated the value proposition of each business function in the respective boxes. Inbound logistics deliver value to operations, which in turn deliver value to outbound logistics. Outbound logistics deliver value to both marketing and sales function, and services and support function. Marketing and sales deliver value to the external stakeholders to meet the core objectives. Services and support delivery value in parallel to the external stakeholders.

Two of the core IT applications that typically exist in all organizations are customer relationship management (CRM) and human resource planning (HRP) systems. We specifically mention them here as they are defined by and for the most important entity for any organization – people. CRM is the core system for external people (say, consumers) and HRP for internal (say, employees). All other systems – finance and payroll, products and services, inventory, sales, et al – are designed based on the structure and nature of these two core systems.

Core objectives are realized and reported by one or more business functions based on the type and nature of business for the enterprise. For example, for a profit-making firm, revenue and margin may be accounted for by finance, whereas for a non-governmental organization, social welfare index may be accounted for by the marketing and sales function.

Mapping Business Metrics to IT Metrics

Corresponding IT entities in terms of applications and data form the basis of the business functions. Hence, the value can thus be derived from the underlying IT systems, and mapped to the business functions using the given DevOps assessment approach.

Following is a representative list of metrics for each of the business functions across the value chain, and the IT metrics mapped to the business metrics; though not necessarily one-to-one. IT implications of business metrics that lead to the respective IT metrics *(text indicated in italics in the table below)* are provided along with the business metrics. While assessing the IT processes in terms of agility – hence, cycle time – within context of the given business function, the metrics below can be used to validate if the process imbibes the corresponding measures; if not, the target state architecture for IT may accommodate one or more of them, given the constraints of people and technology.

Staff functions are not explicitly covered, given that such systems are construed not to be subjected to frequent changes at application and data layers, and are typically hosted on secure and reliable in-house infrastructure. However, we do acknowledge that such systems – as they adapt to technologies such as cloud, containerization, microservices and AI – gradually need to embrace DevOps for factors such as security and reliability as they apply to such newer technologies. Hence, IT metrics on such factors would be still relevant while designing and executing such systems.

Further note that certain terms such as "raw material", "inventory" and "work-in-progress" would need to be interpreted appropriately based on the type and nature of industry. For a few industry verticals, the industry specific implications for DevOps as given in the next chapter would provide you with an understanding of such terms.

Business Function Metrics: *IT Implications*	IT Metrics
Inbound Logistics | Assets and raw materials Low to medium change frequency, quality of input material / data is important	
o % raw materials wasted due to change in requirements: *Delay in application or database changes may result in higher wastage* o % actual raw material changes versus total no. of change requests: *Market-driven frequency of change for IT* o % on-time (by SLA) asset maintenance and repair: *Application integration enabling requests being sent through third party app by personnel*	o Release frequency of raw material management applications to handle third-party or consumer change requests (for say, new product line causing changes to operations' assembly line processes) o Throughput of integration interfaces between asset management application to third-party apps (say, apps from maintenance and repair service providers)
Operations | Core processes, work-in-progress and inventory Medium to high change frequency, both system reliability and quality are key	
o Ratio of work-in-progress (WIP) items utilized versus idle: *Optimal inventory processing through business rules in associated applications* o % on-time completion of finished products versus minimum inventory threshold: *Execution dependency control between product management and inventory applications* o Number of changes to inventory specifications due to say, new product lines: *Application and database release dependency based on frequency of changes*	o Lead time to change for product / service and inventory management applications (say, with client-side app for handheld shop-floor devices) for business rule changes in evaluating product status o API downtime (interface reliability) between product / service and inventory management applications o Lead time to change for inventory management application and inventory database changes o % availability of online portal

- Average time to serve a new customer request; % content served on-time: *Application and database availability*
- Time taken by customers in logging on to the customer portal: *Application and database availability, IT security*
- Average time taken from online customer registration to approval: *IT process optimization and application / database availability, IT security*
- Average time to convert and transmit content / data from one format to another (digital or otherwise): *Extent of IT-led automation for consistent data conversion and related changes*

	- Change success ratio of online system (portal and connected backend applications) – say, CRM or HRP systems – with respect to customer complaints
	- Application and data vulnerability (security issues) for online systems
	- % automation of content / data conversion, retrieval and provisioning in production environment; including changes to content / database schemas and associated applications

Outbound Logistics | Channels and distribution
Low to medium change frequency, both system reliability and security are key

- % channel utilization by product categories: *Transaction workload and application / database scaling requirements*
- % sales conversion by channels: *IT process optimization and reliability*
- Average distribution time of products / services from point-of-origin to point-of-sale: *Application / database pipeline reliability and availability*

	- API downtime (channel management reliability) between channel provider's (third party) application and channel management application
	- % availability of channel management application
	- Lead time to change for channel management application due to business rule changes

Marketing and Sales | Research, branding, advertising, public relations and sales
Medium to high change frequency, availability and data security is important

- % sales conversion by customer sign-ups across marketing channels: *Channel*
- Release frequency and lead time to change for campaign management

availability and reliability of backend integrations o % new customers (or, segments) served versus existing customers: *Need and frequency of application changes* o Conversion ratios by advertising campaign categories and/or customer segments: *Transaction workload, application scaling and integration requirements* o Number of changes to existing campaigns by markets served: *Need and frequency of application changes* o Ratios of new : cross-sell : up-sell opportunities open versus closed: *Third party app integration and release dependencies due to changes*	application to support channels, segments, markets and/or services o Lead time to change for sales management application due to business rule changes on sales categories and segments o % availability for mobile apps (field sales personnel) and CRM o API downtime between customer portal and campaign management application (relevant for on-time cross-sell and up-sell opportunities) o Vulnerability issues for quote management applications (server plus client-side apps with field sales personnel) and CRM
Services and Support | Service desk and technical support Medium to high change frequency, reliability and data security is important	
o % changes to service catalog; new services versus existing services: *Need and frequency for application and databases changes* o % on-time resolution of support and service requests by severity: *IT system availability, reliability and scalability* o Technical issue traceability to business requirements: *Technical debt reduction for code and faster code fixes* o % technical issue auto-resolution, and % automated service workflows: *IT system reliability with self-healing infrastructure*	o Release frequency for service catalog management application and associated databases o Lead time to change for integration APIs o API downtime for: • Third party service request application integration • Robotic agents for auto-resolution or auto-service • Event trigger system integration

o Frequency of recurring technical issues and service requests: *Efficiency of IT processes including application or database fixes*	• CRM and HRP integration with service request workflows o % availability of auto-resolution and auto-service systems

Note that Operations as a business function for any industry typically is the core part that handles the majority of backend and middle layer processing activities. Hence, most of the business metrics concentrate on the operations aspect of the enterprise. For some industries, either or both of the inbound logistics and outbound logistics may exist as part of operations, rather than being independent business functions. Marketing and sales serve as the entry point for customers to know about and avail services of an enterprise, whereas services and support acts as the feedback loop on customer experience for the enterprise.

While discussing on the industry verticals in the next chapter, most of the discussions would be around the line functions, as they primarily define the differences on how the industries work. The staff functions typically follow standard structures across industries, and hence impact on DevOps assessment for the corresponding systems may not vary widely across industries.

DevOps for Select Industry Verticals

While assessing DevOps for several organizations spanning across industry verticals, we found the following to be the common themes which organizations strive for in context of their IT systems, albeit with varying priorities attached:

o   Reducing IT cycle time
o   Increasing availability and quality of applications and data
o   Ensuring system reliability and security

For example, a retail organization may attach a higher priority to reducing IT cycle time with respect to sales for a new product line than say, system reliability; whereas for a banking organization who is facilitating the sale through an electronic gateway, the focus may be more on system reliability and security rather than IT cycle time. However note that the four factors – availability, quality, reliability and security – themselves in turn have a bearing on the core objective of DevOps which is to reduce the IT cycle time. For example, poor quality or system reliability results in repetitive fixes to the applications or infrastructure, hence in turn increases the effective IT cycle time. Similarly, security issues may cause delays, data theft and customer loss, thereby requiring fixes to the system resulting in effectively high IT cycle time. The purpose of this chapter is to show the IT implications in context of DevOps as perceived by the respective industry verticals.

Retail and Consumer Packaged Goods (CPG)

The retail and CPG industry has been at the forefront of the DevOps revolution. Fast adoption of DevOps was fueled by high volatility of the end consumer in an extremely competitive environment, and the challenge of providing mass customized offerings – both products and accompanying services – across the customer segments. Customer experience in terms of little or no waiting time for obtaining the product in hand, the product quality itself (especially the more premium the product, the higher is the expectation on quality) and category-specific accompanying services; led to organizations adopting the following while assessing a DevOps-based approach to IT:

- **Lower time to market** – This entails reducing IT cycle times throughout the value chain, including both business-to-business (B2B) players such as spare parts distributors, and business-to-consumer (B2C) players such as retail showrooms. This would require evaluating DevOps across multiple technology stacks that span across creating customer demand through marketing channels (CRM systems); capturing customer requirements (online portal or mobile platforms); pushing product specifications to retail operations (enterprise resource planning or ERP systems); and finally leveraging the right distribution channels (third party integrations, say using APIs).

- **Quick customization to product specifications** – Retail operations would mainly focus on the specification changes in terms of promotion, pricing and packaging. The IT systems, hence, need to support multiple product releases; even the same product with multiple variations. Such releases induce complex inter-application dependencies in the business logic layer and databases, and corresponding changes that need to reflect on to the presentation layer say, the online portal, in real time.

- **Leveraging multi-channel ecosystems for market penetration** – Successful end consumer reach entail leveraging multiple retail channels effectively to get the product in consumer's hand. Further, a strong service network requires third party service providers on the value chain to ensure a strong brand loyalty. From an IT standpoint, third party application (and database) integration enabled through a Software-as-a-Service (SaaS) based platform and IT orchestration dashboard becomes an important component for assessment.

Media, Publishing and Information Services

The movement towards DevOps adoption in this industry started when majority of such organizations moved towards adopting electronic and digital formats for information communication, from the traditional paper-based and print formats. Such movement at first entailed provisioning large amount of content in multiple formats in the least possible time – if possible, in real time – to consumers of the information; and later evolved into filtered content on-demand to the consumers, anytime, on any platform and at any place. Following are the business requirements and their implications on adopting a DevOps-based approach to IT:

- **Lower time to market** – This entails reducing IT cycle times throughout the value chain, including both B2B (say, content creator) and B2C (say, news channels and publishers) players. This would require evaluating DevOps across multiple technology stacks that span across selection of channels that can reach consumers in real time or near-real time (supplier systems); creation and filtering of content (systems handling large databases and Big Data incorporating machine learning algorithms); and transmission of content through the channels (online portal and mobile platforms).

- **Ensuring channel reliability and security** – Given that the content has to consistently reach the consumers fast – ideally in zero time from point of origin to point of consumption – and the proprietary nature of generated content, channels used for transmission has to be highly reliable ensuring high content accuracy, and highly secure. This entails highly reliable IT backbone (read, pipeline reliability and chaos engineering aspects) and high application and data security practices.

- **High quality of content on-demand** – Quality of content, especially during conversion from one format to another (say, print to electronic; text to image; et al), needs to be consistently ensured, IT systems should imbibe robust quality engineering practices. For on-demand content that need to reach out to specific customer segments, aspects such as secure containerization of content data and related data analytics pertaining to handling of large amounts of unstructured data, may need to be assessed.

Banking, Financial Services and Insurance

The advent of large financial institutions and insurance organizations was to enable or mobilize large financial transactions – either monetary or non-monetary – among people, enterprises and nations. Further, paradigms such as Open Banking and Blockchain technology have brought a greater need of collaboration not only across banking and financial institutions, but also with other industries. DevOps as a practice has become a key enabler to ensure high security, availability and reliability for such transactions occurring across a multitude of systems and processes within the regulatory confines of nation(s) involved. Hence, while assessing IT from a DevOps perspective, following are the implications:

- **Safe and secure financial transactions** – Financial transactions, insurance policy administration, risk modeling and assessment outcomes, and claims need to be encrypted in proprietary formats, however conforming to industry standards, that should have high resilience to data theft. This requires IT processes to ensure complete test coverage and traceability for applications, data and network infrastructure with respect to security. The processes may incorporate machine learning algorithms that can predict and mitigate effectively any unforeseen security vulnerabilities to the data, that too across multiple channels of transaction.

- **Reliability of the financial transaction channels** – Channels such as payment gateways, the associated network layers and other electronic platforms need to ensure high reliability of financial transaction data to prevent data loss or data corruption. Hence, the underlying IT systems need to incorporate feedback loops to detect quality and adequacy of data being transmitted. For any transmission failure, suitable rollback mechanisms need to be in place with options to re-initiate the transaction through alternate channels for highly critical transactions. In case of insurance organizations, system reliability with respect to processing claim settlements on-time, is of essence.

- **Regulatory compliance for financial transactions** – Financial transactions and insurance policy administration are governed by regulatory requirements of the nation(s) in which the participating financial institutions operate, for example, the UK Data Protection Act, Single Euro Payments Area (SEPA) regulations and Sarbanes-Oxley (SOX) Compliance. From an IT standpoint, this implies that the associated databases (and data) should have necessary mechanisms to ensure data security, privacy, quality and integrity. Data integrity needs to be further validated (through say, reconciliation) as part of the financial ecosystem in which transactions take place. DataOps is hence an important aspect of ensuring how operations – including database releases; handling data archival, data environments, data migration and data usage – around data is made highly robust and secure. Further, IT should support dynamic changes to regulatory requirements in real time, necessitating DevOps-led processes for reducing change cycle times.

Manufacturing

Manufacturing industry has long been an adopter of DevOps, more so in terms of bringing in efficiencies through automation and process integration across assembly lines. The concept of lean manufacturing, for long, has inspired the paradigms of Agile and DevOps; a concept that has focused on reducing the work-in-progress, being perceived as waste, eating up precious time and cost across the manufacturing cycle. Time and motion studies towards scientific management from a people standpoint has also been extensively studied in this industry. The main tenets from a business perspective that has implications in IT with respect to DevOps are as follows:

o **Reducing waste from concept to production** – Manufacturing assembly lines seek to keep optimum levels of work-in-progress inventory as such inventory adds to cost over time. Having an optimum inventory also ensures an optimum demand to supply match for finished goods. Practices such as Agile, lean engineering, Kaizen and Just-in-Time manufacturing point to reduction of waste. From an IT perspective, DevOps fully aligns to the aforesaid practices from both people and process perspectives.

o **Reducing manufacturing cycle time through critical path efficiencies** – Manufacturing industry started the practice of scientific studies on optimizing the time taken to manufacture, and at the same time ensure high quality. It included study of the critical path – a quantitative concept we have tailored extensively – to understand what impacts operations the most. Quality engineering imbibed across the path, along with ensuring high reliability of the systems, has been the focus areas of both the industry, and DevOps from IT perspective.

- **Large scale high-end automation to reduce people dependencies** – The industry has embraced robotic process automation with IoT based systems throughout the assembly line value chain. This enables effective failover mechanisms and real time changes to the process due to changed customer demands. From an IT perspective, the underlying IT infrastructure, applications and databases need to adapt to such changes and at the same time, ensure high availability and reliability; by adopting intelligent automation across the pipeline with say, self-healing and auto-scaling mechanisms. Usage of machine learning algorithms (hence, AIOps) and Infrastructure-as-a-Code (IaaC) to build such robust pipelines have been of essence.

Lifesciences and Healthcare

Given the critical nature of products and services of this industry – catering to preservation, rejuvenation and sustenance of human life – ensuring optimal cycle times for say, health emergencies, and high reliability of processes with zero failure rates are the two most important factors that drive the value chain. Specifically for life sciences, innovations around newer diagnosis and treatment machines and methods, and improved drug formulations require efficient and intelligent mechanisms to manage huge amounts of related data. Further, proprietary nature of data demands high data security measures for such organizations. Following are the factors that have implications for the underlying IT systems, and are also relevant from a DevOps perspective:

- **Zero tolerance time and reliability of processes and systems** – This is the most important criterion that determines the credibility and performance of any healthcare institution. Ensuring such high performance standards require IT systems to be not only extremely resilient to failures – both in terms of availability and reliability – but also capable of realizing optimal cycle times to cater to patients. Changes to specific processes need to be addressed by the applications by embracing the least lead time to change. A high test coverage encompassing both functional and non-functional requirements need to be incorporated into the DevOps pipeline.

o   **Support data-driven life sciences innovations** – Constant innovation in areas such as biotechnology, genetic engineering, et al, need to be adopted in near real time across the healthcare value chain. This requires two primary ingredients from an IT standpoint – managing huge amounts of proprietary data and related changes to databases in secure environments (bringing in DataSecOps), and reliable integration to third party life sciences and healthcare organizations for validation, testing, collaborative research, and production rollout workflows. From a DevOps assessment perspective, reliability and security of such systems need to be assessed.

o   **Regulatory compliance** – Due to the critical nature of the industry, government regulations on provisioning of healthcare services, defining of minimum health standards, related insurance and patient data protection services (say, HIPAA regulations), and usage of specific drugs, et al, impose several restrictions to the industry operations. From the IT standpoint, DevOps assessment should focus on change cycle time and reliability to application and data based on such regulatory changes.

Telecommunication and Cable

This industry has been one of the very structured adopters of DevOps, given the presence of large physical networks and being a highly regulated industry. With such large networks to manage, and proprietary and disparate technologies to be integrated for cross-network support, the focus for the industry has been consolidation of services over extensive IT platforms; first as Platform-as-a-Service (PaaS) and then SaaS that can be leveraged by consortium of such organizations. Further, to cater to the organizations that need to go beyond the capabilities of traditional physical network, dedicated cloud services – Telco clouds – are increasingly leveraged to provide the necessary PaaS abstraction. Assessment of IT from a DevOps perspective for such organizations need to cater to the following:

o   **Multiple transmission formats over networks** – Organizations need to be able to transmit data – either as voice or as data (packets), say over the internet – in multiple formats, speed and complying to proprietary and industry protocols. Advent of transmission of written text (say, SMS) in addition to voice and data over say 3G, 4G, 5G or IoT-based networks, have created additional requirements for change. Moreover, data may be transmitted either through physically wired networks or over-the-air (say, wireless), or a hybrid network. From a DevOps standpoint, IT cycle time to manage such changes and ensuring availability, scalability and reliability of the underlying systems, are important aspects of assessment.

- **Handling fluctuating network traffic on-demand** – Customers today utilize telecommunication and cable networks for a plethora of purposes that warrant handling of high fluctuations in network traffic and on-demand transmission of data (say, media content). Adoption of technologies such as Software Defined Networks (SDN) and Network Function Virtualization (NFV), either using Customer Premises Equipment (CPE) or Telco cloud; coupled with security, utilization and reliability of such networks may be the focus of DevOps assessments.

- **Regulatory compliance** – The industry is highly regulated by governments in terms of managing customer interests on one hand, and controlling of broadcasts based on national interests on the other hand. Hence, handling such regulatory changes in real time is an important aspect to comply to. From an IT perspective, ensuring high data security and integrity should be a part of the DevOps target state.

Energy and Utilities

This industry is highly regulated, depend largely on physical energy generation and transmission mechanisms, and segregated by the nature of business operations. The energy sector discovers, generates the fuel from traditional non-renewable and renewable sources of energy; whereas the utilities sector processes and distributes the energy to both industrial and commercial customers, and individual consumers. Hence, they fall on a sequential value chain. Given the nature of the industry, following are the IT implications with regard to a DevOps assessment:

- **High resilience to failure, and facilities security** – Facilities for energy and utilities companies are large physical assets that need to be highly reliable and secure. Operations not only has to have a robust disaster recovery (DR) mechanism consisting of DR installations to meet demand, but also dynamically change its security characteristics based on hot, running and cold sites against security threats; such organizations have clear cut core and demilitarized zones. The IT implication is to have underlying IT components – applications, databases and IT infrastructure embrace reliability and security engineering practices, more so applied to the proprietary software and databases in place. Such practices may also incorporate data from sensors across sites, thereby looking at filtering and managing large amount of unstructured data.

- **On-demand distribution without significant transmission loss** – Organizations in the industry own and manage large scale flexible infrastructure for distribution across large distances on-demand. This allows for no or minimal transmission loss, hence being able to dynamically manage installation characteristics based on type of energy being transmitted. For every new installation or such changes, underlying IT systems need to embrace fast changes to accommodate suitable quality measures based on say, sensor data. Hence, DataOps on Big Data as a discipline becomes important for evaluation of IT.

- **Regulatory requirements and allocations** – The industry is strategic in nature, as it provides necessary fuel to support an entire nation's infrastructure while exploiting precious natural resources. Hence, regulations ranging from extent of resource exploitation, usage of energy, security considerations, hotline management for critical services, and management of sensor data containing sensitive customer information and that of national interests, et al; are thrusted upon the industry players. This requires the underlying IT systems to incorporate such regulatory changes in real time, and also provide analytics on application and data change pipelines, data usage and production system feedback on compliance.

We have purposefully left out a few industries as they typically show one or more of the following characteristics:

- Incorporating or have incorporated industry standard systems and processes that do not typically require a significant rate of change, thereby having established systems to ensure architectural considerations of IT

- Being quite similar to one or more of the above industry verticals that we have discussed here, in terms of IT implications versus the business focus areas

However, given changing business models and paradigms today across industry verticals, with significant impact on the underlying IT and cross-industry collaboration, DevOps may still significantly apply to the other verticals as well. For such assessments, you may refer to the above sections (or the summarized figure below) to derive industry specific needs for DevOps adoption from the specific focus areas we have described.

Industry Verticals Summarized

Retail and CPG	Media, Publishing, Information Services	Banking, Financial Services, Insurance	Manufacturing	Life Sciences, Healthcare	Telecommunication, Cable	Energy, Utilities
Lower time to market	Lower time to market	Safe and secure financial transactions	Reducing waste from concept to production	Zero tolerance time and reliability of processes and systems	Multiple transmission formats over networks	High resilience to failure, and facilities security
Quick customization to product specifications	Ensuring channel reliability and security	Reliability of the financial transaction channels	Reducing manufacturing cycle time through critical path efficiencies	Support data-driven life sciences innovations	Handling fluctuating network traffic on-demand	On-demand distribution without significant transmission loss
Leveraging multi-channel ecosystems for market penetration	High quality of content on-demand	Regulatory compliance for financial transactions	Large scale high-end automation to reduce people dependencies	Regulatory compliance	Regulatory compliance	Regulatory requirements and allocations
Characteristics • Product centric • Physical and digital distribution • IT cycle time is in focus	**Characteristics** • Service centric • Increasingly digital distribution • IT cycle time and quality in focus	**Characteristics** • Service centric • Increasingly digital distribution • Availability, reliability and security in focus	**Characteristics** • Product centric • Physical distribution • IT cycle time and reliability in focus	**Characteristics** • Service centric • Physical distribution • IT cycle time, availability and reliability in focus	**Characteristics** • Service centric • Physical distribution • IT cycle time, reliability and security in focus	**Characteristics** • Service centric • Physical distribution • Availability, reliability and security in focus

Technology and Tools List

The following list is non-exhaustive (both in terms of categories and tools covered) and representative only. We are not necessarily indicating the names of corresponding tool vendors or owners, or their respective trademark notations. Further note that the tool names (and vendor names where mentioned) may not be accurate and are subject to change at the time of publication of this book or later.

The ones in *italics* are not specific tool names, but general technology or solution descriptions that are standalone or accompanied by corresponding tool or package names.

Collaborative document/ content/ knowledge management (KM)						
Confluence	SharePoint	Documentum	Alfresco	Wiki	Joomla!	IBM ECM

Agile story/ issue tracking and collaboration						
Jira	HP ALM/ Agile Manager	IBM RTC	Rally	SmartBear	VersionOne	Pivotal Tracker
Trello	SprintGround	Targetprocess	ALM Octane	*Tracker as part of KM tool*	*Tool with adaptive algorithm*	Bugzilla
IBM RTC	Team Foundation Server (TFS)	Axosoft	Trac	Agilo for Trac	Apache Bloodhound	Helix ALM

Source code editor/ Integrated development environment (IDE)						
OS specific text editor	Eclipse	NetBeans IDE	Visual Studio	Android SDK	Xcode IDE	Objective C IDE
C/C++ IDE	*COBOL dataset editor*	IBM RDZ	IDLE (for Python)	IntelliJ IDEA	RStudio	IBM RAD

216

Code and test quality

SonarQube	FxCop	CM evolveIT	PMD	Checkstyle	Topaz	*Tool with adaptive algorithm*
Cobertura	Kiuwan	StyleCop	CAST	Checkmarx	Coverity	SideCI

Continuous integration

Jenkins	*Scripts (Groovy, PowerShell, Python, etc.)*	Cloudbees Jenkins	CircleCI	GoCD	*Tool with adaptive algorithm*	AnthillPro
Hudson	Team Foundation Server	TeamCity	TravisCI	Buddy	Bamboo	CruiseControl

Continuous delivery/ deployment

XL Deploy	IBM UrbanCode Deploy	Octopus Deploy	Jenkins	CA Nolio	Gearset	AutoRabit

Source code repository

Git	IBM Rational ClearCase	Subversion	BitBucket	Mercurial	GitHub/ GitLab	Endevor

Binary repository

Artifactory	Nexus	Docker Hub	Apache Archiva	ProGet	CloudRepo	Cloudsmith Package

Build and package

Maven	Ant	MS Build	Gradle	Broccoli	Packer	Grunt

Monitoring, data streaming and analytics

Hygieia	Kibana	AppDynamics	Dynatrace	Zabbix	Splunk	Logstash

| Sumo Logic | Graylog | Apache Kafka | ELK (Elasticsearch-Logstash-Kibana) | Nagios | New Relic | Opsview Monitor |

Release management

| XL Release | IBM UrbanCode Release | CA Release Automation | Automic | *Tool with adaptive release planning* | Microfocus Release Control | Basis Transport Expresso |

Functional test automation

| Selenium | HP QTP | IBM RFT | JUnit | NUnit | ZUnit | TestNG |

Non-functional (and mobile) test automation

| JMeter | HP LoadRunner | Fortify | WebInspect | Tripwire | Karma | Jasmine |
| NeoLoad | PhantomJS | TestComplete | Sauce Labs | Perfecto | Mocha | Appium |

Environment provisioning and HCI (Hyper Convergence Infrastructure)

| Puppet | Chef | AWS OpsWorks | AWS CloudFormation | Ansible | Terraform | MS Hyper-V |
| Vagrant | Salt | Dell EMC VxRail | AWS (Elastic) Beanstalk | Docker | VMware | Cisco Hyperflex |

Cloud and container/ cluster management

| Pivotal Cloud Foundry (PCF) | Morpheus | Kubernetes | Apache Mesos | OpenStack | Right Scale | OpenShift |
| InContinuum CloudController | CloudBolt | RedHat CloudForms | Docker Swarm | IBM Cloud (Bluemix) | Scalr | RightScale |

Service workflow

| ServiceNow | BMC Remedy | RemedyForce | jBPM | COPPER | Wexflow | Jira |

Database handling: Automation and management							
Flyway	Liquibase	Datical	DB Maestro	Redgate Software	Apache Spark	Attunity Maestro

DataOps						
DataKitchen	Delphix	Composable Analytics	Ascend	Kinesis	MapR	Qubole
Infoworks	Devo	HPCC Systems	Attunity	Lenses.io	Nexla	StreamSets

Robotic process automation						
UiPath	Blue Prism	Automation Anywhere	Workfusion	IBM Watson	OpenSpan	NICE RPA

Chaos engineering						
Simian Army suite*	Pumba (for Docker)	Blockade (uses Docker)	Chaos Dingo (for Azure)	Tugbot (uses Docker)	Monkey-ops (for OpenShift)	Chaos Lemur
Chaos-http-proxy	MongoDB Atlas	*Chaos Monkey	*Chaos Gorilla	*Chaos Kong (for AWS)	ChaosCat (by PagerDuty)	Chaos Lambda

AIOps	
Python packages	*Neural networks:* scikit-neuralnetwork
	Evolutionary computing: DEAP (Distributed Evolutionary Algorithm with Python)
	Computer vision: NumPy, SciPy, Matplotlib, PIL and Pillow, OpenCV, SimpleCV, Mahotas, Scikit-learn
	Robotics: Python Robot package
	Expert systems: Pyknow

Machine learning	NumPy, SciPy, Scikit-learn, Theano, Tensorflow, Keras, PyTorch, Pandas, Matplotlib
Speech processing:	SpeechRecognition-PyPi
Natural language processing:	Rasa, NLTK, TextBlob, Stanford CoreNLP, spaCy, gensim

DevSecOps: Security as Code						
Tanker (tanker.io)	Continuum Security	Virgil Security	Krypton	Drie	ThreatModeler	Checkmarx
Contrast Security	Immunio	Aqua Security	Dome9 Security	GauntIt	WhiteSource	CA Veracode

Glossary

The terms are described as interpreted and used by the authors; hence, are not necessarily their respective industry standard or formal definitions. The reader is advised to consult formal literature or other sources, as suitable, for such formal definitions.

Activity	A task within a process that takes an input, gets executed and produces an output; as applied to Agile projects, can be a story or a task based on how fine-grained the details are captured for analysis
Agile	Software development methodology that breaks up tasks into short manageable chunks, each producing a logically complete deliverable, thereby enabling fast adaptation to interim changes
Agile Dev	Agile methodology as followed by developers (and testers) only
Agile Ops	Agile methodology where operations team participates; Agile Dev may extend to Agile Ops whereby both Dev and Ops teams participate
Agility	As applied to IT, capability of a team or process to not only deliver software or software fixes substantially faster than traditional methods, but also quickly adapt to changing requirements
AIOps	Incorporating AI capabilities to the DevOps pipeline for making the pipeline itself more resilient to failures, and imbibe machine learning to the pipeline so that it can itself learn, validate, decide and actuate IT tasks with little or no human intervention
Analytics	Information that can be used of decision making, as extracted from systematic analysis of available data and associated metrics
Behavior Driven Development (BDD)	Software development process whereby test cases (written prior to coding as in case of TDD) are based on how the software behavior would be to an external user
Blue-Green Deployment	A ZDD approach whereby there are two production instances running for a software, with only one being live at any point of time

Change	A service request (that translates to a requirement) for a new or enhanced system or software characteristic, behavior or feature
ChatOps	A branch of AIOps that uses conversational intelligent agents to understand inputs in natural human language, interpret, analyze and accordingly actuate IT (or, business) operational tasks
Chaos Engineering	A practice and discipline to deliberately introduce failure conditions in a given IT system – pre-production or production – so that corresponding system behavior can be analyzed and improved upon to withstand such failures; failures may be performance degradation due to high transaction load, system unavailability due to server or network downtime, security compromised, incorrect parameters passed during run-time causing application or pipeline failure, et al
Cluster	Typically one or more nodes that act as machines hosting and running a set of applications, typically on containers
Container	Portable environment that is created to host an application, that include the minimum OS resources and services required to execute the application; it eliminates the need to run an entire virtual machine (VM) or OS to host each application, and can be saved as an "image" that can be reused to quickly re-create the environment
Continuous delivery (CD)	Software engineering practice whereby short development cycles ensure release-ready software chunks that can be released reliably when needed
Continuous deployment	Software release strategy whereby deployment of release-ready software (as enabled by CD) is seamlessly enabled
Continuous integration (CI)	Software engineering practice whereby short changes by developers to the code is immediately tested and added on to the larger code base as suitable
Continuous Monitoring	Software engineering practice whereby software running on specific environments are continuously monitored for detect compliance and performance issues or events

Critical Path	The path within the process network diagram that is considered critical (requiring optimization) based on a set of criteria
Critical Path Method (CPM)	Quantitative method which analyzes a process (as a set of activities) by demarcating the critical and non-critical tasks and optimizing the critical tasks in terms of time, resource and costs
Culture	A set of human behavior – along with associated activities and artefacts – shaped by beliefs, customs, rituals and norms; in an organizational setting, the definition extends to human teams working towards a common goal or a set of goals
DataOps	DevOps practices that focus on development, enhancement, maintenance and support for data and databases – including data operations, data store administration and data migration as applied to both structured and unstructured data
Deterministic	An activity that always generates the same single outcome for a given input, instead of varied heuristic outcomes
DevOps	Operational philosophy that results in better and seamless communication between development and operations groups in an organization, resulting in faster delivery cycles, better quality of deliverables, and higher reliability of underlying systems
DevSecOps	An extended paradigm of DevOps whereby IT security also becomes the responsibility of both the Dev and Ops teams
Dynamic Programming	Quantitative method in which a problem is broken up into shorter chunks (sub-problems) that are optimized recursively in terms of say, time and cost
Event	It has two meanings based on the context: (a) a deviant change in system state that is captured by monitoring processes, say a software failure or CPU overload, (b) as applied to our critical path analysis, a state (denoting a specific outcome) that either leads to an activity or is a result of an activity

Float Time	The idle time that an activity within a path may have, either due to waiting for another activity to complete or for manual reasons; for the purpose of our analysis, the former cause applies
Functional Requirement	A software requirement that depicts the behavior of the software (as appears to an external user) in terms of functions specific to a set of inputs and outputs
Game Theory	Quantitative method in which a mathematical model is derived based on conflict (and cooperation) factors between rational decision makers (or, "players")
Heuristics	An algorithm or logic that produces varied outcomes for a given input, some of which may be relatively good or bad based on the context, however may not be optimal
Immutable Infrastructure	Infrastructure that can be created and destroyed (and re-created quickly) on-demand based on changed system conditions; implies that the hosted software would be re-deployed each time any change occurs
Incident	A record created in a workflow system due to the occurrence of an event that may need a specific resolution of fixing of the associated issue
Infrastructure as Code	The tasks pertaining to infrastructure (and environment) provisioning and management can be coded (using specific technologies/ tools) to automate such tasks
Intelligent automation	Using automation software (or software chain) that is capable of adapting to changed system states by altering its own behavior based on context
IT Service Management (ITSM)	The framework describing the process (comprising of steps, tasks, teams and technologies/ tools) used to monitor, manage, fix and improve software; typically in a production environment
Kanban	A methodology used by Agile teams to manage a continuous flow of work by visualizing the entire workflow vis-à-vis the actual progress

Known Error Database (KEDB)	A repository of problem records for which root causes may be known but corresponding permanent fixes are pending
Lead Time	The total time taken by an activity in a process
Linear Programming	Quantitative method in which a linear function is drawn on several variables, which is then maximized or minimized for say, output or costs
Load Balancing	Distribution of workload across cluster of compute resources comprising of say, computers, network components, containers, etc.
Machine Time	The time taken by automation (say, by an automation tool) of an activity in a process
Markov Process	Quantitative method in which a mathematical model is derived based on probabilities of occurrence of a future outcome (assuming that it cannot be accurately predicted based on current behavior)
Metrics	A measure computed using specific variables' outcomes that indicates performance of a process or system under given conditions over a given scale or range
Microservices	An application architecture approach whereby a large application is developed as comprising of modular components or services
Node	A logical collection of IT resources managing one or more containers; associated services enable intra- and inter-container communication, network configuration, etc.
Non-functional Requirement (NFR)	A software requirement that depicts the operation of the system (including the environment where the software is hosted) in particular conditions; this is typically architecture driven
NoOps	"No Operations"; a state whereby the IT environment is completely abstracted from the underlying infrastructure, resulting in apparent irrelevance of an operations team to manage technologies and tools in-house
Path	A series of events and connected activities within a process network diagram that starts at an initial event and ends at a final event

Pipeline	Considering the analogy of multiple product releases over an assembly line in manufacturing, a pipeline is a collection of software engineering practices, typically automated, to make one or more version(s) of the product or solution release-ready; each version on a pipeline requires specific tasks to be completed by different roles in the team as the code moves over the pipeline
Pipeline as Code	The software delivery pipeline can be coded (using specific technologies/ tools such as CI servers) to automate the tasks that need to be executed by the team
Problem	An incident categorized as recurring due to an underlying system issue that has not been resolved or fixed
Process Network Diagram	Graphical representation of a process comprising of events (states), activities (tasks connecting events) and related details; used for critical path analysis as applied to our assessment approach
Process Time	The manual time taken by human personnel executing an activity in a process
Release	The process of deploying software on to a given environment
Scrum	Agile development methodology that uses cross-skilled focused teams ("Scrum", as in rugby) comprising of developers, designers, testers and ops; thereby enabling high agility in software delivery
Scrum Board	Visual display of the progress (open items, work-in-progress and completed items) of a Scrum team during a sprint
SecurityOps	The Ops team that embodies additional responsibility of overseeing IT security requirements (monitoring, assessing, defending)
Self-healing	An algorithm or system that has the capability to diagnose failures on its own and adapt to changed conditions or resolve such failures to keep the system in running state
Service Request	A software or infrastructure change request, not necessarily arising due to an issue, that needs to be catered to as a service

Software Development Life Cycle (SDLC)	The framework describing the process (comprising of steps and associated tasks, teams and technologies/ tools) used to develop, test and release software
Sprint	Short consistent incremental cycle used in Agile Scrum software development methodology that produces a meaningful working chunk of the software
Test Driven Development (TDD)	Software development process whereby test cases are written first before actual code development starts; hence, the test cases would fail for the first time (prior to code being written against them)
Traceability	In view of an IT process, the ability to trace back any issue or problem to its corresponding test cases, code and further to requirements
Value Stream	Value stream is an analysis technique, described as part of lean management methods, that analyzes current state of a process (comprising of events) and designs a future state based on reduction or elimination of wastes across the series of events
Zero Downtime Deployment (ZDD)	Software deployed in such a manner that it remains online/ in production usage without any downtime; this is made possible through say, blue-green or container-based deployment

References

1. Aho, Alfred V., John E. Hopcroft, and Jeffrey D. Ullman. *Data Structures and Algorithms.* Reading, MA: Addison-Wesley, 1983. Print.

2. Kim, Gene, Kevin Behr, and George Spafford. *The Phoenix Project: A Novel about IT, DevOps, and Helping Your Business Win.* Portland, OR: IT Revolution, 2018. Print.

3. Kulkarni, Parag, and Prachi Joshi. *Artificial Intelligence Building Intelligent Systems.* Delhi: PHI Learning Private Limited, 2015. Print.

4. Kulkarni, Parag, and Pradip K. Chande. *IT Strategy for Business.* New Delhi: Oxford UP, 2008. Print.

5. Mishra, K. L. P., and N. Chandrasekaran. *Theory of Computer Science: Automata, Languages and Computation.* New Delhi: Prentice-Hall of India, 2010. Print.

6. Ross, Jeanne W., Peter Weill, and David C. Robertson. *Enterprise Architecture as Strategy: Creating a Foundation for Business Execution.* Boston, MA: Harvard Business School. Print.

7. Vohra, N. D. *Quantitative Techniques in Management.* New Delhi: McGraw Hill Education (India) Private Limited, 2010. Print.

Abstraction	184
Activity	71, 83
Admin	173
Administration	200
Agent	163
Agile	44, 71, 105
Agility	6, 7
AI	163
AIOps	163, 211
Analytics	39, 48, 170, 208
API	188
Application	41, 52, 79, 127
Architect	133
Architecture	97, 106, 111, 120
Archival	13, 177
ARM	188
As-Is	97
Assessment	16
Automata	10
Automation	7, 12, 39, 49, 51, 100, 103
Auto-resolve	130
Availability	42
B2B	208
B2C	208
Backup	175, 177
Banking	8, 208
Behavioral	170
Benchmark	9
Binary	187
Branching	178
Build	14, 51
Bursting	189
Business	29, 135, 141
Capital	121
Captive	42
Cases	141
Change	6, 123
Chaos	14, 156
ChatOps	164
CLI	188
Cloud	187
Code	13
Collaborative	20, 126
Competitive	8
Configuration	20, 118
Connector	83
Consolidate	147
Consultant	133
Consulting	133
Container	183
Continuous	11, 14, 157
Correlation	171
Cost	48, 114, 165
COTS	190, 193, 197
CPE	213
Crashing	69
Criteria	80
Criticality	31, 69, 72, 84, 89
CRM	200
Cross-train	46, 122
Culture	18, 21, 39, 42, 43, 89, 93, 106, 116, 142, 145
Cyclic	158
Data	13
Database	13
DataOps	31, 170, 214
DataSecOps	212
DDL	176
Deadlock	158
Debt	194
Defect	51, 123
Delay	89
Demilitarized	214
Dependency	12, 88
Derivable	92
Deterministic	12
Dev	5, 16
DevOps	5, 7
DevSecOps	45
Digital	144
Dimension	39, 122
Documentation	20
Domain	160
Downtime	125
DR	192, 214
Dummy	83
Duration	88, 89
EC2	188
Eliminate	92
Energy	213
Engineer	103
Engineering	7, 12, 15, 91
Enhance	92
Enterprise	198
Entity	67
Environment	14, 176
ERP	207
Error	158
ETL	178
Evolutionary	164

Failover	211
Failure	6, 128, 156
Feedback	181
Final	86
Finance	200
Firewall	167
Float	68, 87, 88, 89
Function	201
Functional	13, 51
Geographic	41
Grid	171
Hacker	167
Handbook	47
Hardening	186
Heatmap	33, 142
Heuristic	7
HIPAA	212
Hotline	214
HRM	200
HRP	200
Hypervisor	178
IaaC	211
Immutability	14
Immutable	185
Implementation	100, 103, 143
Inbound	200
Incident	15, 52, 129
Industry	206
Infinite	158
Information	67, 84, 91
Infrastructure	5, 52, 100, 120, 127
initial	86
Initial	83, 86
Injection	158
Inorganic	144, 147
Input	72, 84
Insurance	8
Integrity	158, 209
Intelligent	163
Inter-group	20
Intra-group	20
Inventory	201
Kanban	45
Latency	8, 158
Layer	29
Layered	120
Leadership	135
Lean	91, 210
Learning	165
Legacy	190, 193
Logistics	200
LPAR	194, 195
Mainframe	193
Maintainability	43
Manpower	121
Manufacturing	210
Marketing	200
Markov	65
Masking	175
Master	180
Material	67, 69, 84, 92
Mean-time-between-failures	50
Mean-time-to-repair	50
Media	8, 207
Meeting	79, 134, 136
Merging	178
Metadata	170
Metrics	39, 50, 121, 122, 125, 127, 201
Microservices	13, 16
Migration	178, 190
Modeling	174
Modernization	193
Monitoring	14, 15, 160, 168
MTBF	195
MTTR	195
MVP	179
Network	86, 98
Neural	164
NFV	213
Non-functional	13, 51
NoOps	25, 183, 190
Objective	38, 91
Offshore	42
Onshore	42
Operations	200
Ops	5, 16
Optimal	56, 98
Optimization	7, 12, 91, 121, 131
Outbound	200
Output	72, 84, 89
PaaS	212
Parallelism	16, 92
Participant	79
Patch	177
Path	66, 80, 86, 89, 91, 98
Pattern	22, 111
People	106, 125
Performance	52, 122
Periodicity	160
Persistent	178

Personalization	171
Pipeline	10
Port	186
Portal	207
Portfolio	32, 41
Postpone	93
Pre-assessment	38
Predecessor	71
Predictability	12
Predictive	170
Prepone	91, 92
Presentation	137
Prioritization	32
Process	39, 47, 86, 122
Procurement	118
Propensity	107
Protocol	186
Quality	13, 91, 127, 174
Quantitative	21, 64
Quarantine	175
Questionnaire	38, 71, 80
Readiness	31, 39, 60
Recurring	89
Redundancy	13, 175
Release	14, 42, 123
Reliability	13, 43, 52, 91, 127, 156
Report	57, 138
Requirement	6, 173
Requirements	12
Resilience	157
Restore	157, 175, 177
Retail	8, 206
Retrieval	13
Review	137
Rework	124
Risk	140
Roadmap	140
Robotic	211
Role	72, 109
Rollout	6, 123
SaaS	207, 212
Scalability	43
Scanning	175
Schema	178
Scope	40
Score	21, 41, 55, 57, 106
Scrum	44
SDN	213
Security	43, 45, 167, 186
Self-healing	14
Self-orchestration	19
Self-service	190
Sensor	171, 214
SEPA	209
Serverless	188, 190
Software	5
SOX	209
Speech	165
Spike	189
Sprint	13, 45
State	67
Story	71
Summary	149
Support	200
TCO	187
Technology	39, 48, 72, 89, 118, 127
Telco	212
Telecommunication	8, 212
Tempering	186
Tenet	7
Test	51, 128
Throughput	8
To-Be	97, 100
Toggle	179
Tool	118
Toolchain	10
Topology	21
Traceability	52, 124
Transaction	208
Transformation	19, 84, 142, 144
Trunk	179
Utilities	8, 213
Utilization	131, 143
Validation	136, 137
Value	199
Variation	112
Velocity	125
Vendor	42, 135
Veracity	171
Versioning	177
Virtualization	14
Visibility	43
VM	185, 188
Volume	178
VPC	191
Waste	6, 39, 91, 124
Weight	57
Workflow	5, 48, 124

Printed in Poland
by Amazon Fulfillment
Poland Sp. z o.o., Wrocław